OLD SOUL
YOUNG SOUL

THE PATH FROM SEEKING TO STILLNESS

CIRAK

All rights reserved. No part of this book may be reproduced by any mechanical, photographic, or electronic process or in the form of a phonographic recording, nor may it be stored in a retrieval system, transmitted, or otherwise copied for public or private use without the publisher's prior written consent.

The author does not dispense medical advice or prescribe any technique as a form of treatment for physical, emotional, or medical problems without the advice of a physician, either directly or indirectly. The author's intent is only to offer information of a general nature to help you in your quest for emotional and spiritual well-being. Should you use any of the information in this book for yourself, the author and the publisher assume no responsibility for your actions.

Cirak and the tree ring logo are registered trademarks of Cirak Inc.
Soul Pool photo by Zoltan Tasi on Unsplash

Editor: Michael Cirak
Website: cirak.com

Copyright © 2025 Cirak 1st Edition ISBN: 978-1-7350140-7-4

The Soul Pool

Emerging from Source, a new soul is catapulted into life by the re-entry of another soul's completed journey. Fueled by the sheer excitement of discovery and backed by the wisdom of the collective consciousness of those who went before it, the new soul embarks on its journey of self-actualization, only to return one day and contribute back to the soul pool.

– *Cirak* May 4, 2008

Contents

Foreword	1
Core Practice	5
SOCIAL	9
1. Culture	11
2. Media	17
3. Personas	23
4. Rank Illusion	29
5. Peer Pressure	35
6. Social Anxiety	41
7. Bullying	47
8. Academic Pressure	51
9. Body Image	57
CAREER	63
10. Money	65
11. Scarcity	71

12.	Career Choice	75
13.	Job Search	81
14.	High Achiever	87
15.	The Imposter	93
16.	Toxic Workplace	97
17.	Work and Life	103
18.	Burnout	107
19.	Job Loss	111
20.	Retirement	115
FAMILY		119
21.	Birth	121
22.	Adolescence	127
23.	Parents	133
24.	Black Sheep	139
25.	Dating	145
26.	Love	151
27.	Marriage	157
28.	Pregnancy	163
29.	Infertility	167
30.	Abortion	171

31.	Parenthood	177
32.	Breakup	183
33.	Infidelity	187
34.	Divorce	193
35.	Empty Nest	199
MENTAL		203
36.	Knowledge	205
37.	Planning	213
38.	Procrastination	219
39.	Expectations	223
40.	Comparison	229
41.	People-Pleasing	233
42.	Self-Esteem	239
43.	Self-Love	243
44.	Overthinking	249
45.	Creative Block	259
46.	Perfectionism	263
47.	Reactivity	267
48.	Anxiety	275
49.	Stress	281

50. Depression	287
51. Failure	293
52. Purpose	299
EMOTIONAL	305
53. Heartbreak	307
54. Forgiveness	311
55. Conflict	317
56. Trauma	323
57. Feeling Lost	327
58. Hopelessness	331
59. Trust	335
60. Anger	341
61. Abandonment	347
62. Boundaries	351
63. Grief	355
64. Guilt	359
65. Shame	363
66. Jealousy	369
67. Loneliness	373
68. Boredom	379

69. Feeling Stuck	383
PHYSICAL	387
70. Body	389
71. Sleep	395
72. Pain	399
73. Injury	403
74. Illness	407
75. Diagnosis	411
76. Food	415
77. Meat	421
78. Addiction	427
79. Gender	433
80. Body Alterations	439
81. Aging	449
82. Death	455
SPIRITUAL	461
83. Awareness	463
84. Thoughts	471
85. Attachment	479
86. Identity	483

87.	Intelligence	489
88.	Listening	497
89.	Stillness	503
90.	Acceptance	509
91.	Imagination	517
92.	Manifestation	523
93.	Flow	531
94.	Spiritual Bypass	537
95.	Psychedelics	543
96.	Regression	553
97.	Multiverse	559
98.	Meaninglessness	565
99.	Meditation	571
100.	Presence	577

OLD SOUL
YOUNG SOUL

THE PATH FROM SEEKING TO STILLNESS

CIRAK

Foreword

An old soul is often described as someone who demonstrates maturity, insight, and perspective that is typical of someone much older. They come across as deep, timeless, and wise beyond their years—not just in biological age, but in soul age. It's as if they carry the energetic imprint of many lifetimes.

Old souls approach life with introspection, empathy, and a natural sense of detachment from superficial pursuits. They are less focused on status, artificial stimulation, or proving themselves to others—and more drawn to reflection, inner peace, and alignment with something more real and enduring. They have access to broader perspectives and deeper dimensions. They flow with events and intuit the best course of action.

This stands in stark contrast to their behavior in earlier stages of their evolution, when they were still a young soul.

Young souls still have many basic lessons and experiences ahead of them. They are driven to seek happiness through achievement and outcomes, are deeply attached to their thoughts and emotions, and try to control the people, places, and things around them. They are constantly comparing what is happening to what they think should be happening. They become consumed by doing things "the right way" and are always concerned with what others think of them. They operate more at the surface reality—not because there's anything wrong with that, but because their life experience hasn't yet shaped them in more profound ways.

The impact soul age has on how a person experiences various life challenges is enormous. This book covers the 100 most common ones.

You might feel inclined to think of being an old soul as superior and a young soul as inferior. But in reality, awareness exists as a spectrum across many different areas of life. In some areas, you might be highly aware, while in others, you have severe blind spots. You might have a fulfilling career but struggle with meaningful relationships. Or you might be extremely creative but wrestle with attracting abundance.

Whatever it may be, it is imperative to steer clear of value judgments. Soul age is not about right or wrong, better or worse. The purpose of this book is not to make you feel guilty, and certainly not to shame you. It's designed to help you reflect on your life, foster acceptance of your past, and cultivate greater awareness as you move into your future.

That said, you can expect the topics in this book to challenge you. They'll push you to leave your comfort zone and take a closer look at who you are, the choices you make, and the lifestyle you lead. Seeing your blind spots isn't always pleasant. The inner critic may roar, and avoidant behavior may surface. If that happens, remind yourself: discomfort is the feeling of growth. There would be little point in picking up a new book if everything in it confirms what you already believe.

As such, this book is an invitation to find a more awakened view of yourself and life. It is a comprehensive reference for the most common circumstances you are likely to face. You may read it front-to-back, or jump directly to the chapters you feel most called to. Either way, you should set an intention to meet these pages with honesty and openness. The point is not to convince you of anything that doesn't resonate. It's to bring the light of awareness to any rigid thought-forms you may be mindlessly living by. But for that, you need to be willing to re-evaluate everything.

Ready? Let's begin.

Core Practice

Throughout this book, you'll be invited to sit with your feelings, observe your sensations, and release energetic blockages. But what does that actually mean in practice? The following walks you through a simple but powerful technique you can return to any time a chapter stirs something within you.

Working With Sensations

As you read the following pages, you will encounter topics that inevitably trigger you. When you feel strong emotions, set the book aside, close your eyes, and direct your attention inward. Where do you feel the trigger in your body? Locate the exact spot. A lot of emotions live in your stomach. Anxiety in your chest. Heartbreak in your heart. Grief in your lungs. Or constriction in your throat from not speaking up. There can also be tightness in your jaw or shoulders from carrying stress.

Wherever it may be, begin by observing the sensation directly—not your story about it, but the raw, physical appearance in your body. What shape does it have? What size is it? Is it fluffy like a cloud, or more dense like a rock? Can you see the boundaries? If so, are they clearly defined or more blurry? Can you sense a temperature, texture, or even a color? Let the observing part of your mind describe the feeling through the power of association. There's no need to fix or analyze it—only to notice. Stay present with the sensation until it begins to shift, release, or even dissolve. Even a slight reduction in intensity is a sign of energetic movement.

During this exercise, whenever you find that your mind has drifted, simply notice it and bring your attention back to your sensation. Focus on doing this as swiftly and smoothly as possible. You may experience frustration that you're not able to keep your mind still. Should this happen, practice accepting the reality of the moment as it is. *My mind has drifted.* Then return your attention to where you last left off in your body.

IMPORTANT: If the emotional charge ever feels overwhelming, back off and give yourself space. You can return to it later. Instead, practice self-observation with smaller triggers until you build up your capacity. This technique requires gentleness and discernment. Consider working with a trained somatic coach if deeper, more long-term support is needed.

Regardless of your life stage, it is highly recommended that you begin or deepen a daily meditation practice. A powerful place to start is the Thought Awareness meditation found at cirak.com/resources. Practicing once or twice daily—ideally in the morning and before bed—will help you develop a spacious awareness around your thoughts. The greater the gap between your thoughts and your awareness of them, the greater your freedom to choose your response. This alone can dramatically transform how you move through life.

For an even deeper practice that amplifies your inner voice, explore the Body Awareness meditations on the same webpage. Based on ancient Vipassana teachings, this technique teaches you how to observe sensations without reacting to them. Over time, you retrain your nervous system to remain grounded and non-reactive in even the most challenging situations, so you can act clearly, efficiently, and wisely.

Thought Awareness and Body Awareness meditation provides a powerful one-two punch for personal transformation: clarity of mind and connection to body.

You are encouraged to keep this page bookmarked so you can easily reference it at any point.

SOCIAL

Chapter I

Culture

Young Soul

Culture feels like truth itself. You inherit it without ever realizing it's optional. The values, rules, and rituals you grow up with are not seen as agreements but as reality. You don't ask whether they're right for you, because questioning them feels like betrayal—a risk of exile from the only belonging you know. At this stage, identity is fragile, and culture offers the scaffolding: what counts as success, how to behave, what emotions are safe to show. It feels easier, safer, even natural to follow what's already been stamped with approval.

But adoption becomes identification. You don't just accept your culture's preferences—you treat them as universal law. If someone thinks or lives differently, it seems wrong, misguided, even dangerous. Other ways of being threaten your own sense of stability. Rather than seeing them as variations, you dismiss them as errors. Culture becomes both compass and cage: guiding you toward belonging, while invisibly narrowing who you're allowed to be.

The lens is installed before you even know you're looking through it. That's why it feels so normal. Even when its rules seem outdated or hypocritical, you obey them—not out of conviction, but out of fear. Fear of judgment, ridicule, rejection. The need to fit in binds you more tightly than the rules themselves. You suppress your own instincts to maintain the comfort of approval.

Eventually, cracks appear. You feel the strain of self-censorship, the unease of saying what you're supposed to rather than what's true. You notice the gap between who you sense yourself to be and who your culture allows you to be. What once felt like safety begins to suffocate. The price of belonging starts to feel too high.

You begin to see how culture not only shapes your external life—work, marriage, money—but even scripts your inner world. It tells you which desires are valid, which emotions are shameful, which dreams are realistic. You may even confuse its voice for your own. But something in you resists. *This can't be all there is.*

At this stage, separating out often comes clumsily through conflict, rejection of tradition, or chasing counterculture identities. You try on alternatives not always because they fit, but because they're not what you were given. And while this may look chaotic, it's part of the loosening process. The young soul begins to realize that identity borrowed from culture will never be enough.

This is the first turning point: realizing culture is not *the* way, but *a* way. The moment you see its relativity, you begin to sort through the beliefs you inherited. Some you keep, some you release. It's the quiet start of inner freedom—not rebellion for rebellion's sake, but the recognition that your soul requires more space than culture alone can provide. And with that realization, the young soul begins the slow work of becoming an old soul.

OLD SOUL

As an old soul, you've likely felt estranged from culture for as long as you can remember. Its noise and rules always seemed too small, too shallow for the depth you carried. You may have learned to play along, but never quite belonged. Even while performing the rituals, you sensed: *this is not the whole of life.*

Now you see culture for what it is—a set of agreements, useful but provisional. Language, food, art, rituals, even laws: all ways humans coordinate with each other. They can be beautiful expressions, but they are not reality itself. They live on the level of form, while your essence belongs to the formless. Culture provides shape; the soul provides depth. You can honor both without confusing one for the other.

Participation becomes conscious. You may join in a festival for the joy it brings, or decline a custom that asks you to betray your integrity. You no longer need conformity to secure connection, because you know true belonging arises in presence, not performance. You recognize that culture can amplify love or stifle it, but never define it.

You begin to notice that culture is not monolithic. What once looked like "the way things are" now reveals itself as many overlapping tapestries—regional, generational, subcultural. This helps dissolve the illusion of absolutes. You can walk fluidly among them, appreciating their textures without being claimed by any of them.

Where the young soul resists culture through defiance, you meet it through compassion. You don't need to prove your freedom by rejecting tradition—you embody your freedom by choosing consciously, again and again. Even while others feel bound, you can join lightly, without getting entangled.

What once felt like an unquestioned authority, you now enjoy the flavors of shared life without mistaking it for your identity. Culture becomes another container for your presence practice. Every interaction with it—whether joining in or stepping away—becomes an opportunity to remember who you are beyond it.

Culture Chart

Cultural conditioning runs wide and deep. It's one of the primary lenses through which you view life. Sorting yourself out from it becomes a central part of your journey. This chart shows how culture affects young vs old souls.

Young Souls	**Old Souls**
Culture feels like truth itself—unquestioned	Culture is one lens among many—not ultimate
Beliefs and norms inherited wholesale	Beliefs consciously chosen by inner alignment
Conformity equals safety and belonging	Authenticity valued over approval
Difference seen as threatening or wrong	Difference welcomed as diversity
Identity defined by roles and labels	Identity rooted in essence, not labels
Fear of rejection keeps expression contained	Inner alignment outweighs fear of exclusion
Outdated rules followed to avoid judgment	Rules adapted or released via inner guidance
Culture acts as compass and cage	Culture appreciated as form; spirit remains formless

Prompts

1) What cultural values or traditions have shaped how you see yourself?

2) Which cultural rules do you follow out of genuine alignment, and which out of fear of judgment?

3) How do you react internally when you encounter a belief or lifestyle different from your own?

4) What aspects of your culture feel like a safe home, and what aspects feel like a cage?

5) Have you ever questioned a cultural "truth" and decided to live differently? What happened?

6) How do you balance honoring your roots with staying true to your own path?

7) What role does belonging play in your willingness to conform to cultural expectations?

8) In what ways has your culture shaped your ideas of success, love, or identity?

9) What traditions or customs do you keep because they genuinely enrich your life?

10) What would your life look like if you were free from every cultural expectation you've inherited?

Chapter 2

Media

Young Soul

Media becomes the atmosphere you breathe without noticing. It shapes how you think, feel, and define reality, long before you suspect it's doing anything at all. As a young soul, you're impressionable, so you take the flood of content as life itself: news, entertainment, social feeds, gaming. They all whisper the same illusion—that real life is happening "out there," and unless you consume, react, and keep up, you'll be left behind. You become convinced that without constant exposure, you are incomplete.

Entertainment pretends to relax you, but mostly sedates you. The binge, the scroll, the clip—they simulate enjoyment, even meaning. But when the screen goes dark, emptiness sets in. Your body feels heavy, your mind overstimulated. What you thought was leisure was really avoidance. Instead of inhabiting your own life, you got lost in someone else's.

News is perhaps the most deceptive form. It calls itself information, but its true purpose is persuasion. Narratives are curated, fear is amplified, and repetition installs belief. Rarely do you pause to ask: *Who benefits from me feeling this way?* At this stage, you confuse exposure with awareness. To "stay informed" is to stay entranced, locked in cycles of outrage and dependency.

Social media deepens the trance by turning your identity into a projection. You build a digital self for applause and think visibility brings value. Every "like" feels like a sip of water, but leaves you thirstier. The more you polish your image, the further you drift from your essence. You become addicted to affirmation while being starved of authenticity.

Gaming offers the final illusion: mastery without growth. In digital worlds, you can win instantly, control outcomes, and avoid the slow, awkward process of becoming. The trophies mean nothing, but they save you from facing the one character you came here to level up: yourself.

At its root, the young soul uses media not as a tool, but as a way to avoid feelings of lack. You reach for screens to fill space, regulate mood, and postpone silence. You fear what you might feel without them. Media becomes a substitute for inner life—a noisy distraction that keeps you from noticing your own presence.

Even when you try to be discerning—choosing "smart" podcasts or documentaries—you still consume passively, rarely questioning the vibration of what you take in. You think the louder you are, the more meaningful your message. In truth, you're only reinforcing your dependency on external noise.

OLD SOUL

As an old soul, you've felt the hollowness that follows the glow of the screen—the sense of time lost, attention drained, spirit dulled. You don't need to reject media entirely, but your relationship has inverted. Where once it consumed you, now you choose how—or if—you engage. You'd rather nourish yourself than numb out.

You know media is never neutral. Every story, clip, and post carries a frequency. You're not just absorbing content—you're absorbing the energy of its creator. That's why you've become vigilant. You choose voices that uplift your frequency, that open your heart, that remind you of the infinite beyond the screen.

The news cycle reveals itself not as information, but as orchestration. Its frames and omissions are too obvious to ignore. You no longer take headlines at face value because you can feel the energetic signature behind them.

"Breaking news" breaks your flow more than it informs your soul.

Social media loses its grip once you stop making your self-worth dependent on it. You may still share, not for likes, but to spread your message of light. You scroll lightly, like a guest passing through, without residency. Even low-vibe content can be witnessed without entanglement.

You begin to honor attention as sacred currency. Every click, every view, every reaction is an offering of your attention. And you no longer give that offering casually. If something drains you, you step back. If something enlivens you, you lean in. You curate your inputs not for entertainment, but for resonance.

Over time, you find you need less. What once felt like deprivation now feels like freedom. The silence between media becomes more valuable than the content itself. The less you consume, the more you create. The less you react, the more you respond. You consume less, experience more. Media becomes a tool, not a trance. Where once you sought escape, you now seek enrichment. And slowly, the simplest moments—a walk, a silence, a real conversation—become more compelling than any screen can.

Media Chart

Media is one of the most all-pervasive forces in the world. The following chart contrasts different attitudes towards media of young souls vs old souls.

Young Souls	Old Souls
Media as stimulation and escape	Media as tool for awareness and connection
Consumed unconsciously, driven by habit	Engaged with intentionally, chosen with discernment
Validation sought through likes, followers, views	Expression flows without attachment to metrics
Comparison and envy amplified	Discernment and inspiration cultivated
Overexposure to noise, news, and trends	Selective intake, aligned with inner clarity
Identity shaped by external narratives	Identity rooted in inner truth, media treated as form
Dopamine-driven scrolling for distraction	Present, embodied use to learn or share
Fear of missing out drives consumption	Freedom to step back without loss
Time fragmented, focus scattered	Time honored, attention protected
Media dictates mood and thought	Awareness shapes relationship with media

© 2025 Cirak

PROMPTS

1) What kind of media do you consume most often? How do you typically feel afterward?

2) Where does media consumption help expand your worldview? Where does it make it shrink?

3) Do you engage with any of your media habits for comfort or distraction?

4) What is your motivation to share something online? Do you want to feel seen or validated?

5) How do you respond emotionally to the news? Is it empowering or overwhelming?

6) What would a more conscious relationship with media look like for you? Which kinds of media feel nourishing or soul-affirming to you?

7) If you're a content creator, how can you use media as a tool for truth, beauty, and being of service?

8) If you had to design your ideal media "diet," what would it include—and exclude?

9) How might your inner world change if you became more selective about the media you allow in?

Chapter 3

PERSONAS

YOUNG SOUL

From an early age, you learn to present yourself in ways that fit expectations. You sense what earns praise, what avoids punishment, what keeps people pleased—and you adjust. You become the achiever, the pleaser, the rebel, the charmer. Each is a costume tailored to fit the environments you grow up in. At first, it feels smart, even protective. You feel safer, more valued, more in control.

But costumes harden into masks, and masks into identity. You forget where the performance ends and the real you begins. You say yes when you mean no, laugh when you want to cry, stay agreeable even when you disagree. These behaviors win approval, so you keep repeating them. Yet beneath the surface is the quiet ache of self-betrayal.

Masks protect, but they also imprison. They distort intimacy, filter communication, and leave you strangely lonely even in a crowd. People connect with your mask, and you with theirs—leaving everyone unseen. Deep down, you carry the fear that if your real self were exposed, no one would stay.

Letting go feels terrifying. Who will you be without the mask? What if rejection comes? What if you don't even like who you find underneath? So you double down on pretending. But pretending grows heavier with time. The smile strains, the success rings hollow, the relationships crack. You suffocate beneath the weight of who you are not.

Eventually, something breaks through: a betrayal, a burnout, a breakdown. For a moment, the mask slips. But the world doesn't end. Instead, reality sharpens. A strange relief emerges. A clarity. And with it, the first desire to be seen as you are.

The transition is never elegant or smooth. You stumble, overshare, retreat. Sometimes you put the mask back on when fear resurfaces. But something has shifted: pretending feels worse than rejection. And who exactly is being rejected, anyway—the mask, or you?

You begin to notice other people's masks too. The tension in their voices, the practiced smiles, the subtle avoidance of truth. Judgment softens. You see everyone as improvising, trying to be loved. And you realize: dropping your own mask gives others permission to do the same.

So you make different choices. You speak even when your voice trembles. You show up without filtering every mood. Sometimes it's received well, sometimes not—but you feel more alive either way. For the first time, your soul, not your mask, is steering your life.

And while the world may not always reward authenticity, your being does. You sleep deeper, breathe easier, laugh from the belly. You may not know fully who you are yet—but you know who you are not. And that is the beginning of old soul freedom.

Old Soul

As an old soul, you've worn masks across lifetimes—and know that none of them are real. They once served their purpose: survival, protection, belonging. But you've also felt the emptiness of false identity. Every role eventually dissolves, leaving the same awareness shining underneath.

You've played roles well—leader, lover, artist, healer. But you no longer mistake them for your essence. You are not the story, but the presence aware of the story. That recognition brings a liberating detachment. You don't need to impress, persuade, or be understood. You just need to be.

When old masks try to return—wanting to seem smarter, kinder, more spiritual—you catch yourself. You recognize the impulse as fear, not truth. And you choose presence instead of acting a part. You've discovered that nothing is more magnetic than being real.

You don't demonize personas. You see them as survival strategies. You have compassion for those still caught in the cycle. You know how frightening it feels to live without armor. But you also know the cost of wearing it too long: disconnection, depression, disease.

You also begin to notice how collective personas shape entire cultures—nations showing off strength, religions projecting purity, families portraying harmony. You see that it's all a universal play of masks. Even culture itself is a mask—an inherited costume passed from generation to generation. Its gestures, traditions, and rituals can be beautiful, but they are not essence.

This recognition dissolves judgment even further. It allows you to honor the form while remaining free from it, participating without being possessed by it. You stop wishing people were different and start trusting the larger unfolding: every mask, whether personal or collective, eventually cracks under the weight of truth.

Your compass now is radical honesty—especially with yourself. Instead of asking, *Will this make me liked?* you ask, *Is this true?* You stop editing yourself to appease. You stop shrinking to keep others comfortable. Your presence itself becomes an invitation for truth.

In relationships, you lead with authenticity. You ask real questions. You listen with your whole being. You love without conditions because you know you are love. And from that ground, those who stay in your life are those meant to be there.

Even the identity of "authentic" becomes suspect. You see how the mind can make another mask out of sincerity. So you cling less and less to self-images, even noble ones. You allow yourself to evolve, to shift, to dissolve into undefinable presence.

This brings a profound joy—a sense of home no role can provide. You no longer hear applause. You no longer fear rejection. You no longer measure yourself in relation to others. You simply live as who you are.

That doesn't mean you float above life in perfection. You may still cry. You may still doubt. But you do so without shame or censorship. You let your body tremble, your voice break, your heart spill. What matters is not how you appear, but how truthfully you show up. And in the irony of spirit, the less you try to be radiant, the more you shine.

PROMPTS

1) What masks do you wear around certain people, and why?

2) What parts of yourself do you hide or mute in settings like the workplace or in public?

3) What role does fear play in your decision to wear or remove a mask? Which mask feels the heaviest to maintain?

4) When you look at others, can you sense when they're wearing a mask? How does that affect your connection?

5) Are there times when you're performing a role unconsciously, even to yourself?

6) How do you discern between a tactful strategy and self-betrayal in communication with others?

7) When was the last time you were fully yourself with someone? What made that possible? How did it feel?

8) What emotions come up when you imagine dropping all social masks?

9) What would change in your life if you allowed yourself to be fully authentic?

Chapter 4

Rank Illusion

Young Soul

Rank illusion begins with the belief that your worth must be proven—and that proving it requires comparison. As a young soul, you measure yourself against others: their clothes, careers, partners, popularity, possessions. Cultural standards of success slip in unnoticed and, without realizing it, your self-esteem becomes hostage to showing constantly updated and improved results.

This anxious state feels normal. Everyone seems to be chasing the same things, and society rewards those who play well. The job title. The car. The house. The acclaim. You call it motivation, ambition, growth. But underneath, it's fear of falling behind, fear of being unseen. Every success only sets the bar higher. There is no arrival, only the gnawing sense that you're never enough.

What you don't yet see is that the world you're competing in is arbitrary. The rules were made up—usually by those who profit from them. They're designed to keep you striving, never resting, never free. Rank anxiety convinces you that love and respect must be earned, that your self-worth depends on your output. Even your rest becomes strategic—you relax only to recharge for the next push. Life feels like an endless audition where you never get the part you really want: your true self.

The turning point often comes with fatigue, emptiness, the realization that no trophy, title, or applause has ever delivered peace. You begin to wonder: *What would life be without this pressure?* You notice how much joy, rest, and authenticity you've traded for a fragile sense of superiority that never lasts. For the first time, you suspect that the ladder itself may be the problem, not the difficulty of climbing it.

You start to see how the chase distorts your relationships. Friends become rivals. Colleagues become threats. Even loved ones become benchmarks to measure against. Instead of connection, rank illusion leaves you isolated—always trying to prove, never able to relax. The very recognition you crave distances you from the intimacy you long for.

Eventually, you glimpse the truth: the whole ladder is imaginary. Its rungs exist only because everyone agrees to climb them. Freedom doesn't come from reaching the top—it comes from stepping off entirely. And only you can do that. When you stop trying to impress and begin to express, life slowly becomes yours again.

OLD SOUL

As an old soul, you've brushed up against rank anxiety before—maybe even climbed the ladder for a while. You might have worked tirelessly to be seen, praised, celebrated. Not necessarily out of vanity, but because you hadn't yet recognized just how deeply you were conditioned to live for outcomes. But in time, you saw through it: the arbitrary rules, the fleeting high of recognition, the fading applause. None of it lasted. You know now that no amount of acclaim can fill an inner void. Only alignment with truth can.

So you've stopped trying to outrun your self-doubt with achievements. You see clearly that your value doesn't come from what you do, but from who you are—your presence, your energy, your light. You've discovered that the deepest form of success is resonance: the sense of being in harmony with your own soul, regardless of how others measure it.

You still pursue mastery, but now it's for the joy of creating. You serve others—not to be noticed—but because being of service nourishes your soul. Your ambition has shifted from lack-driven to love-based. And in doing so, everyone around you benefits. The energy you once poured into competition now flows into creation, collaboration, and contribution. What once narrowed your life now expands it.

What's more, you see how the illusion of rank actually blinds people to their own gifts. In chasing someone else's idea of success, they ignore the unique beauty only they can bring. But when you step out of comparison, your energy becomes available for authentic expression. In that freedom, your very being becomes an offering to the world.

When you're surrounded by striving, the rank illusion may still appear convincing. But now, you can leave it intact for those who need it. You remember what's true for you.

The challenges of navigating a society designed by and for young souls becomes a constant reminder that, ultimately, your presence itself is your power. Not your CV. Not your possessions. Not your follower count. Just you—clear, grounded, radiant without trying.

Rank Illusion Chart

Comparing yourself to others is such a simple trap to fall into. It doesn't cease, even at later stages of life, unless you bring some serious awareness to it. The following chart illustrates how young souls and old souls handle the temptation of rank illusion.

Young Souls	**Old Souls**
Worth tied to proving and comparison	Worth inherent in being, not outcomes
Self-esteem hostage to results	Peace rooted in presence and alignment
Success measured by titles, possessions, and applause	Success measured by resonance, joy, and authenticity
Every success raises the bar higher	Every creation arises from love, not pressure
Rules of the "ladder" assumed real	Rungs of the ladder seen as imaginary
Friends, colleagues, even loved ones become rivals	Relationships seen as collaborations, not competitions
Rest treated as strategic recharge	Rest honored as nourishment and presence
Fear of falling behind drives ambition	Trust in timing and flow guides ambition
Recognition pursued at the cost of intimacy	Authentic expression creates deeper connection
Life feels like an endless audition	Life becomes freedom to express your true self

© 2025 Cirak

PROMPTS

1) What does "success" mean to you, and where did that definition come from?

2) What areas of your life are most affected by comparison or competition?

3) Have you ever achieved something others admired, but still felt empty or unsatisfied? What did that reveal?

4) How do you feel when others are celebrated or admired more than you? What story arises inside?

5) What would it feel like to stop trying to impress anyone, even yourself?

6) What has rank anxiety cost you in terms of joy, rest, or authentic self-expression?

7) When do you feel most like yourself, and does that version of you care about recognition or rank?

8) Who in your life sees and values you without needing you to prove anything?

9) What inner truths have you discovered about your worth that no longer depend on others?

10) What would change in your life if you redefined success as alignment, not approval?

Chapter 5

Peer Pressure

Young Soul

Peer pressure isn't always overt. Often, it appears in glances, silences, raised eyebrows, or the unspoken pull of group energy. As a young soul, your sense of self is still forming, so you scan others for cues on how to be, adjusting your behavior to feel safe. You're not trying to be false. At this stage, you're just trying to get through each day without unnecessary drama.

Lacking a true inner compass, you grab onto external markers of what's acceptable, desirable, or worthy. Roles form around you: the agreeable one, the entertainer, the quiet one. In a world where belonging feels synonymous with survival, peer pressure doesn't feel like pressure—it feels like the obvious path.

You start adopting traits, beliefs, and ambitions that aren't really yours. You laugh when something isn't funny. You stay silent when something feels wrong. You go along with plans that violate your instincts. The safety of the herd numbs your curiosity, and agreement becomes your substitute for connection. Slowly, silently, you become a stranger to yourself.

Every time you override your truth, tension accumulates. A tightening in the chest, a fog in the mind, a heaviness in the gut. You dismiss these signals as the price of fitting in. But they add up. They build a version of you others may accept, but that you no longer recognize. The nervous system begins to equate silence with safety, approval with self-worth, even as your soul grows restless beneath the weight of conformity.

When choices come from the outside in, the life you build—relationships, career, causes—feels hollow. You're not deliberately lying, but you're not fully alive either. You're curating a self that's acceptable to others at the expense of your own soul. And the toll is clear: muted joy, a constant edge of loneliness, and the haunting sense that you're living someone else's script.

The wake-up call usually comes as exhaustion, burnout, or meaninglessness that can no longer be ignored. You finally ask: *Who am I beneath all this pretending?* You begin to notice when you're posturing or appeasing, and how discomfort arises whenever you try honesty. To your surprise, the small act of saying *no* becomes freeing.

With that, courage grows. You realize peer pressure is not just external—it's internalized. It's not others keeping you small, it's you pressuring yourself to stay acceptable. The moment you stop doing that, true connection emerges—not from agreement—but from authenticity.

OLD SOUL

As an old soul, you've lived enough lifetimes to know the cost of betraying yourself. You've played the roles, won the applause, and swallowed your truth to belong. And at this point, you simply refuse to pay that price again. Self-respect outweighs social approval.

That doesn't mean you're immune. Peer pressure still whispers in subtler forms: the temptation to tone yourself down, to censor your clarity, to dim your brilliance so others feel comfortable. The urge to go along can still surface, but now you notice it. You observe the sensations in your body, release what's there, and return to your truth. You know in true harmony there is no room for self-abandonment.

A new form of pressure may arise—not about acceptance, but about how you're perceived. You don't want to seem arrogant, aloof, or unrelatable. While compassion matters, you've learned that over-accommodation is just another form of self-diminishment. Trying not to outshine others may look kind, but it subtly denies the light you're here to share.

Your task now is quiet strength: honoring others without betraying yourself. You no longer impose your views, but you don't withhold them either. Boundaries and honesty come without apology. People feel your integrity, and that presence becomes more trustworthy than conformity ever was. Even in silence, your energy communicates clearly: you are rooted in yourself, and therefore safe to be around.

You see that peer pressure is simply the echo of collective fear—the fear of being different, of standing alone, of not being enough. By staying grounded in your truth, you dissolve that fear for yourself, and in doing so, you give others permission to do the same.

You also notice how your steadiness brings balance to the whole room. It's not that you try to persuade others or posture. You simply keep your pace, tell the truth gently, and hold your boundaries with firm kindness. The more you relax into what's real for you, the more others feel like they can do that for themselves. Your ease becomes proof that belonging doesn't require agreement, only presence.

Eventually, peer pressure loses all relevance. You may still sense it, but it no longer governs you. You're not playing to the crowd anymore—you're living from the soul.

Peer Pressure Chart

In a world where you must get along with people at varying levels of awareness, it can be tricky to first discover your truth, separate out, and then maintain and grow it despite finding yourself on the fringes of society. The following chart shows how young souls vs old souls respond to peer pressure when they encounter it.

Young Soul	Old Soul
Seeks approval to feel secure	Guided by inner alignment, not opinion
Follows the crowd to avoid rejection	Stands alone when truth requires it
Fears judgment and social exclusion	Sees judgment as projection, not truth
Conforms to be liked or validated	Expresses truth regardless of outcome
Changes behavior to fit in	Listens to inner knowing before acting
Believes fitting in means safety	Knows authenticity is safety
Compromises values for belonging	Soul values above social acceptance
Avoids conflict to maintain image	Allows conflict if it serves truth
Acts from fear of not being enough	Acts from clarity of being whole
Identifies with persona roles	Lives as presence, not performance

© 2025 Cirak

Prompts

1) Are there particular people or environments where you notice yourself shrinking or self-censoring? What do you fear would happen if you were fully yourself there?

2) When you feel pressure from others, how does it show up in your body? Are there specific sensations that alert you to self-abandonment?

3) Do you ever suffer from FOMO? If so, how much does it influence your choices or self-worth?

4) What values or truths do you feel called to embody more boldly, even if it makes others uncomfortable?

5) How do you distinguish between genuine connection and the illusion of belonging through conformity?

6) Have you ever paid a price for being authentic—and was it worth it?

7) In what areas of your life do you still seek external approval? What's behind that?

8) What would it feel like to live from your truth without fear of judgment?

Chapter 6

Social Anxiety

Young Soul

Social anxiety is a classic young soul challenge because your sense of self depends heavily on how others perceive you. Even ordinary situations can trigger fear of embarrassment—being called on in class, speaking up in a meeting, standing out in a group. At its worst, just being in public and feeling watched can feel unbearable.

You don't yet recognize that this fear is rooted in identification with thoughts about what others might be thinking of you. Thoughts about who you should be. Ironically, you're anxious about being watched by people who aren't actually watching—because they, too, are caught in their own self-conscious spiral. But when you're fused with your thoughts, you believe you're the only one feeling this way.

Any belief you accept unexamined can become overwhelming and turn into a mental heath issue. Thoughts are inconsistent, messy, and fickle. Without awareness, you're likely to mistake them for truth. And then you live in fear of shadows your own mind has projected. Most phobias form this way: thought believed without question. Even everyday worries—like being without your phone—can spiral into full-blown anxiety.

Each time you believe a fearful thought, your body tightens, your chest constricts, the gut drops, and mind fogs. You interpret these signals as proof of danger, when they're actually evidence of mental identification. The loop feeds itself: thought fuels sensation, sensation fuels more thought. Without awareness, this cycle becomes your reality. You start living in anticipation of judgment, rehearsing every move in your head, as though life were a performance scored by others. The weight of imagined eyes follows you everywhere.

The shift begins when you remember: *I am not these thoughts.* You are not even the feelings those thoughts trigger. You are the awareness holding them both. Anchoring in that awareness breaks the cycle. Fear loses power when you stop giving it belief. What once felt like exposure slowly reveals itself as opportunity: a chance to return, again and again, to presence. Each moment of recognition is a small liberation, and over time those moments accumulate into maturity.

OLD SOUL

As an old soul, you may still feel overwhelmed in groups—but not from fear of judgment. What weighs on you is energetic density. You feel the subtle currents in a room: the tension beneath conversations, the emotional residue people carry, the scattered thought-forms that buzz like static. If your own reserves are low, just being in chaotic energy can leave you drained.

One of the gifts of old soul awareness is the ability to design a life that honors your sensitivity. You stop pushing yourself into crowds just because it's expected. You no longer override intuition to prove you're adaptable. Solitude and silence become your safe havens. A single aligned conversation becomes more nourishing than a hundred noisy encounters. You no longer act from avoidance. You move in alignment.

This doesn't mean you reject the world. You still engage, but without chasing outcomes. The fear of missing out dissolves when you know your worth isn't tied to being seen. You allow the world to remain what it is—messy, loud, beautiful—because you've allowed yourself to be.

Now, social settings become less about surviving others and more about sensing energy. You can walk into a room and feel its emotional climate within seconds. Instead of being destabilized, you use that awareness to choose:

where to stand, who to engage, when to step out. Presence becomes your shield, clarity, and anchor.

Your peace no longer hinges on circumstance. It is chosen. That choice lets you move freely: sometimes entering the crowd, sometimes stepping back, but always centered in yourself. What was once anxiety becomes discernment. You don't fear the energy of others—you simply decide which energies you'll welcome into your field.

In that freedom, social life becomes less of a threat and more of a dance—one you join or sit out from without apology, because you are who you are, independent of your environment. Whatever may ensue around you, you remain whole.

And eventually, what once drained you begins to transform. With practice, you can even turn your sensitivity into service—holding space, stabilizing energy, or quietly transmitting calm into a room without saying a word. You no longer need the crowd's approval, yet your presence uplifts it. What was once the source of your greatest discomfort becomes a way for love to flow through you.

Social Anxiety Chart

Social points of engagement are all around, and any triggers you may have are likely at the center of your day-to-day experience. Developing greater awareness is therefore essential. The following chart contrasts how young souls vs old souls deal with social anxiety.

Young Soul	Old Soul
Feels exposed and judged in social situations	Feels spacious and grounded, not defined by others
Self-image depends on external approval	Self-image arises from inner alignment and self-acceptance
Attention collapses inward, obsessing over appearance	Attention expands outward, present with others and the environment
Body tightens; energy contracts and withdraws	Body relaxes; energy flows openly and naturally
Overthinks every word and gesture	Responds authentically without rehearsing or self-editing
Sees social rejection as a threat to identity	Sees social dynamics as temporary and not personal
Avoids or escapes social situations to feel safe	Chooses interactions intuitively, engages without fear
Believes others are evaluating or criticizing constantly	Recognizes most people are absorbed in their own experience
Tries to control the impression they make	Lets presence and natural energy speak for itself
Freedom comes from dissolving the need for approval	Freedom comes from resting in being, not performance

Prompts

1) Describe a typical situation where social anxiety arises. Where in your body do you feel the tension? Close your eyes and locate the sensation in your body. What happens when you observe it without trying to change it?

2) Reflect on how often you believe your thoughts without questioning them. How might your experience shift if you saw them as passing clouds?

3) In what ways do you try to control how others perceive you? What would happen if you didn't?

4) Have you ever experienced being fully present in a group setting without fear or self-consciousness? What allowed that to happen?

5) What people or places nourish your sense of peace and authenticity? Which ones drain or destabilize you?

6) What boundaries do you currently set to protect your energy? What boundaries are you afraid to set?

7) What does it feel like in your body when you override your intuition to fit in or avoid judgment?

8) What would it look like to design a life that honors your sensitivity while remaining open to deep connection?

Chapter 7

Bullying

Young Soul

Bullying often plays a big role in a young soul's journey—whether you're on the receiving end or the one inflicting it. Your sense of self is still fragile and externally defined. You don't yet know who you are beyond how others treat you. The sting of bullying feels personal and permanent and seems to confirm your deepest fear: that something is wrong with you.

If you've been bullied, you may carry those wounds into adulthood—wounds that shape how you relate, trust, and even physically carry yourself. You might become a perfectionist, a people-pleaser, or someone who stays small just to avoid being seen. You build a persona to protect yourself and start living from defense or self-denial, instead of truth, love, or freedom. Even long after the bullying stops, you may replay the voices of those who shamed you, as if they are your own.

If you've been the bully, it usually stems from painful emotions you didn't know how to process, so you projected them outward. Anger, shame, or insecurity felt unbearable to hold, so you pushed them onto someone weaker, hoping the release will bring relief. But it never does. The cycle repeats until awareness grows—usually through guilt, isolation, or by being humbled.

Whether you were bullied, the bully, or both, the opportunity is the same: to become someone who doesn't pass pain forward, but who can process and release it fully. The task is not to erase what happened, but to notice where those experiences still live in you—and to do the inner work to come out of it.

You begin to see that breaking the cycle is not only possible, but essential to your own freedom. To break the cycle, you are being asked to grow in empathy, courage, and self-worth. Because you can only ever treat others the way you treat yourself.

OLD SOUL

As an old soul, bullying leaves an early imprint. You may have felt like an outsider from the start. Your sensitivity, depth, or energetic presence made you an easy target. You didn't fit the mold, and others sensed that. Without the tools to understand or defend yourself, you may have first internalized the pain before learning to transmute it into empathy and strength of character.

You see now that bullying was never about you—it was others projecting their discomfort with themselves onto you. They couldn't sit with their own wounds, so they displaced them. Your work has been to release the part of you that carried their pain as proof of your unworthiness. You've learned to transcend the abuse and recognize that pain needs a witness, not a host.

Having been bullied has given you the insights and compassion to be the kind of person others feel safe around. It puts you in touch with your humanity and that of those who hurt you. That doesn't mean you should invite them back into your life. It just means you've released the charge, practiced forgiveness, and found freedom. Instead of cycling through resentment, you become a quiet proof that it's possible to move beyond harm without denying that it happened.

You also see that bullying is not an isolated act but part of the human curriculum. Every culture, every age group, every family system has some version of it. What you once took as a personal wound, you now understand as a collective shadow playing itself out. This deepens your compassion and sharpens your discernment. Instead of asking *Why me?* you ask *What does this show us?*

That shift turns your pain into service—not through martyrdom, but by embodying the safety, empathy, and clarity that the world itself longs to learn. In your presence, others sense a refuge—the very thing you once longed for. What was once cruelty becomes the soil of your kindness, and what was once shame becomes the ground of your strength.

Prompts

1) Were you ever bullied? What do you still carry from past experiences that needs healing?

2) Are there ways you've internalized bullying through self-criticism, perfectionism, or shame?

3) Did you ever stand up for yourself or others despite fear? What gave you the courage in that moment?

4) How do you hold compassion for those who hurt others, without enabling or excusing them?

5) How has the experience of bullying shaped the way you read a room or sense unspoken dynamics?

6) How can you embody the safety and presence you once longed for, both for yourself and for others?

Chapter 8

Academic Pressure

Young Soul

How you handle external pressure—especially in highly structured environments like modern academia—is one of the clearest indicators of your soul age. As a young soul, you're quickly swept up in the drama. The collective urgency of others adds to the illusion that the stress is real and justified. But it's not just normal stress—it's the sheer weight of the institution itself. A massive system tells you what matters, how to succeed, and who you should become. Questioning that isn't just difficult—it feels unthinkable.

From an early age, you're told that education is the key to success and happiness. That it's the one thing that will get you ahead. So you follow the steps, meet the expectations, and wait for the promised reward. But the more you progress, the clearer it becomes: there is no finish line. Each stage of education becomes a gatekeeper to the next—with every test, every grade, every evaluation seemingly carrying life-or-death consequences for your imagined future. The fear of messing up doesn't just threaten your academic standing—it threatens your identity, your self-worth, and all your hopes and dreams.

Over time, the path is so deeply internalized that you no longer realize it's optional. You don't question whether it's aligned—you just keep getting grades and degrees. Graduation becomes your purpose, achievement your identity, and stress your constant companion. You absorb the beliefs and ideologies of the system without even noticing. Your creativity gets squeezed into formats, your intuition silenced under terms of engagement. Even your joy becomes graded. The academic world isn't just a phase you move through—it becomes the lens through which you see reality.

When you leave school, this mental structure becomes your framework for navigating adult life. You continue chasing goals, seeking validation through output, measuring worth by metrics, and making decisions through logic rather than intuition. You enter workplaces or relationships still waiting for the invisible examiner to hand out your grade. And because the system taught you to equate effort with self-worth, you keep overextending long after the class is over. You may find success, but it's never really yours. You're doing it for those whose conditioning you perpetuate.

Only when your old soul begins to stir—through burnout, failure, or the ache of emptiness—do you begin to ask the deeper question: *What if none of this was ever mine?*

OLD SOUL

An old soul sees education for what it is—a useful tool to impart social structure, not universal truth. You recognize that institutions help organize society, but they are not more important than your health, your joy, or your divine blueprint. You understand that no single degree or title can capture your full potential—and that true learning happens outside the classroom, in the unfiltered curriculum of everyday life. If a subject doesn't genuinely interest you, no amount of prestige, praise, or parental approval can make it worth your time.

You also know that pressure doesn't equal purpose. Pursuing something just to meet expectations will only drain your spirit, cloud your clarity, and create unnecessary suffering—for yourself and those around you. You've learned that genuine curiosity generates its own stamina, while obligation quickly degrades into resentment. You don't need to be exhausted to prove your commitment. You don't need to suffer now to be happy later. If the path isn't alive now, it isn't the path.

That doesn't mean you reject education altogether. You simply approach it consciously. You choose environments, teachers, and learning styles that nourish your curiosity and individuality. You might question every syllabus, reframe every metric, or skip traditional credentials altogether. For you, learning must serve life—not the other way around. Education becomes a resource you draw from, not a box you live inside.

Even when immersed in a formal system, you don't lose yourself in it. You remember that grades cannot capture who you are and that other people's opinions—no matter how reputable they may be—are not your truth. You know you can only speak authentically through that which you have felt, that which you have been destined to explore. From that place, you can care deeply about your work without making it your identity. You can participate without conforming. You can succeed without betraying yourself.

You also sense that life itself is the ultimate classroom. Every challenge, failure, and quiet observation teaches you more than a test ever could. You start to measure success not by accolades or certificates, but by how fully you can meet each moment with awareness and integrity. In this way, education becomes less about accumulation and more about refinement—polishing the soul, not so much the resume.

The time will come when you become the teacher. Not because you followed all the rules, but because you learned how to be true to yourself. Your authority doesn't come from letters after your name, but from the light in your being. That becomes your greatest education—and your greatest gift to the world.

PROMPTS

1) Have you ever defined your value by your grades, school, or degrees? How does that conditioning still live in you?

2) Do you hold your children or younger relatives to similar standards? What effect does that pressure have on them?

3) Did following the prescribed path actually result in the life you were promised? What unexpected twists taught you more than school ever could?

4) If you're considering further education, are you choosing it from alignment or fear? What signs of truth or compromise are you noticing?

5) What would it look like to pursue education purely for joy, growth, or soul-led interest—not for approval or status?

6) Have you ever abandoned a path that looked good on paper but felt wrong in your body? What happened when you trusted your deeper knowing?

7) What beliefs about education did you inherit that no longer resonate with you? Are you ready to let them go?

8) What would it mean to redefine intelligence, success, or mastery on your own terms?

Chapter 9

Body Image

Young Soul

Every soul starts out infatuated with their body. It's the ultimate externalization of identity. You believe you *are* the physical form you see in the mirror. Add to that your name, your home, your social class, and instantly a story forms—a story of who "you" are and where "you" come from. That story becomes the foundation of your worldview. Everything you experience in life is filtered through that constructed identity.

It's no surprise, then, that one of the first ways you measure yourself against others is through appearance. Whatever the norms, standards, and trends of your particular era or culture may be, the need to belong leads you to define your worth by how closely you match those external ideals. The distance between you and the ideal becomes the battleground where your self-worth lives and dies.

While all souls wrestle with bodily identification, young souls tend to carry the attachment well into adulthood and beyond. At any given stage, you might see yourself as too young, too old. Too thin, too thick. Too short, too tall. It never ends. The desire to "fix" your body can become obsessive—leading to compulsive shopping, excessive training, eating disorders, or cosmetic alterations. And when your confidence, mental health, and happiness depend on your looks, the beauty and media industries are quick to profit from your insecurity.

As long as you live in your head, you'll find it hard to like yourself—because the head only sees parts, not wholeness. It can only compare, not accept. True self-love begins the moment you stop staring at your reflection for confirmation and turn inward toward felt experience. When you taste presence, even briefly, you realize your aliveness is far more beautiful than any image.

Old Soul

Even as an old soul, some identification with the body is inevitable. The descent from formlessness into form is so sudden, so dense, that embodiment itself can feel like a shock. The difference is, you return to your authentic self more quickly.

You remember there's nothing wrong with you, that you are whole exactly as you are. You know you're not your mind or body. You honor your form, care for it, and treat it as sacred—but you don't mistake it for your essence.

That doesn't mean you ignore health or neglect physical needs. On the contrary, you care for your body because it's the vessel through which the formless expresses itself. You eat well, sleep deeply, and move regularly—not to fix, impress, or fit in, but to remain tuned, grounded, and receptive.

You know that your clarity, creativity, and capacity to love depend on how well your body is cared for. Instead of being a problem to solve, the body becomes an ally—offering signals, sensations, and rhythms that guide you into balance.

As such, you see your body as an energetic vehicle—a soul-interface through which Source gets to experience this dimension with you as co-creator. What your body looks like, what gender it is, where it's from—these are details, not definitions. They don't touch the power you feel when you're aligned with flow.

From this perspective, beauty radiates less from symmetry and more from vitality. Your presence shapes your appearance.

Ultimately, anything you identify with gains control. Anything you don't identify with loses its grip on you. When you remember yourself as awareness, the body is freed to be what it always was: not your prison, not your trophy, but your sacred companion in this brief and miraculous journey.

Body Image Chart

The following chart contrasts how young souls vs old souls deal with body image.

Young Soul	Old Soul
Seeks validation through appearance	Honors body as sacred vessel
Compares body to ideals and trends	Accepts body's uniqueness and rhythm
Uses body as a tool to control or attract	Treats body as a channel for presence
Feels shame or pride based on looks	Feels reverence regardless of form
Alters body to feel worthy or safe	Attunes to body for truth and intuition
Treats body as separate from soul	Sees body and soul as integrated
Avoids aging, flaws, or imperfection	Welcomes change as part of design of life
Attaches meaning to beauty standards	Detaches meaning from physical form
Fears being judged or unseen	Fears nothing—radiates from within
Believes body defines identity	Knows body reflects, not defines, essence

© 2025 Cirak

Prompts

1) How much do your looks matter to you? How much time do you spend grooming yourself? Are you enjoying your body—or putting on a mask to cover up insecurity?

2) Which parts of your appearance have you struggled to accept—and why? Can you separate inherited judgments from your true feelings?

3) Do you view diet, fitness, skincare as ways to support your energy—or as attempts to become "enough"?

4) What would it feel like to take care of your body out of reverence, not rejection?

5) When do you feel most embodied and alive in your body? What activities or environments support this?

6) How does social media affect the way you perceive your body? What would change if you didn't compare?

7) What messages did you receive about your body growing up? Are they still running your life?

8) Can you see how the glow of mental, physical, and spiritual health makes every body type attractive?

CAREER

Chapter 10

Money

Young Soul

To a young soul, money represents the ultimate form of power, freedom, and validation. It's the key that unlocks the doors to happiness, comfort, and self-worth. It promises security from fear, admiration from others, and control over your life. You may spend much of your energy chasing it, believing that once you have enough, everything else will finally fall into place.

This pursuit is fueled by the belief that success is measurable, visible, and external. You tie your identity to your bank account, possessions, or accomplishments. Financial pressure feels like personal failure. Debt becomes not just a burden, but a reflection of inadequacy. You push harder, make compromises, and say yes to things that drain you—all to fix an inner sense of lack that money promises to solve, if not directly, then by association.

The concept of ownership captures this illusion perfectly. You crave things—not just for their utility, but for what they symbolize. A house, a car, a designer bag, the latest device. These objects become extensions of your self-worth. And yet, the satisfaction is short-lived. The thrill fades almost before you can enjoy it, and the cycle restarts—each new purchase promising completion, each one leaving you emptier than before. It's a treadmill that never stops—unless you step off.

Eventually, you do. The constant need to prove yourself through wealth takes its toll. When money feels scarce, you panic, make impulsive choices, or drown in shame. When you feel behind, you compare yourself to others, chasing an imagined standard that keeps the rat race alive. Even when you reach your goals, the peace you hoped for doesn't last. You've done what the world said would make you happy, but your life remains restless.

As always, disillusionment marks the beginning of a deeper journey. You begin to ask new questions: *Why am I still anxious when things look good on paper? What have I been trading for security?* You begin to notice that money doesn't actually soothe your fear—it amplifies it, because now you're terrified of losing what you've gained.

Debt starts to look less like failure and more like feedback. It reveals where you've been unconscious—financially and energetically. Financial pressure becomes a mirror that shows how much your peace depends on control. You begin to ask: *What would it mean to trust life instead of constantly trying to manage it?*

You might slow down, simplify, choose differently. Not because you've given up on wealth, but because you're redefining what wealth is. Instead of needing to buy new things, you prefer the freedom that comes from letting go. You discover that wealth isn't what you accumulate, but what you no longer need.

You find your footing in a new way of living—one that values alignment over output, presence over pressure, and enough over more. You stop trying to buy your freedom—and start learning how to feel it from within. That shift is the beginning of old soul wisdom.

OLD SOUL

As an old soul, you've already seen through the illusion that money buys happiness, that success guarantees fulfillment, or that owning more means being more. You know better—not just intellectually, but experientially. You've chased, acquired, and still felt empty. That's what woke you up.

Now you see money as energy—a neutral, flexible force that reflects your relationship with trust, service, and self-worth. You neither worship nor reject it. You work with it consciously. You recognize that abundance isn't about numbers in a bank account but about the openness of your heart. When you live in contraction, even wealth feels scarce. When you live in trust, even modest means feel abundant.

Financial pressure no longer terrifies you. It reminds you that even spiritual beings must meet life with practical integrity. You feel the tension between worldly demands and soul truth, but you meet that tension the same way you meet every moment—with sheer presence.

Debt, too, becomes a teacher. You feel its energetic weight, not as shame, but as a sign that something is out of balance. You simplify, recalibrate, and move forward with grace. You've stopped trying to avoid the lesson and started listening to it.

Ownership no longer seduces you. You don't cling to things, titles, or image. If they come to you as part of creation, great. But you understand that you don't truly own anything—not even your body. Everything is borrowed. Everything is temporary. And that knowing frees you from the illusion of permanence. Rather than hoarding, you know that money flows to where it can serve.

You may still enjoy beauty, comfort, and luxury—but they no longer define you. You could let it all go tomorrow and still feel whole. You travel light, energetically and spiritually. You use money not to look rich or feel superior, but to support healing, creativity, generosity, and truth. Wealth, for you, is no longer measured in possessions but in the depth of your peace, the clarity of your choices, and the freedom of your soul.

Ultimately, you're not here to own more. You're here to transcend the physical dimension by dissolving your attachments to lack, fear, control, and limiting beliefs. You don't free yourself by expanding and consolidating your material footprint, but by becoming more aware of what serves your higher calling. In that state, there is only infinite abundance.

Prompts

1) Where in your life is the pursuit of money dominating your choices, and where is it supporting your truth?

2) How do you define "enough" financially, emotionally, and spiritually? Where are you still chasing more, and what do you hope it will give you?

3) What emotions arise when you feel financial pressure? What old stories might those feelings be tied to?

4) How do you react to debt? With shame, denial, or awareness? What is it here to teach you?

5) In what ways have you tried to prove your worth through money, status, or possessions?

6) What would change if you no longer needed to own something to feel secure or complete?

7) What would it feel like to truly trust that life is supporting you, even when money feels tight?

8) What role does being of service play in your current definition of wealth?

Chapter II

Scarcity

Young Soul

As a young soul, scarcity is one of the earliest illusions you encounter in the physical world. Everywhere you look, you see lack: not enough time, not enough love, not enough money. You're faced with competition, hierarchy, and limitation, leading you to believe that for one person to win, others must lose. Unless you fight for your piece of the pie, you'll wind up empty-handed.

This belief drives a frantic way of living. And not just materialistically speaking. Scarcity-consciousness creeps into all areas of your life. You start to cling to more attention, more security, more validation. You overwork, overthink, overcommit. The fear of missing out drives your choices. Simple rest feels unsafe. Because if you slow down, someone else might take what you've worked for. And if you let go, everything might fall apart. Your body runs on adrenaline, your mind runs in circles, and your spirit runs on empty. Exhaustion becomes your baseline, but you call it normal.

Scarcity becomes your mental framework. You approach relationships from need, not from completeness. You chase success from fear, not from joy. You expect struggle, so you get it. The world mirrors your belief that there isn't enough—and that you aren't enough either. Even when you get what you want, you're too anxious to enjoy it because you fear losing it.

Whether you gain, succeed, or receive, instead of peace a new fear arises: what if it disappears? Satisfaction gets postponed again, pushed into the future, always one step out of reach. Life becomes a constant bargaining game—you promise yourself you'll relax once you hit the next goal, but peace never arrives.

Eventually, you realize no amount of money, control, or accumulation can create the safety you long for. Every outcome just leads to more striving. Only in grief, illness, or burnout do you pause and turn to look inward. *What if scarcity is just a belief I inherited? What if life isn't withholding, but it's me holding myself back?*

You begin to imagine a different way—the way of an old soul.

OLD SOUL

As an old soul, you've experienced scarcity in many forms—financial, emotional, relational. You've known the anguish of believing you're not enough as you are. But over time, you've realized that scarcity is just that—a belief.

You begin addressing it in the body as much as the mind: slowing your breath, observing sensations, noticing that when the nervous system is at ease, there's a felt sense of "enough." From that groundedness, the old story of lack loses its authority. You learn that abundance isn't a number—it's a nervous system at rest, a heart that trusts, a soul that's connected to Source.

Since then, you've stopped measuring your worth by what you have. You no longer chase love, approval, or success to feel valid. You understand now that "not enough" is not healed by having more—it's healed by no longer giving thoughts of lack your attention. After all, that which you give your attention to, you become.

So, you've begun to live in rhythm with life, accepting that abundance has seasons and that stillness is the most potent place of co-creation. You trust the winter as much as the harvest, knowing both serve your unfolding. You don't panic during dry spells, because you've lived enough cycles to see the harvest always returns.

As such, you give without fear of depletion, receive without guilt, and let go without a sense of loss. You don't need to cling to things to feel safe. You no longer view possessions as extensions of identity. You stop counting what's missing and start noticing what's here. You live in sync with resources, with love, with time. Abundance is not what stays, but what flows.

Prompts

1) Where in your life does scarcity show up? In time, money, attention, love? How does it affect you?

2) What early experiences made you feel like there wasn't enough safety, approval, affection, or support?

3) How do you act when you're afraid of not having enough? Do you grasp, hoard, compete, or fall apart?

4) When you rest or slow down, do you feel guilty? Why?

5) Can you think of a time when life supported you in an unexpected way? What did that teach you?

6) What does "enough" feel like in your body? How can you return to that state when fear arises?

7) What new belief about abundance are you ready to embrace?

Chapter 12

Career Choice

Young Soul

When you don't know yourself, you look outward for direction. You listen to what others think you should do. You chase outcomes, believing they'll make you happy later. You choose paths that promise security or recognition, assuming those things will lead to fulfillment. You plan out your whole life as if you can control what will matter to you in the future.

You may pursue a career because your family insists on it. Because it looks good. Because it pays well. Even if it doesn't inspire you, you keep moving forward—learning skills, proving yourself, fitting into expectations. You build a reputation, form a routine, and become financially dependent on it. And by the time you realize it doesn't quite fit, that there might be other things you prefer doing, the hole feels too deep to climb out of. It's still possible, of course. But life gets complicated quickly when inner clarity is missing.

When you're disconnected from your inner truth, your choices become driven by fear, lack, and the illusion of control. You repeat unconscious patterns. You stay in roles that don't light you up. Your body feels heavy, mornings feel like battles, and the joy you once imagined never arrives. Self-worth becomes tangled with job titles, paychecks, and approval. You wonder why you feel trapped—but that's what happens when every step is based on avoiding discomfort, not following joy.

Eventually, frustration builds, and you hit a wall. The safe life begins to feel suffocating. The cost of "success" shows itself: anxiety, fatigue, emptiness. And still, every choice holds a lesson. Every detour helps you know yourself better—if you're willing to pause and reflect.

Awareness doesn't come overnight, of course. It takes time to unlearn what you've absorbed from others. But more and more, choosing a career becomes less about the position and more about the relationship you have with yourself. *Is this who I am? Is this who I'm meant to be?*

When these questions arise, give yourself permission to slow down, tune in, and choose again. Life is not linear. You're not behind. No paycheck can purchase peace if there's no resonance. The most important career move you'll ever make is choosing you.

OLD SOUL

As an old soul, you've learned to listen to your body, your intuition, and your energy. You spend less time on things that drain you, and more on what brings you to life. You no longer chase status or salary alone. You seek creative flow, soul fulfillment, and meaningful contribution. How you show up at work is an extension of how well you know yourself.

At this point, ignoring your inner voice is no longer an option. It's too loud and clear. You've become uncompromising in your alignment. You set boundaries, protect your peace, and trust divine timing. You no longer choose based on appearances or pressure. Instead, you decide based on what resonates. Not what makes sense, but what feels true. Not what serves you, but what serves something greater than yourself.

Leaving a job, should you choose to do so, no longer comes from reactivity or restlessness—it comes from a deep knowing that this chapter is complete. You honor what has been, bless it, and move on when the time calls for it. In fact, you look forward to creating space for something new to arrive. Transitions may still bring fear, but you recognize fear as a surface ripple, not a reason to ignore truth.

And when you feel stuck, you don't just blame your job—you turn inward. You examine how you've been showing up. You ask: *Am I present—or just focused on the outcome?* You understand that *what* you do is secondary. *How* you do it is primary. Every role becomes a mirror of your state of consciousness.

Even a simple job—sweeping floors, filing documents, answering calls—can become luminous when done with awareness. Work stops being about identity and becomes a field for practice. You stop looking for the job to give you meaning, and instead you infuse meaning into every job you hold.

You also stop trying to "find your purpose" as if it's hiding somewhere. You embody it in each moment. You bring your frequency into every interaction. You stop looking for the job to give you meaning—and become the person who creates meaning by how you show up.

Career Choice Chart

The job is where you spend a big chunk of your time. Make it count. The following chart illustrates how young souls vs old souls choose their careers.

Young Souls	**Old Souls**
Driven by external approval and expectations	Driven by inner alignment and resonance
Choose paths for security, prestige, or recognition	Choose paths for joy, flow, and contribution
Identity tied to job title, salary, or reputation	Identity rooted in presence, not position
Fear of failure or disappointing others guides choices	Intuition and truth guide choices
Stay in roles that drain spirit out of obligation	Leave roles when the soul feels complete
Career seen as linear ladder with fixed milestones	Career seen as fluid, evolving path
Success measured by comparison and external metrics	Success measured by authenticity and inner fulfillment
Fear-based compromises create resentment and stagnation	Boundaries protect peace and support vitality
Purpose seen as something to "find" in a job	Purpose embodied in every role through presence
Career defines self-worth	Self-worth defines career choices

© 2025 Cirak

Prompts

1) What originally motivated your current career path? Inspiration, pressure, fear, or default?

2) In what ways has your work supported your growth? In what ways has it dulled your spirit?

3) If you knew for sure you wouldn't fail, what line of work would you explore? Why?

4) What would change in your life if you stopped trying to make others proud or comfortable with your choices?

5) What qualities, environments, or communities bring out the best in you? Are they present in your work now?

6) What false definitions of "success" are you ready to let go of?

7) If your career were a spiritual practice, what lesson is it currently asking you to learn?

Chapter 13

Job Search

Young Soul

Job searching is one of the most stressful experiences in a young soul's life. You send out dozens of applications, only to have them vanish into a black hole. Every silence feels like rejection. Every generic response email deepens the sense that no one wants you. Your confidence begins to erode. You start to imagine the worst—that you'll never get hired, never be valued, never find stability again.

The longer it drags on, the more worthless you feel. You start to dread opening your inbox. You become stuck between anxiety and paralysis. Waiting becomes its own kind of suffering. And because your identity is so tied to productivity and employment, being "in between" jobs can feel like an endless void. Days blur together, nights full of restlessness, and the absence of structure feels like an indictment. You forget that you are more than your resume.

Ironically, during this time when you're not working and have extra time to rest, you may spend more time worrying instead of healing. Instead of enjoying the expanded freedom you have, you stress about how soon you can jump back on the hamster wheel. You don't use the space to nurture neglected parts of yourself—you use it to judge yourself even more. You forget that life is still happening, still unfolding, even when your career isn't.

Instead of treating this period as a golden opportunity to reflect, create space, and expand your self-knowing, you treat it like a penalty box. You try to "earn" your way out of limbo by working harder at being chosen. But the harder you push from fear, the more drained and disoriented you feel.

You start believing your value lies in being picked, forgetting that no application or interview can define your essence. Rejection feels personal. Time feels like it's running out. And everything starts to feel like it depends on getting that one offer—even if it's less than ideal.

With enough soul maturity, you begin to wonder: *What if this isn't punishment? What if this gap is actually a gift?* That shift in perception marks the beginning of old soul wisdom. That's when having a job doesn't define your value. It's what you do with the pause that does.

Old Soul

As an old soul, you understand that a job is not just about being chosen—it's about choosing where your energy belongs. You're not simply seeking employment. You're seeking a place that supports alignment. You know the difference between settling and resonating. And you won't trade your peace for a paycheck.

That changes everything. Job searching becomes all about discernment. You use the space between roles to reflect, recalibrate, and reconnect. You let your higher self reassert itself. You notice what energizes you and what depletes you. You revisit dreams you put off during your last role. You don't rush the process—you let it unfold. Waiting itself becomes a practice of trust, a lived reminder that your worth is not on pause.

You remember that not every opportunity is a match—even if it pays well or sounds impressive. You no longer chase titles or safety. Your next role should reflect who you've become—not just who you used to be.

You approach your search as a spiritual practice. You research not just companies, but founders. Not just roles, but values. You notice how leaders speak, how teams communicate, and whether integrity is woven into the culture. You trust your gut—not just the job description. You know that you are interviewing them as much as they are interviewing you, because the exchange of energy will shape your days and your spirit.

And when it comes time to interview, you're grounded. You're not there to impress—you're there to explore resonance. You no longer see rejection as failure. You see it as divine redirection. You know there are endless doors in life. You bless the ones that fall away and walk through the open doors with grace.

Most of all, you trust that the right opportunity will feel mutual. It won't require you to shrink, hustle, or betray yourself. It will invite you forward, speak to your soul, and meet you with respect. You recognize that the right role doesn't demand that you prove yourself—it reflects back the truth that you belong.

Prompts

1) Do you know yourself? The better you know yourself, the better your decisions. Nothing exemplifies this better than when choosing where to work next. If you are not clear to the best of your ability what you're good at, what inspires you, and where you see yourself going, you will not only waste your time on jobs that aren't a good fit, but

you will also rob yourself of finding the ones that fulfill your potential.

2) Are you selective? It's too easy to use online job boards to apply in bulk. A Young Soul thinks that all that matters is getting a job – any job. An Old Soul recognizes that you're playing with your life. You will spend most of your time at work, meeting people who could become friends or lovers, and most certainly turn into leads for the next job. Finding an organization that aligns with your values is imperative. That includes considering the size, market positioning, and product vision. Look at how much care they put into promoting that vision on their website, in their brand, press releases, and interviews with company leadership. Company values typically trickle down from their founder(s). So make sure you really resonate with their mission.

3) Have you done your research? Job descriptions often lack details about company culture. Contact current or former employees, check online forums, social posts, and profiles of the people you would be working with. Even if your skills are a match, if you don't enjoy the atmosphere, work style, or attitude towards personal growth, you might take a job and, 6 months later, hate your life. Then you're in the pickle of do you stay miserable or do you quit, deal with the politics, mark on your record, and start your search all over. Each time you quit, it takes a toll

psychologically. So, do your research upfront. Life gets complicated if you don't act with clear intent.

4) Are you growth-minded? Only apply for jobs that leave enough room for growth. You need to fulfill your current role, but you also need a sense of expansion. If you get too pigeonholed, your horizon shrinks, and limiting beliefs take hold. During the interview, and even outside of it, ask about growth opportunities. Remember, you're interviewing them as much as they are interviewing you.

5) Do you know your worth? Have you ever sold yourself short? If you don't feel like the company honors your time at a rate that is fair in the industry, resentment will grow. Also, it's not just about cash. Get creative in the ways you work out a package everyone can feel good about.

6) How do you typically feel during job searches? Empowered, anxious, hopeful, disoriented? What's underneath those feelings?

7) What messages about work, value, or success did you absorb growing up? Are those messages still running your choices?

8) Have you ever taken a job out of fear rather than alignment? What did you learn from that experience?

9) Where are you still trying to prove your worth through your job title, salary, or resume?

Chapter 14

High Achiever

Young Soul

As a young soul, being seen as a high achiever feels like a strength. You're praised for your drive, admired for your discipline, and rewarded for your results. Achievement becomes not just what you do, but who you are. It gives you structure, identity, and a persona to inhabit. You don't realize that underneath it all, you're being driven by an unconscious fear—fear of falling behind, being ordinary, or feeling unseen.

Your self-worth becomes tethered to achievement. You feel valuable when you're being productive, successful, or validated—and useless when you take a break. Slowing down makes you anxious. The moment one goal is met, another replaces it. You're always building something: a career, a reputation, a future version of yourself that will finally be enough. And yet, something feels off. You feel numb, disconnected, or resentful. There's often a physical toll—sleep and exercise get neglected, fatigue and depression keep surfacing. But you brush it all aside. Rest feels dangerous. Questioning the status quo feels like weakness. So you double down and push harder.

Even in your quieter moments, the achiever's voice doesn't let you rest. It whispers that you should be doing more, that others are ahead, that your value is slipping if you're not producing. Joy starts to feel conditional—granted only after the next milestone. But milestones move like the horizon: always just out of reach. Deep down, you sense the emptiness beneath the chase, though you may not admit it yet. What looks like ambition on the outside is often a restless anxiety within—an inability to simply be.

Eventually, you realize you're not just physically tired—you're spiritually drained. The rewards no longer satisfy. The applause feels distant. The endless striving feels, well, endless. You begin to see that what you're really seeking isn't success—it's peace. It's ease. It's flow. But flow doesn't come from trying to make things happen. It comes from letting things happen.

This realization doesn't make you less capable or accountable—it makes you wiser and more consistent. The turning point comes when you stop equating effort with value and begin listening to what feels right. You stop trying to win the race and start questioning whether the race was ever yours to begin with. That's the beginning of the transition to becoming an old soul.

Old Soul

You've worn the high achiever hat before—in this life and likely many that came before. You know how to work hard, exceed expectations, and lead. But now, your relationship with achievement has changed. You're no longer motivated by pressure, but by presence. You're no longer trying to prove yourself—you want to feel yourself. Alignment and authenticity matter more than outcome, because you know the best results come when you're relaxed, intuitive, and connected to the moment—not grasping for control or approval.

As an old soul, you meet challenges head-on. But you stay heart-based, not mind-bound. You show up with discipline, but without rigidity. You've stopped chasing fixed ideas and started listening for right timing. You're no longer obsessed with productivity. You care more about aliveness. When something feels forced, you pause and reflect. When it flows, you ride the wave.

You still have high standards—even higher, in fact, now that you see and think clearly. But the emphasis has shifted from outcome to process. From reward to fulfillment. From self-critical to self-assured. From high achiever to aligned creator. You're no longer trying to manufacture momentum. You let it grow naturally by getting out of your own way. You rest when your body asks, and say no when something doesn't resonate. You let success happen through you, not because of you. And when old achiever patterns resurface, you meet them with awareness. You choose not to abandon yourself again.

You still create, lead, and contribute, but without the compulsion to prove anything. Your work is no longer a negotiation for worth; it's a natural overflow of who you are. This shift brings a paradox: when you no longer cling to achievement, you often achieve more—because your actions are rooted in clarity, joy, and service. You're less interested in how high you climb, and more in how deeply you're aligned. For you, the true "high achievement" is living in sync with your soul.

Being a high achiever wasn't wrong. But being identified with it was limiting. Now you achieve from feeling complete. From your co-creative connection to Source. And that's your greatest accomplishment of all.

High Achiever Chart

It's easy to lose yourself in the doing, no matter what stage of your journey you're at. But how you go about it makes all the difference. The following chart illustrates how young souls vs old souls experience high achievement.

Young Souls	Old Souls
Driven by fear of failure or insignificance	Driven by love, clarity, and alignment
Seeks external validation and recognition	Moves from inner calling and self-respect
Measures worth by results and status	Measures success by integrity and flow
Pushes through exhaustion and resistance	Honors timing, energy, and cycles
Controls every outcome to feel safe	Surrenders to process while acting with precision
Needs goals to feel purposeful	Is purposeful with or without goals
Identifies with success and achievement	Is rooted in presence, not identity
Burns out chasing endless milestones	Stays resourced by working from stillness
Avoids vulnerability and imperfection	Leads with humility and authenticity
Fears slowing down—confuses it with failure	Knows slowing down often leads to mastery

© 2025 Cirak

Prompts

1) What messages did you receive growing up about success, productivity, or achievement? How have they shaped your identity?

2) How do you feel when you're not actively pursuing anything? What emotions arise in the absence of productivity?

3) Are your current goals truly aligned with who you are now?

4) What deeper need or unhealed wound might be hiding beneath your ambition?

5) When do you feel most at peace—and does that version have a place in daily life?

6) What would your life look like if your self-worth wasn't connected to what you produced?

7) What fears arise when you consider resting more, simplifying, or saying no to overcommitment?

8) What small changes could help you move from pressure to presence in your work this week?

9) What would it mean to redefine success as alignment, not accomplishment?

CHAPTER 15

THE IMPOSTER

YOUNG SOUL

Imposter syndrome is the experience of feeling like a fraud—even when you're capable, qualified, and successful. You think you're not as talented or worthy as others believe and fear one day they'll find you out. As a young soul, you are especially prone to this experience because your sense of identity is still externally defined. Your confidence is tied to credentials, titles, seniority, social approval, and the illusion that there's a "right" way to do things.

This insecurity often comes to the surface when you step into a new level of responsibility. Suddenly, you feel like you're making things up—and in truth, you are. But that's not failure. That's the nature of co-creation. You just haven't yet learned to trust your presence, spontaneity, and intuition.

At this stage, the unknown feels threatening. Repeating what is already established feels much safer. You haven't cultivated deep inner guidance, so the idea of being seen in real time—before you feel ready and polished—is terrifying. You try to mask the fear with preparation, control, or office politics, not realizing that these strategies only amplify the self-doubt. The more you chase flawless delivery, the more fraudulent you feel.

Comparison only magnifies the pressure. You measure yourself against peers, mentors, or imagined ideals, assuming they know what they're doing while you're just faking it. But what you're comparing is your private uncertainty to their curated outer image. Of course you always come up short.

The truth is, everyone is improvising. There is no perfect script. The sooner you release the imaginary standard, the sooner you begin to work with what is real—your actual insight, your lived experience, your presence in the moment. Imposter syndrome is not proof that you are inadequate. It is proof that you've been living from pretense instead of authenticity.

In that sense, the imposter is not your enemy but your teacher. It shows you the exhaustion of control and the futility of pretending. It calls you to show up without needing to "know," to discover that your worth isn't in performance but in presence. And by taking that leap, what you once feared becomes the thing that sets you free.

Old Soul

As an old soul, you've learned to welcome the unknown. You no longer expect life to unfold according to a plan, because you know any plan is too small for the mystery. You trust that a Source-led life takes care of everything. Whatever the situation, when you are rooted in awareness, the right words, ideas, and actions will arise.

You've also outgrown the assumption that anyone fully knows what they're doing. Most people are simply repeating what worked before, improvising from habit, or clinging to borrowed experience. You know that while experience can guide, it cannot come up with something new. The mind recycles. Presence creates.

Because of this, you no longer waste energy rehearsing, anticipating, or worrying about how you appear. You show up and respond to what's there. You allow mystery to inspire you. You live attuned to what life is asking right now, which makes your expression alive, fluid, and magnetic. Confidence no longer comes from proving yourself, but from serving the moment.

And when old insecurities do surface, you no longer take them personally. You see that the voice of doubt belongs to the false self, not to who you are. The one who is unsure is not the one who is aware.

Your relationship to the imposter has transformed. You no longer fight it, hide it, or scramble to correct it. You see through it. You know there was never a fraud to begin with—only the mistaken belief that you had to *be someone* instead of simply being. And in that recognition, the imposter dissolves, leaving only authenticity, clarity, and the freedom to express without pretense.

Prompts

1) What messages did you receive growing up that made you question your worth or competence?

2) How comfortable are you with the unknown? Co-creating with life requires comfort with mystery.

3) What would it look like to trust your intuition instead of trying to prove your knowledge?

4) In what areas of your life are you still pretending? What are you afraid would happen if you stopped?

5) What does real confidence feel like in your body? How is that different from pretending?

6) What's one small way this week you can begin to show up more authentically—even if you feel unready?

Chapter 16

Toxic Workplace

Young Soul

You haven't yet developed enough self-awareness to notice the conditioned behaviors that shape your decisions—especially fear, lack, and control. These unconscious patterns drive your actions, and when placed in the collective dynamics of a workplace, the result is often tension, competition, and conflict. Wherever many people gather to collaborate, the energetic incongruities get amplified. If you bring reactivity, resistance, and unresolved wounds, the environment will mirror them back to you with uncanny precision.

Instead of pausing to reflect, you judge. Instead of listening, you react. You see yourself as right and others as wrong, and this rigid stance fuels the power struggles that slowly erode the team's well-being and your own. The more you defend or assert, the more others push back. The workplace grows combative, emotionally unsafe, and energetically chaotic. Yet you don't realize you're part of the equation—that your own inner fragmentation contributes to the outer dysfunction.

Once a workplace tips into toxicity, it rarely heals from within. The dysfunction hardens. Trust disappears. Leaders rotate in and out. Passive aggression replaces honest dialogue. And yet you may stay—lured by promotions, guilt, comfort, or fear. You tell yourself it's temporary. You tolerate the red flags. You numb yourself with drinking, scrolling, binge-watching—anything to escape what your soul already knows: this is not where you belong.

If you ignore the signs, your body will intervene. Burnout, migraines, digestive issues, and anxiety flare up. You dread Sundays and fantasize about quitting. And as so often happens, a crisis becomes the only way a young soul finds the courage to leave.

Even then, you may tell yourself it's failure. But it isn't. It's an invitation. Your soul is learning to honor its boundaries, to value peace over appearances. In time, these painful lessons ripen into personal growth. You learn to pick up on red flags sooner, to say no faster, and to stop trying to fix what doesn't want to be healed. That shift—choosing self-respect over self-denial—is the doorway into old soul wisdom.

OLD SOUL

You're familiar with toxic workplaces—in fact, they're some of the most potent accelerators of self-awareness. They help you draw the line between collective demands and your own needs. They teach you the difference between healthy pressure and chronic stress. They show you what you want by clarifying what you don't.

You recognize the signs before they escalate: closed-door meetings, hollow pep talks, the creeping exhaustion that spreads through the team. But instead of spiraling into blame or taking sides, you pause and ask a deeper question: *What is life showing me here?*

As an old soul, you've cultivated the awareness to move through complex spaces with composure. You see that people are always projecting their inner wounds. You notice how fear moves through systems, how emergencies get institutionalized, how drama feeds itself when no one interrupts the cycle. Your steadiness becomes a stabilizing presence, even when others are unraveling.

But you also know the limits of endurance. Holding space for lower frequencies takes energy. Wisdom includes discernment. You may try to bring light for a time—offering clarity, embodying calm—but when truth is punished and dysfunction is rewarded, you don't cling. You step back. You no longer sacrifice your peace to maintain appearances. You understand that not every environment is meant for you.

Before you exit, you still reflect. *What in me tolerated this? What did I come here to learn?* You don't leave to escape—you leave to grow. Every difficult workplace becomes a training ground for clarity, sovereignty, and self-trust.

What once felt like punishment now reveals itself as curriculum. No environment is wasted if it brings you closer to your own alignment. And with each lesson, you become less afraid of leaving and more devoted to honoring where your soul truly belongs.

And over time, you come to see that even the most toxic spaces had their place in your path. They sharpened your discernment, deepened your compassion, and strengthened your capacity to stand in truth.

What once drained you now equips you to recognize resonance instantly—and to walk with confidence toward the environments, people, and callings that match the frequency of your soul.

Toxic Workplace Chart

When there's disharmony at your company, it can affect people in different ways. The following chart illustrates how young souls vs old souls deal with toxic workplaces.

Young Souls	Old Souls
Workplace tension feels personal and threatening	Workplace tension seen as projection of others' wounds
Reacting, judging, defending, escalating conflict	Pausing, observing, discerning, staying grounded
Staying in dysfunction out of fear, comfort, or guilt	Leaving when misaligned, honoring boundaries and truth
Culture feels fixed, unchangeable, and suffocating	Culture viewed as energy flow—shifting or resisted
Burnout, anxiety, and physical symptoms ignored	Body's signals honored as guidance to change
Passive aggression and politics normalized	Direct communication and inner clarity prioritized
Focus on proving worth or gaining promotion	Focus on preserving peace and energetic integrity
Trying to fix what doesn't want to heal	Offering presence, then stepping back when change is resisted
Blaming environment as punishment	Recognizing environment as curriculum and mirror
Crisis as collapse and failure	Crisis as initiation into sovereignty and self-trust

© 2025 Cirak

Prompts

1) Have you ever stayed in a toxic workplace longer than your body or intuition wanted you to? What kept you there?

2) What physical or emotional symptoms do you experience when you're in an unhealthy work environment?

3) Do you feel responsible for fixing dysfunctional environments, even when it's not your role? Why?

4) What energetic cues or red flags do you tend to ignore when a workplace is no longer aligned?

5) What belief systems (about success, loyalty, or endurance) make it harder for you to walk away?

6) How do you typically cope with workplace stress—and are those coping mechanisms helping or harming you?

7) What would it look like to make decisions based on inner peace instead of outer rewards?

8) In what ways has your definition of a "healthy workplace" changed over time?

9) What is your soul asking you to prioritize in your next work environment—and are you listening?

Chapter 17

Work and Life

Young Soul

As a young soul, "work-life balance" sounds like something you're supposed to want, but not something you genuinely embrace. You're still defining your worth through what you produce, still chasing success as the ultimate measure, and still learning how to listen to your body. The next promotion calls louder than your nervous system. The drive to prove yourself overrides the need for self-care. As long as your body holds up, rest feels indulgent while overwork feels noble.

You've likely been taught—implicitly or explicitly—that hustle is a virtue. That sacrifice now will earn you freedom later. But the promise of "later" keeps moving, and it always arrives blurred. Your lifestyle gets scrambled, your mind scattered, but still you keep pushing. You say yes even when you're empty, and you wear your exhaustion like a badge of honor. Rarely do you pause to ask: *Is this even the life I want?*

The longer you stay on that track, the more you fear that if you stopped long enough to feel your truth, you might have to change. When questions arise about the system, you assume the problem must be you. If you're tired, you think you need to be stronger. If you're behind, you think you need to go faster. Your calendar is full, but your spirit runs on fumes. You cling to vacations, weekends, or retirement as your escape hatches—yet even then, guilt often overshadows your rest.

Even when your body cries out, you override it. Caffeine when you can't focus. Pills when you can't sleep. You keep suppressing symptoms instead of listening to them. For most young souls, it takes a major crash to spark the deeper inquiry: *What is all this really for? When did I lose my peace? How did I get so far from joy?*

The answers don't arrive in a single flash. But the very act of asking means something in you has shifted. A quieter, old soul wisdom is awakening—the part of you that no longer wants to sacrifice life in the name of work, but longs for a truer balance within.

Old Soul

As an old soul, you've lived through the imbalance before. You know what it's like to serve a culture that worships productivity while your spirit longs for rest. You've learned—sometimes painfully—that your energy is not endless. If you misplace it, life begins to reflect your disconnection back at you.

You no longer confuse busyness with purpose. You've seen through the myth that more is better. You let your body's rhythm guide you. You consult your inner compass before you say yes. You honor the seasons within—not just the deadlines outside. You've stopped trying to force balance and started tuning into it. Sometimes it calls you into creating. Sometimes it calls you into stillness. Always it calls you into alignment.

And yes, imbalance still happens. In times of expansion, ambition can take over and you drift into old habits of striving. In times of retreat, you may lose track of practicalities. But you no longer panic. You allow each season to express itself, trusting that life rebalances when you stop resisting—and when you cultivate regular practices to restore presence and clear energy before you fray.

You've come to see that true productivity arises only from presence—and presence cannot be faked. To be aligned is to be effective. To be scattered is to waste energy, no matter how much effort you pour in.

Ultimately, you understand that your real work is awareness itself. Everything else—career, family, money, health—is simply the classroom. Whether you're resting or creating, teaching or parenting, it's all happening within the same field of consciousness. As long as you keep tuning into that field, life organizes itself into balance. And what once felt like a battle between "work" and "life" becomes the single movement of being.

Prompts

1) What beliefs do you subscribe to about work, rest, and play? How do those beliefs play out in your life?

2) What parts of your balance have you been sacrificing for the sake of "success"? What has it cost you?

3) What does rest look like for you—and do you actually let yourself feel it?

4) Where do you keep overriding your rest in favor of saying yes to more work?

5) When was the last time you were truly rested and how did that affect your happiness and output?

6) What small change could you make this week to support both your work and your well-being?

Chapter 18
Burnout

Young Soul

In most work environments, effort is rewarded with money, promotions, and praise. Naturally, you internalize this system. You begin chasing outcomes, imagining there's a finish line that, once crossed, will finally deliver the peace you're looking for. But that finish line never comes.

You blame yourself. You become absorbed in trying to control the path—planning every detail, mapping every step, rehearsing every move. You believe sheer effort guarantees results. You overthink, over-plan, and override your intuition. You push past your body's signals. You dismiss fatigue, frustration, and anxiety as obstacles to conquer. You take pride in sending company emails at midnight. Stress feels like the necessary tax of success.

But each time your form dips, recovery takes longer. The drive to get up and face the grind each day fades. You're no longer fueled by inspiration, but by fear—fear of falling behind, being seen as weak, or losing control. You ignore the symptoms of burnout until they bring you to a standstill. Exhaustion, irritability, emptiness. When it hits, it hits hard—derailing your health, your work, and your sense of self.

Burnout doesn't just slow you down physically. It halts your creativity, clarity, and severs your desire for living. You can't co-create from depletion; you can't feel joy when your system is in survival mode. It becomes an uncompromising teacher: your mental-physical well-being is not optional.

If you're attentive, you learn. You start to notice the early signals—your fading focus, your shallow breath, your reluctance to face the day. You realize burnout was never punishment; it was your mind and body begging you to listen, asking you to value rest, simplicity, and balance as much as results. This is where the shift begins—the moment you promise yourself not to abandon your body and spirit again.

Old Soul

You've known the sharp edge of burnout before—and the long, heavy recovery that follows. Now, you no longer gamble with it. The moment you notice the early signs—tension in your jaw, dread creeping into the mornings, a dip in your natural creativity—you pause. You listen. You adjust. Nothing is worth the cost of your peace, your health, or your connection to Source.

You've abandoned the belief that stress is proof of importance. You no longer chase validation through over-commitment. Your body has become your compass. When it says rest, you honor it immediately. You know that sustainability is not laziness, but wisdom. It is what allows you to serve more fully, to create with more flow, and to meet life from presence rather than depletion.

Of course, old habits may return—perfectionism, people-pleasing, subtle fears of not being enough. But now you meet them with awareness. You stay vigilant, observing your sensations, anchored in self-trust. Rest and work have become partners in your rhythm. Renewal is not a luxury—it's part of your devotion to life.

Your spiritual practices help keep you aligned. Meditation, breathwork, stillness—all serve as touchstones to return you to center. And when you slip, you don't judge yourself. You notice, accept, and re-align.

Life no longer feels like a series of frantic sprints. It has become a steady unfolding. You work when inspiration calls. You rest when stillness arises. You've discovered that true productivity is not born of pressure, but of peace.

And peace can only be felt when you are here, now, allowing life to move through you.

PROMPTS

1) Have you ever experienced burnout? What toll did it take—physically, mentally, spiritually?

2) What beliefs were you carrying that led you to override your needs? Where did those beliefs come from?

3) What signals does your body give you when you're approaching burnout? How can you better respond?

4) Where in your life are you still pushing through exhaustion instead of honoring your limits?

5) If you're burned out now, what would it look like to create a safe space of full rest around you?

6) What fears come up when you slow down? What do you think you'll lose? What might you gain?

7) What practices help you stay grounded in your body and attuned to your needs?

8) What one promise can you make to yourself today to prevent burnout from returning?

Chapter 19

Job Loss

Young Soul

When you lose your job, your first instinct is often to scramble, update the resume, scroll job boards, send out bulk applications. The urge to fix the situation immediately is overwhelming. It isn't just about money—it's about identity, routine, and self-worth. Without work, you feel like you've lost your anchor.

This reaction makes sense. You've been conditioned to believe that productivity equals value, that gaps on a resume are shameful, and that unemployment equals failure. So you chase the next opportunity quickly—not because it inspires you, but because the silence feels unbearable. Much of your self-esteem still hinges on how others perceive you, and without a title or role, you fear being judged as irrelevant.

If you look closely, though, you'll see what lies beneath the panic: grief, self-doubt, disorientation. These emotions rarely get permission in main street culture. Instead of pausing to feel them, you rush to cover them with action. Rather than using the break to sit in stillness, you do everything possible to jump back onto the treadmill.

Of course, survival matters. If you're truly living paycheck to paycheck, securing income is necessary. But if there's even a little breathing room, you don't need to rush. You can let this gap become a sacred pause rather than a penalty. A chance to grieve what has ended, to recalibrate your direction, to remember who you are beyond titles and tasks.

Losing your job doesn't mean you're fallen behind. It means a chance to catch up with yourself. Sometimes life clears a path so you can see what you've been too busy to notice. What feels like disruption is often the very doorway into expansion.

Old Soul

When you lose your job, you no longer confuse it with losing yourself. Your identity has loosened from titles and positions. You recognize the gift of space that others might fear. You welcome the pause, the reset, the rare opening where obligations fall away and the inner life can expand.

Even if practical adjustments are required—downsizing, budgeting, simplifying—you trust your capacity to adapt. You've learned that fewer possessions bring more freedom, and that time is worth more than money. Instead of grasping at the next role, you let life reorient you.

You use this space to reflect on where you've been, what you've outgrown, and what wants to emerge. You resist the urge to fill the gap too quickly. You stay in the unknown long enough for a deeper clarity to arise. You know that transition itself is part of the teaching, shaping you as much as any new opportunity will.

Not everyone understands. Some may see your stillness as laziness or your trust in mystery as recklessness. But you no longer measure your life by their lenses. Their discomfort only shows them what they have yet to face. You remain steady, honoring the gift that has been placed before you.

As an old soul, you see job loss not as disruption but as divine intervention. What looks like an end to others, you recognize as a doorway into greater freedom, deeper authenticity, and a path that only reveals itself once the old has been cleared away.

PROMPTS

1) What emotions came up when you first lost your job? Are you still carrying them? Where do you feel that energy in your body?

2) What part of your identity was tied to this job or title? Who are you without it?

3) What did you love about this job—and what parts didn't fit?

4) What beliefs about success, productivity, or stability are surfacing now? Are they true?

5) What lessons or patterns are being revealed through this job loss?

6) If fear wasn't in the way, what kind of work would feel expansive, meaningful, or joyful?

7) Who in your environment triggers guilt about taking space? Can you hold compassion for that?

8) What are you ready to release—and what are you now open to receiving?

Chapter 20

Retirement

Young Soul

Retirement can feel like both a reward and a shock. After decades of striving, achieving, and saving, you may have pictured this chapter as one of ease—but when it finally arrives, unexpected emotions surface. Without the daily rhythm of work, you wonder: *What is my purpose now? Who am I without my job?*

The freedom feels exciting, yet strangely disorienting. The structure that once gave shape to your days is gone. That openness can feel both exhilarating and unsettling. You might fill the space with travel, hobbies, or side projects—maybe even return to work when an old employer calls—anything to avoid sitting with yourself in stillness.

The same tendencies carry over into this new space. You compare yourself to others: how they're "succeeding" at retirement, how fulfilled they appear. You wrestle with guilt from inactivity, confusion from feeling useless, or pressure to prove you're still relevant. After all—you want this chapter to feel meaningful, too.

You may bounce around ideas, entertain half-hearted attempts at productivity, and keep busy for a while. But eventually you realize retirement isn't an end to meaning. Like all major pauses in life, it's an invitation to redefine yourself—or more precisely, to let go of old definitions. You begin to explore joy beyond achievement, passions that waited for time and space, fulfillment that isn't measured by output or constrained by deadlines.

Slowly, you understand that this chapter isn't about accomplishment at all. It's about stepping into your values more deeply than ever, with perspective and wisdom that weren't ready until now. And with that, you enter your unhurried becoming, learning that true meaning never came from being busy—but from simply being.

Old Soul

You see retirement not as an ending, but as a return—to your roots, your essence, your soul. You've given your energy generously to outer purposes for so long. Now life invites you inward. The spaciousness feels like a blessing, not a loss. Finally, there is time to wake up freely, listen deeply, reflect honestly, and move with intention.

RETIREMENT

You honor the journey—what you built, how you served, how you grew. Yet you don't cling to titles or achievements. They were roles your soul played for a time, and now something more authentic is calling. You don't always know what it is—and yes, at times that feels scary—but you trust the path that has brought you here has prepared you for what's next.

Moments of grief may arise—grief for routines ended, identities released, or dear ones who didn't make it this far. But you know grief is also only part of clearing space.

Looking back, you rest in the quiet knowing that you did your best. You've done enough. And still, life—like it always does—is asking you to let go of the past and keep leaning forward.

Retirement becomes a sacred space for your spiritual practice. An invitation to be fully present, to create from love alone, to share your wisdom without expectation. You may tend a garden, write a memoir, guide others quietly, or simply enjoy your breath. Whatever form it takes, you cultivate the peace and joy that arise from letting everything and everyone just be.

And in time, you realize: you were never just your work. You were always a soul in motion.

PROMPTS

1) How has your work shaped your identity—and how is that identity shifting now?

2) What emotions arise as you enter or imagine retirement? What part of yourself is asking to be rediscovered?

3) What passions or dreams have you postponed that now feel ready to emerge?

4) Where do you feel tension between rest and the need to stay productive?

5) What does fulfillment mean to you now—and how has that evolved?

6) How can you create a daily rhythm that nourishes your body, mind, and soul?

7) What new roles or expressions of service feel aligned in this chapter?

8) How can you release the need to prove your worth—and simply enjoy being?

9) If your higher self were guiding this next chapter, what would it gently invite you to trust?

FAMILY

Chapter 21
Birth

Young Soul

Everyone enters the physical dimension with an imprint of their spiritual origin. But as a young soul, you forget quickly. The spectacle of the material world seduces you—the infinite variety of sights, sounds, shapes, and stories pulls you into identification with form. It's exhilarating to inhabit a body that grows and changes, to sense the world through your eyes and ears, to believe this vast playground was made just for you. Under such thrilling circumstances, it's easy to disconnect from your true essence.

And so you do. Conditioning begins almost immediately. You take things at face value and believe whatever you're told—while assuming others think as you do. You absorb subtle messages about success, worth, conformity, and competition. Curiosity gives way to fear of failure. Passion gets replaced by ambition. Wonder is reduced to knowledge. Self-discovery takes a back seat to wanting to win.

Living from this surface reality without guidance from your higher self breeds frustration, confusion, discord, and overwhelm. You reach for things that numb and distract: food, screens, sex, substances, busyness. Anything to silence the growing disarray and emptiness.

But this amnesia is part of the curriculum. You have to lose yourself to find yourself. The blind patterns that arise from disconnection eventually lead you home. But as a young soul, you don't see it that way. When things fall apart, you assume you've failed. But in truth, they're falling into place. It may not be *your* plan, but it is *the* plan.

The sooner you accept that growth is inherently uncomfortable, the sooner your existence begins to make sense. You're not here to avoid—you're here to evolve. Each breakdown, each crack in the illusion, brings you closer to remembering who you are.

Old Soul

As an old soul, you forget at birth as well. The shock of finding yourself embodied stuns everyone, regardless of how evolved. But the big difference compared to your younger soul peers is that you find your way back more quickly. Even in childhood, a quiet awareness persists—that life is sacred, that something deeper is unfolding beneath the surface. You may not be able to name it, but you sense it.

While others are enthralled by the drama of the world, you notice the stillness beneath the noise. You question things early. You feel when something is off, even if you don't yet know why. Though you may get swept up in conditioning for a while, the veil doesn't stay thick. Something in you remembers.

That memory shapes your path. You don't stay on the beaten track for long—it doesn't feel true. You feel others' motives. You pick up on undercurrents. You're aware when something is pretense versus real. You begin to navigate by intuition rather than approval, and your life diverges from the collective norms. You're less afraid of the unknown—not because it isn't daunting, but because you trust the unfolding.

You've lived enough lifetimes to know that trying to control life only makes it feel more out of control. So you let go sooner. You return to presence faster. And when the unexpected arrives, you hold space for the blessing it may conceal. That's the gift of soul memory—it allows you to live lightly, yet deeply.

You understand now that every birth is a forgetting, and every lifetime an invitation to remember. The forgetting hurts most when you resist it. The remembering comes sooner when you surrender. You're no longer here to conquer the world—you're here to remember what's real, even as you walk through what isn't.

PROMPTS

1) How have formative experiences negatively shaped your self-image? Notice where you feel activation in your body. Can you stay present with those sensations until they soften or release? (Avoid traumatic memories that require deeper therapeutic support)

2) Can you recall formative experiences that contributed to a positive sense of self? How does this feel in your body? Can you stay with that sensation, too? Notice how your system responds to being fully met with positive emotion.

3) What are three core soul lessons you feel you came here to learn? How are these themes still playing out in your life?

4) If you've never explored past lives, ask yourself: Does it feel possible to learn all you need to in just one lifetime? Why or why not?

5) When you reflect on your patterns, do you tend to move through challenges quickly and with awareness, or do you get stuck in loops? Are there areas of life where you're more fluid and adaptive, and others where you're more rigid and entangled?

6) How easily do you get swept up in surface distractions? What helps you come back to your center?

7) In what ways do you still try to control life, and what happens when you try? What shifts when you let go?

8) Recall a time something didn't go to plan, but turned out to be a blessing. What did it teach you about surrender?

9) What sensory experiences make you feel most connected to your spiritual origin? Music, nature, silence, dreams, certain people? How can you bring more of that into daily life?

10) If you could whisper one message to yourself at birth, knowing everything you now know—what would it be?

CHAPTER 22

ADOLESCENCE

YOUNG SOUL

By the time you reach adolescence, the amnesia has taken over. You've long forgotten who you are and why you're here. The spiritual dimension feels like a dream, and the physical world takes center stage—dazzling, confusing, and intense. Your top priority is to establish belonging: socially, culturally, geographically. You crave safety in numbers, templates to live by, and a sense of control over the unfamiliar terrain of emotions. The easiest way to feel secure is to fit in.

And so you do. You submit to the norms of your group, the rules of your culture, and the "truths" of your upbringing. Your beliefs feel like absolute facts, and you avoid anything that threatens them. Questioning feels dangerous because you're still in the truth-building phase, not the truth-stripping one that comes later. Rather than explore what you actually believe, it's safer to absorb what others do and follow in placid agreement. Teenagers aren't wired for authenticity—they're wired for adaptation. Being different is not on the to-do list.

As a young soul, you carry the belief systems from these years well into adulthood, where they harden into identity and shape how you experience the world. At some level, you might know they aren't *you*. The longer you cling to one version of reality, the more you suffer when life inevitably refuses to follow your script. Still, in your teenage years, you're nowhere near ready to release them. There's comfort in narrowness. There's identity in ideology. There's even a sense of power in rebellion.

Whether you're a teen or an adult, as a young soul you rarely take growth into your own hands. You're mesmerized by distractions, driven by comparison, and tethered to others' opinions. The desire to belong outweighs the desire to know yourself. Your identity is built on external reflection, not internal resonance.

Only when life stops cooperating—when plans collapse, friends betray, or your carefully constructed sense of self crumbles—does the light of awareness begin to flicker. Confusion, loss, and disillusionment pry your grip from the steering wheel and nudge you toward your higher self. Cruel or not, that's how life works. You resist growth until you can't anymore. And that's okay. Each breakdown becomes part of your awakening. Suffering isn't punishment—it's evolution into an old soul.

Old Soul

As an old soul, adolescence shakes you, too. Hormones, identity, longing, and confusion sweep you into the storm. But you recover more quickly. The distractions of youth may tempt you, but they don't root deeply. Social approval doesn't hold your attention for long. You may stumble into self-doubt, rebellion, or escape, but you don't stay lost there. Something inside you already longs for depth.

Still, being an old soul in a young body has its own challenges. Your emotional intelligence outpaces your environment. You see through illusions your peers still worship. You question systems your elders uphold. You feel the dissonance of a world that doesn't match your frequency. Sometimes you feel like an outlier, even an alien, in your own family. You know you don't fit, but you don't yet know how to live that truth.

At the same time, your wisdom hasn't fully ripened into confidence. You don't yet have the life experience to fully trust your intuition, the courage to speak your truth without hesitation, or the independence to design your life freely. Your body is still changing. A part of you is still waiting for you to grow into yourself. This tension—seeing through what isn't real while still depending on it—can feel disorienting, frustrating, and lonely.

But you know you can't bypass the human experience. Your task is to honor your incarnation, not resist it. To live your curriculum, even when you already sense something beyond it. You accept the awkwardness, the longing, and the constraints of youth as training grounds for greater wisdom.

Being awake early in life is both a challenge and a gift. It opens access to higher frequencies of awareness and manifestation. You get to co-create not from fear or control, but from wonder, gratitude, and the simple joy of being alive. You learn to walk in two worlds at once—living your human life while listening to your soul, letting it guide you through the chaos.

Slowly, you learn to trust what you've known all along: the wisdom is already within you. Adolescence is simply the fire that tempers it.

ADOLESCENCE CHART

Your teenage years can have a big impact on how your adult life takes shape. Your soul age tends to make itself known and set the stage for things to come. The following chart illustrates how young souls vs old souls move through adolescence.

Young Souls	Old Souls
Conformity to group norms feels necessary for safety	Inner questioning arises despite social pressure
Beliefs absorbed from parents and peers as absolute	Beliefs examined and updated through intuition
Identity tied to fitting in and external approval	Identity begins forming around authenticity and awareness
Rebellion plays out as reaction, not true independence	Rebellion transforms into discernment and deeper alignment
Easily swept up in distractions and comparisons	Distractions lose their grip more quickly, presence restores balance
Fear of being different keeps expression suppressed	Acceptance of difference leads to trust in inner voice
Truth seen as fixed, one version for everyone	Truth sensed as layered, flexible, and personal
Growth resisted until suffering forces change	Growth embraced earlier through willingness to surrender

© 2025 Cirak

Prompts

1) What was adolescence like for you—misunderstood and isolated, or supported and seen? What beliefs about yourself were formed during this time? Which ones still shape your life today?

2) How did your social circle during your teen years influence your values and behavior? Reflect on your current circle—does it elevate you, drain you, or keep you in the same frequency?

3) What expectations do you carry about young people that stem from your own upbringing? Are they healthy? Are they outdated?

4) If you could go back and parent yourself as a teen, what would you do differently? What kind of support would you offer your younger self?

5) What parts of yourself did you hide or downplay in order to fit in? Are you still doing this in any area of your life today?

6) Recall a moment from your adolescence when your intuition was strong, but you ignored it. What did you learn from that?

7) What beliefs from adolescence are you ready to question, update, or release entirely?

CHAPTER 23

PARENTS

YOUNG SOUL

As a young soul, you expect your parents to be perfect. When things go wrong in your life, or when you feel insecure or inadequate, you are quick to blame them. You compare your upbringing to others, imagining how different things might have been if only you'd been born into another family. At times you may even feel indignant that they brought you into the world without your consent—a protest that carries its own cosmic irony.

This longing for perfect parents runs deep. If you grew up with a single parent or without biological parents in the picture, you might think that *any* parent would be better than none. The ache of absence can feel unbearable, and you idealize what was missing. But not all presences are nourishing. Sometimes the absence of a destructive parent is its own strange form of grace. Still, as a young soul, you cling to fantasies of what could have been, instead of learning to live with what is.

The mind loves hypotheticals. It imagines different childhoods, different parents, different outcomes. But no matter how vivid the story, it won't change reality. And reality—not fantasy—is the curriculum of your soul. Your task isn't to rewrite the past. It's to feel it, accept it, and grow from it. Making peace with imperfect or absent parents is one of your first and deepest lessons.

You may never receive the kind of love you hoped for from your parents. And that's the whole point. Your disappointments become your openings for growth. You begin to see that love flows not *from* things, but *through* all things—even imperfect vessels. Your parents—biological or adopted—are one conduit. And the very wound they leave behind is what forces you to dig deeper.

Ultimately, the greatest healing doesn't come from being loved flawlessly by others, but from establishing your own connection to the love that flows from within, the love of Source itself.

OLD SOUL

You no longer expect perfection from your parents. You understand that parenthood is one of the most demanding spiritual assignments on Earth. To raise a child is to devote vast amounts of energy to another soul's journey—often at the cost of your own. Parenting, of course, can awaken profound growth, but it also consumes the very time and space needed for inner work. Knowing this, you release the old judgments and see the complexity of the path your parents walked.

You've come to accept that your parents were never meant to complete you. They were the gateway for your entry into this world—your point of origin for this lifetime. Their limitations may have hurt, but they also launched you into the exact karmic trajectory you needed. That includes both the blessings and the challenges. Ultimately, everything has its place.

Even if their flaws are obvious, you've learned to love them exactly as they are. You've stopped demanding that they be different. You've stopped trying to edit the past. You hold your parents in reverence not for their perfection, but for their participation in your soul's unfolding. You recognize that across lifetimes, roles shift: parent becomes child, child becomes teacher. Everyone is learning, everyone is growing.

You also understand that your parents' journey isn't finished. Their soul is evolving just like yours, and your own healing can catalyze theirs. Many of the wounds you tend to in yourself are the unresolved patterns of your lineage. By doing the work, you're not just healing your own life—you're clearing the field for your entire family tree.

With this perspective, every interaction becomes sacred. When you meet your parents with kindness instead of blame, you uplift the space between you. The more you grow, the more permission you give others to grow—even those who raised you. You stop dividing the world into villains and victims. You stop replaying grievances. You release the belief that your happiness depends on others being a certain way. And in that release, you begin to taste the vastness of unconditional love—the kind that heals forward, backward, and beyond.

Prompts

1) What beliefs or emotions do you still carry about your parents? Where in your body do you feel these old imprints? Can you sit with those sensations without resistance?

2) Are there any grudges or unspoken resentments lingering in your family? What is the deeper need or wound beneath them? How would it feel to be the one who initiates healing—not by changing the past, but by releasing resistance to it?

3) Reflect on your fantasies or 'what if' stories about your parents. How often do you revisit these? What would happen if you gave up trying to rewrite the past and instead took insights from what actually happened?

4) In what ways have your parents' limitations shaped your strengths? Are there qualities you've developed because of—not in spite of—their flaws?

5) Consider how your parents were raised. What generational patterns or traumas might they have inherited? How does that change your understanding of their behavior?

6) What have you projected onto your parents that might not actually be true? Are there any stories you're ready to retire in order to meet them as they are?

7) How have your own judgments of your parents mirrored judgments you hold about yourself? What happens when you offer compassion to both?

8) In what ways have your parents tried to love you, even if imperfectly? Can you recognize the form their love took—even if it wasn't the form you wanted?

9) If you could speak to your parents soul-to-soul, without defense or blame, what would you say? What would you most want them to know—and what are you ready to release?

Chapter 24

Black Sheep

Young Soul

The younger your soul, the more being an outsider unsettles you. You want to belong—not just socially, but existentially. You prefer to stay within the swim lane that family, culture, or tradition assigned to you. Doing things the way they've always been done provides a deep sense of satisfaction and safety, and you assume that if something has lasted this long, it must be right. The idea of rocking the boat feels not just uncomfortable, but dangerous. Questioning the norm could unravel your whole reality. *Why would I want to do that?*

Even when you catch glimpses of your uniqueness, you suppress them quickly. It's safer to blend in than to risk being cast out. Should someone dare to break from convention, you might instinctively dismiss them—perhaps by quoting experts, leaning on tradition, or defending the familiar. Their nonconformity feels threatening because it awakens possibilities you're not yet ready to face.

Hence, you surround yourself with others who validate your existing beliefs, not realizing you're just avoiding growth. You don't see this as fear—you see it as loyalty, responsibility, maybe even morality. But underneath, what's really being preserved is your comfort zone. You carry the subconscious hope that some savior, some group—like your family, your culture, or your religion—will guide your life for you, make the hard decisions, and save you from the perils of having to carve out your own path.

When you do notice differences within yourself, you often interpret them as flaws to be corrected rather than signs of blossoming individuality. You compare, correct, and conform, hoping that sameness will equal acceptance. But sameness never really satisfies—it only suppresses what's real. The longer you try to hide your authentic colors, the more restless your soul becomes.

The moment will come when you taste authentic self-expression—even in tiny ways. That's when something begins to shift. Gradually, the discomfort of blending in becomes heavier than the risk of standing out and the "black sheep" label is born.

Old Soul

As an old soul, being a black sheep is no longer something you resist or complain about. It's something you honor and even revel in. You've lived long enough to see that conformity and comfort only keep you stuck. The path toward your authentic self is through separation and individuation.

Knowing this doesn't make it easy. Being the one who sees through the illusion often comes with loneliness. You might be the only one in your family who questions inherited beliefs, who doesn't chase traditional success, or who lives according to inner guidance instead of external rules. But with time, you no longer feel a need to justify it. Your blossoming connection to your inner truth is strong enough to withstand the drag of the group.

Most group identities—family, tribe, religion, ideology—create safety by limiting what's allowed. But you didn't come here to stay safe. You came to awaken. And awakening invariably involves some form of exile. To get your self back, you must break away from the crowd. Not just physically, but in your beliefs, too. No belief system, no tradition can own you if you really want to be free.

As you grow into this role, you see that the label "black sheep" was never a curse but a signpost. It marked you as the one meant to lead—not by dragging others, but by embodying freedom. You discover that the very solitude you once resisted becomes your sanctuary, giving you the clarity and strength to walk paths others fear to tread.

Still, walking this path can feel heavy at times. It's not easy staying present while others resist or ridicule your choices. Lower frequencies often try to pull you back into the old script. That's why finding other awake black sheep is essential. Not to form another group, but to enjoy resonance without restriction—sharing the insights and adventures of your journey freely without pressure to conform.

You understand now that being the black sheep isn't about rebelling against the system. You can let the system be what it is without it touching your freedom. You trust that the more aligned you are in yourself, the more others will join you when they're ready. Your role is no longer to change or convince, but to be fully, freely, and unapologetically you.

BLACK SHEEP CHART

Being different and being yourself are inexorably intertwined. And while most would never admit to being a follower, conformity is still one of the most powerful social forces. The following chart contrasts how young vs old souls handle being a black sheep.

Young Soul (Outcast Identity)	Old Soul (Sovereign Soul)
Feels misunderstood or defective	Sees difference as liberation
Tries to fit in, earn love, prove worth	Lives authentically, free of approval
Feels pain, shame, resentment	Feels peaceful, free, confident
Blames society for rejection	Accepts self fully, lets others be
Seeks belonging outside oneself	Finds belonging in inner wholeness
Defensive and reactive to criticism	Detached and compassionate
Contracts, hides true self	Expands, radiates authenticity
Difference feels like a curse	Difference becomes Source alignment

© 2025 Cirak

PROMPTS

1) Do you currently identify as a black sheep? If so, what has helped you embrace that role—and what still makes it challenging? If not, are there aspects of yourself you've been suppressing in order to belong?

2) Think of someone in your family or community who thinks or lives very differently from the group. How do you feel about them? What assumptions or judgments arise in you—and what might you learn by listening to their perspective?

3) Reflect on the ways you've conformed in the past. Which choices were rooted in fear or habit rather than your truth? What might it look like to find back to yourself in those areas?

4) Where do you still feel pressure to belong or be accepted by others? What is the cost of that pressure—to your energy, your creativity, your peace?

5) What kinds of support or community would feel most nourishing to you now? Most of the time, your biological family is here to teach you lessons. They're not your soul tribe. Where can you find a community of more like-minded?

6) Have you been fighting battles that are no longer necessary? Are there places you can release the need to explain yourself or convert others?

7) What are the spiritual gifts of being a black sheep? How has it shaped your capacity to see clearly, feel deeply, or live authentically in a material world?

CHAPTER 25

Dating

Young Soul

Dating, as a young soul, often feels like a high-stakes game you believe you're supposed to win. The rules aren't always clear, but the rewards are: attention, attraction, approval. You measure your desirability by how many views and swipes you get, how much you're wanted. If you get interest, you feel validated. If you don't, you take it personally. From the beginning, the dynamics are intense—the chase, the uncertainty, the thrill of being desired, of potentially finding "the one." Romance becomes another race to the finish line. But increasingly, when dates don't work out, it doesn't just sting—it gnaws away at your confidence and identity.

As a result, you start to edit yourself. You mold your personality to fit the preferences of the person in front of you. You mirror their interests, temper your needs, and ignore red flags. You're showing your best side—the one you think they want to see—not your authentic one. You do this not because you lack intelligence or real beauty, but because of deeply rooted programming. There is the fear of being alone. The fear of being unworthy. The fear of missing out on intimacy, trust, or the image of a perfect partnership or family. Approval becomes a prize. Rejection becomes a threat. You begin to believe that connection is something you must earn by being more likable, more attractive, more easygoing. In the process, you abandon your authenticity, thinking it will bring you closer—when all it really does is distance you from both others and yourself.

You may also confuse emotional intensity with safety. You're drawn to those who evoke strong feelings, even if those feelings come with inconsistency, anxiety, or confusion. When someone is distant or hard to get, winning them over becomes your mission. You're not necessarily drawn to people who are good for you, but to people who make you feel alive—even if it's through chaos, drama, and the triggering of old, familiar wounds. Subconsciously, you think love needs to be pursued, that validation means progress, and that passion automatically equals compatibility. You chase what's elusive—not realizing that calm, peace, and quiet resonance are where true connection lives.

There is also the trap of comparing yourself endlessly, measuring your value against who your date has seen, who else might want them, or who you imagine they truly desire. Dating apps amplify this mindset, turning intimacy into a competition, as if love were a marketplace. This fuels insecurity and scarcity, pushing you to keep performing, keep proving, keep striving to be chosen. You don't yet see that this treadmill is self-created, and that the real question isn't about being picked—it's about whether you are present enough to choose yourself.

As always, you learn through experience. When the highs no longer compensate for the crashes, you begin to recognize a pattern—that in trying so hard to be wanted, you keep losing yourself. This is where the shift begins. You start to pay attention to how you actually feel—not just how you make others feel. Dating becomes less about being picked and more about standing in your truth. Instead of asking, *Do they like me?* you start asking, *Do I like myself when I'm with them?* And just like that, dating becomes a mirror—which it was all along. And seeing life as a mirror is the threshold into old soul consciousness.

Old Soul

As an old soul, dating can feel like stepping into an arena where everyone is pretending to be someone they're not. A parade of polished images and curated masks. You, however, crave something deeper—not just commonality or compatibility, but genuine connection. And yet, you find yourself wading through clever bios, filtered photos, and rehearsed banter. You sense quickly when someone is leading with a promise rather than presence. And it drains you. Small talk feels hollow. Mind games feel insulting. You're not looking to be entertained—you want to be met. Not just emotionally or intellectually, but energetically. Heart to heart. Soul to soul.

Of course, you know this because you've already lived the other side: the pursuit of passion, the allure of the unavailable, mistaking potential for reality. You've witnessed how much time and energy gets wasted in chaotic entanglements with people who don't know themselves. And so you no longer give your energy to intellect, chemistry, or charm unless they're matched with consciousness. You want someone who can be still with you, hold silence with you, tell the truth with you. Someone who can match your inner peace, not just your outer interests. You're willing to wait for that. You're not willing to choose from scarcity. You know the difference now between being alone and being lonely.

Still, even with your wisdom, old wounds may linger. You may have been told you were "too much," "too sensitive," or "too intense"—usually by those unwilling to meet their own depth. You've tasted connection that felt profound, only to watch it dissolve into abandonment. So now, your heart is open but discerning. You no longer settle for one-sided affairs. You want reciprocity, where each partner takes turns holding the lantern for the other.

You've also learned to read energy beyond words. A date isn't just about what is said—it's about the silences, the eye contact, the subtle vibrations exchanged. You know instantly when someone is present with you versus when they are still lost in pretending. And you'd rather walk away early than spend months trying to excavate depth in someone who hasn't yet touched their own. This clarity saves your energy, and paradoxically, brings you more peace than endless attempts at "making it work."

As an old soul, your need for spiritual connection leads the way. You understand that differences in soul maturity will eventually push apart an otherwise promising match. But when you meet someone who is also walking the path, the relationship becomes part of the path—a container for growth rather than an escape from it. And should you find yourself pulled into old patterns, you use the experience to refine your resonance. You observe sensations, notice where you over-give, where you still crave validation, where childhood traumas still speak. You know that every connection—whether lasting or fleeting—is a reflection of your own inner state.

PROMPTS

1) What role does dating play in your self-worth?

2) Have you ever ignored your intuition just to keep a connection alive?

3) What do you tend to chase in dating, and what deeper need is that tied to?

4) What patterns keep repeating in your dating life?

5) How do you respond to rejection, and what beliefs does it activate?

6) What qualities in a person help you feel safe, seen, and heard?

7) How do you distinguish between chemistry and compatibility?

8) What would dating look like if you removed pressure from the process?

9) Who would you need to become to attract the kind of love you truly want?

Chapter 26

Love

Young Soul

Out of all the external things you believe will make you happy, love feels like the ultimate key to complete you. The world reinforces this idea everywhere you look—songs, movies, social media, advertisements, even your friends echo the same story: find "the one," and everything will finally make sense. You get pulled into the spectacle, convinced that somewhere out there is a missing piece. You invest significant time and energy chasing people who can fill the gaps you haven't yet learned to fill yourself.

Instead of learning to sit with your own company, you search for someone to validate you, choose you, fix you, make life feel whole. You may call it love, but it's often a transaction in disguise: *If you give me attention, I'll feel valuable. If you stay with me, I'll feel safe.* You don't consciously mean to use another person, but because you feel disconnected from yourself, their affection becomes a lifeline. And when the spark of new attraction comes, the thrill is intoxicating—momentarily silencing your inner emptiness.

This kind of love is deeply conditional. It depends on how the other person shows up, what they give, how they speak, how they behave, and whether they keep reflecting your worth back to you. If they stop giving in precisely the way you need them to, the "love" quickly flips into fear, resentment, or despair. Rejection feels like annihilation—not because they failed, but because you unknowingly placed your survival in their hands. No human being can and should carry that weight.

Relationships at this stage are primarily for healing. You're drawn, almost magnetically, to people with wounds that complement your own. Together, you replay unfinished business: abandonment, control, insecurity, longing. If enough awareness is present, these relationships can become classrooms where you begin to glimpse your patterns. If not, they become cycles of blame, eruption, and exhaustion from which it becomes increasingly difficult to extract yourself.

Deep down, what you're actually seeking is the love within yourself. But you don't yet see that. You think it lives in their eyes, their arms, their words. You imagine that if you can just be enough, if you can earn it, the ache will finally stop. This is the illusion: that love is something external, something you must win or deserve, instead of something that awakens when you turn inward.

Eventually, experience humbles you and you realize that no relationship can rescue you from yourself. The absence you feel is not a partner—it is your own unattended heart. Slowly, you begin the real work of self-acceptance, of tending to your being, of discovering that love is less about possession and more about presence. And when love arrives again, you'll be ready to meet with all of yourself.

OLD SOUL

As an old soul, you no longer look for love to complete you. You've learned that love isn't something outside to be acquired, but something within to be uncovered. By befriending yourself, by dissolving the shame and judgment that once clouded you, you've found that your heart already overflows. From this fullness you invite companionship—not as a cure for loneliness, but as a celebration of wholeness.

The pitfalls of conditional love have fallen away. You recognize that what most people call love is a bargain for security or a re-living of old wounds. But you are no longer interested in bargaining. Love, for you, is two beings walking in truth, not to fix each other, but to amplify what's already alive in them both.

Your relationship becomes a sacred container to expand into together—into joy, into clarity, into devotion. The more aligned you both are to yourselves, the freer the love flows. Passion is no longer a fire that burns hot and fizzles out; it is the consistent warmth of two souls devoted to life itself.

You understand that love is not merely a bond between two people—it is a current, a divine stream, flowing through everything. When you and your partner live in alignment, you feel yourselves as conduits of that current. Your devotion to one another is inseparable from your devotion to Source. The relationship is not about what you get, but about how fully you can share presence, truth, and tenderness.

And so, love ceases to be the story of finding "the one." It becomes the story of remembering the One within everything. You no longer cling to love as a possession, nor fear its loss as an ending. You let it move through you, unforced, uncontrolled, unrestricted. In this state, your relationship with each other becomes an act of devotion to the divine.

Love Chart

Infinite love is found at the core of everything that exists and is available to all—if only you approach it a certain way. The following chart illustrates the difference between how young souls and old souls experience love.

Young Souls	Old Souls
Love seen as missing piece—someone else must complete me	Love seen as overflowing state—already whole within
Conditional: based on what partner gives or how they act	Unconditional: flows from authenticity and presence
Intensity mistaken for intimacy, attraction mistaken for destiny	Clarity between passion and compatibility, depth over drama
Relationship as transaction—validation in exchange for attention	Relationship as devotion—shared resonance and growth
Fear of abandonment drives control or self-betrayal	Trust in self and Source allows freedom and openness
Partnership expected to fix loneliness or pain	Partnership expands joy and creativity already present
Drawn to complementary wounds—cycle of fixing and being fixed	Attracted by shared consciousness—cycle of co-creation
Identity tied to being chosen or desired	Identity rooted in Source connection and self-love
Love fades when expectations aren't met	Love deepens through presence, honesty, and growth
Seeking rescue through another	Inviting companionship in walking the path together

© 2025 Cirak

PROMPTS

1) When you've fallen in love in the past, what were you really looking for?

2) What parts of yourself do you believe would be easier to love if someone else loved them first?

3) What fears or insecurities tend to show up in your relationships?

4) How do you imagine being in love would feel if you already felt whole on your own?

5) Where have you confused passion for compatibility, or intensity for intimacy?

6) Can you love someone without trying to fix them?

7) How do your current or past relationships reflect your relationship with yourself?

Chapter 27

Marriage

Young Soul

As a young soul, marriage is seen as a milestone—a box to check, a symbol of success, proof that you've finally been chosen and are therefore worthy. It feels like an accomplishment, a social credential, even a badge of legitimacy. Sometimes you pursue it as an achievement, sometimes you inherit it as an unquestioned family expectation. Either way, the assumption is the same: marriage will make you whole.

More specifically, behind this pursuit is the subtle belief that marriage will fix something—your loneliness, your lack of confidence, or a relationship that feels incomplete. With an eye on the roles and responsibilities that follow, you may even hope marriage will give you a safe identity to hide behind, saving you from facing yourself directly.

At this stage, you still assume that love is sourced from others. A partnership is expected to deliver the peace, validation, or sense of belonging you haven't yet cultivated within. The wedding is imagined as a gateway into "happily ever after," but when the celebration ends and life continues, you discover that the promise of lasting fulfillment isn't magically fulfilled. On the contrary, the very insecurities you hoped marriage would dissolve come to the surface.

For young souls, marriage acts as an accelerator of growth. You attract someone who activates your wounds, mirrors your blind spots, and disrupts your illusions. Believing you've chosen harmony, you often find yourself in long-term confrontation with your own patterns. You may blame and attempt to change your partner—or twist yourself to meet their expectations. Either way, the love remains conditional, based on how well each of you compensates for the other's fears.

There comes a point, when the distance between who you are and who you pretend to be grows unbearable. Some couples maintain appearances, preserving the facade for status or stability. But eventually, the truth breaks through: no marriage can thrive if it's built on the belief that someone else is responsible for your happiness.

Marriage doesn't complete you—it reveals you to yourself. It uncovers what's unresolved and demands your absolute honesty. If you can stay with that discomfort, if you dare to tell the truth, marriage transforms from a fragile agreement into a container of profound growth. It stops being about appearances, and begins being about awakening.

OLD SOUL

As an old soul, you no longer mistake marriage for a milestone that will rescue you from yourself. You're not looking for someone to complete you—you're inviting someone awake and willing to walk beside you in a shared evolution. Marriage becomes a conscious choice: companionship by resonance, devotion over dependency.

To you, marriage is a field where love matures, where truth deepens, and where devotion to Source is expressed through another soul. You care less about appearances and convention than about whether your bond amplifies authenticity, purpose, and presence—two lives tuned to a higher current.

You enter union without illusions, but not without tenderness. Having faced your shadows, you no longer demand another to soothe your wounds. You bring your fullness. You offer love without hooks or manipulation. Challenges don't frighten you; they invite dialogue, reflection, and shared presence. Even discomfort becomes a doorway to deeper intimacy.

Still, marriage is not without tests. People change. Old patterns resurface. Silence can linger longer than it should. Yet you trust the process and return, again and again, to the core question: *Are we still serving the Divine through each other?*

With a conscious partner, marriage is less routine and more co-creation. Together you build not just a household, but a frequency. Your union becomes a living transmission—felt more than declared—of a love that steadies those around you.

You also honor sovereignty within commitment. Boundaries are not barriers but forms of self-care. You choose each other daily through small practices: honest check-ins, swift repair, shared rituals that keep wonder alive, laughter that lightens the serious work of growth. Gratitude becomes a consistent theme and service extends beyond the two of you, letting your love contribute to something larger than yourselves.

In its highest form, marriage is not about belonging to another; it is a merging of energies, a collaboration with life itself.

Marriage Chart

Whether you let being married break you or build you depends on the lens of awareness you bring to the equation. The following chart compares how young souls vs old souls approach marriage.

Young Souls (Contractual Marriage)	Old Souls (Soul Partnership)
Based on roles, expectations, and social norms	Rooted in presence, freedom, and conscious choice
Seeks security through structure and legal binding	Seeks connection through continual mutual alignment
Suppresses truth to maintain harmony	Speaks truth even when it's uncomfortable
Avoids change to preserve the agreement	Embraces change as part of soul growth
Fears loss and clings to commitment	Trusts the flow and lets love evolve
Identifies with "husband" or "wife" as fixed identity	Sees partnership as a living dance, not a title
Measures success by longevity or appearances	Measures success by depth, growth, and authenticity
Blames partner for unmet needs or emotions	Takes full ownership of one's inner world
Seeks control through compromise or sacrifice	Seeks coherence through honesty and alignment
Stays together out of fear, guilt, or duty	Chooses togetherness from joy, resonance, and love

Prompts

1) What does the word "marriage" bring up for you? Is there hope, fear, resistance, longing, or something else?

2) What are you secretly hoping marriage will fix in your life? What parts of you still feel unresolved?

3) Have you ever entered a relationship with a fantasy in mind? How did reality compare?

4) What did you witness or absorb about marriage growing up? Which of those beliefs are you still carrying?

5) Do you associate marriage with safety, identity, pressure, or freedom? Why?

6) How would you show up differently in marriage if you felt completely whole on your own?

7) What role does spiritual growth play in your idea of an ideal relationship?

9) What kind of marriage would reflect the most honest, creative, and loving version of you?

10) How can you begin practicing the qualities of divine partnership—presence, truth, devotion—within yourself, starting now?

Chapter 28

Pregnancy

Young Soul

On one hand, you may see pregnancy as the most natural decision in the world—an experience you can't imagine missing. It appears to be the ultimate milestone: a way to fulfill a role, a purpose, a long-awaited expectation. Beneath the surface is often a quiet hope—that this experience will complete something in you. Even the father, or intended parents walking the path of surrogacy, may carry a powerful longing for this chapter, whether they experience it physically or not.

Pregnancy also carries the emotions of stepping into the unknown. Hope, fear, excitement, and pressure all arise at once. Every choice—what you eat, how you move, how you prepare—can feel weighty with consequence. You compare yourself to others, wondering if you're doing enough, or if your experience measures up. *Is the way I'm feeling the way I'm supposed to be feeling?*

When challenges arise—physical discomfort, emotional swings, fears about change—you may feel overwhelmed or unprepared. In response, you might try to control the uncontrollable. You read every book, follow every rule, buy every gadget, cling to every reassurance. But as with all things in life, the more tightly you grip, the more exhausting it becomes.

Whether this is your first time and everything feels new, or whether you've experienced it before and bring less anxiety, at some point you realize your body—like life itself—is wiser than your plans. As you relax your sense of perfection, you open more fully to trust in your body, in the process, in your evolving self.

And here lies the deeper truth: pregnancy is not just about growing a child—it's about growing yourself. Every symptom, every fear, every joy becomes part of your own transformation.

Old Soul

As an old soul, pregnancy is not merely the creation of life but the co-creation of spirit with matter. You feel the soul of your child long before it arrives, and you honor its presence as a teacher as much as a gift. Each flutter, each wave of fatigue, each shift in your being becomes a message from beyond what you can anticipate.

You know that pregnancy is never meant to be straightforward. It is designed to awaken you—stirring ancestral energies, karmic memory, and hidden thresholds. Alongside the joy, you may feel unexpected grief for the life you're leaving behind, or the identities dissolving as you cross into a new chapter. But rather than resist, you allow it all. You let each emotion sculpt you into who you are becoming.

More than ever, you listen inward. You are in sync with the rhythms of your womb, with intuition, with the subtle instructions of the body. You understand that this soul chose you with divine precision. Rather than control the journey, you hold space for mystery. You make room for the unseen. You become a bridge between worlds.

Still, sometimes you may catch yourself hoping this sacred passage will make you feel more worthy, more transformed, more whole. When expectations fail to match reality—and they always will—you remember to soften. Instead of resisting, you surrender. You let the mismatch deepen you. And in that letting go, compassion, fluidity, and awareness blossom.

Ultimately, pregnancy is not about achieving a perfect outcome but about embodying devotion to the life within you, to your own unfolding, and to the great current of creation flowing through it all. It is less about becoming a parent and more about becoming fully present to life itself.

Prompts

1) What hopes, fears, or beliefs are you carrying about pregnancy, and where did they come from?

2) In what ways is this pregnancy asking you to grow, emotionally, spiritually, or relationally?

3) Are you trying to control this experience, or allowing it to shape you? What would surrender look like?

4) What does it mean to be a vessel for new life? How does it affect your sense of identity and purpose?

5) What old stories about motherhood, birth, or womanhood are you ready to unlearn?

6) What would it look like to listen to your body as your primary guide? What messages has it been offering?

7) In moments of discomfort or fear, how can you trust in your body, your intuition, and the soul of your child?

Chapter 29

Infertility

Young Soul

As a young soul, infertility can feel like a personal failure, a shame you carry in silence. You may find yourself thinking, *Why me? What did I do wrong?* You might see your body as broken, or yourself as somehow less worthy than others who conceive with ease. The inability to create life can feel like a rejection from life itself—from your body, from love, from the future you had imagined.

It doesn't help when there's pressure from every direction—family expectations, cultural narratives, your own inner timeline. You may feel isolated, watching others step into parenthood while you're left behind, questioning your purpose. You try to stay hopeful, but the rise and fall of every cycle becomes an exhausting emotional rollercoaster.

When your identity is still rooted in outcomes, infertility feels like the world is withholding love from you. You might pay for expensive treatments, grasp for answers, or blame yourself—trying to force what isn't ready to arrive. You long for certainty, a way to control your future. And when nothing works, grief and resentment can cloud your connection to your higher self.

But even here, the experience begins to soften you. Slowly, you start to separate your worth from what your body can or cannot do. The question begins to shift from *Why can't I?* to *What else am I here to give, create, and nourish?*

You begin to realize that reproduction, creation, and legacy take many forms. Life is always inviting you to birth something—whether a child, an idea, or a more expansive version of yourself. And from that space, healing begins and peace returns. You are not giving up—you are surrendering to a deeper journey.

Old Soul

As an old soul, infertility is not a verdict but an invitation into profound soul-work, into surrender beyond what the mind can negotiate. You understand that life is never withholding meaning—it is revealing it in unexpected, even if sometimes painful ways.

Though the ache of not conceiving may cut deep, you hold the grief with sacredness. You don't push it away or try to mask it. You allow both the longing and the lesson to live side by side. You understand that creation is not confined to the physical—that your spirit is still here to give life, whether through children, wisdom, art, service, or presence. You don't ask, *Why is this happening to me?* You ask, *How does life want to express itself through me?*

That doesn't mean you shouldn't explore medicine, surrogacy, or adoption. But you do so from a different place. No longer driven by desperation, you act from devotion. You listen to your body, your energy, your timing. You don't force outcomes. You follow intuition. And if the child never comes in the form you imagined, you trust that love will still find a way to move through you and into the world.

You begin to redefine what it means to be a vessel. You realize that motherhood—or fatherhood—is not a title. It is a vibration. It is the capacity to nurture, to guide, to embody love as a living frequency. And this capacity remains, whether or not you hold a child in your arms.

From this space, you can honor yourself not for what you produce but for the life you embody. And you see, with greater clarity, that your soul's purpose has never been limited to biology—it has always been to bring more love into form.

PROMPTS

1) What emotions are most alive for you in this journey—and how can you honor them without judgment?

2) What meaning have you attached to your fertility? What old stories about worth, purpose, or identity are being challenged?

3) How do you hold space for both longing and acceptance at the same time?

4) What does your body want from you right now: rest, trust, forgiveness, care? Where can you invite more gentleness into how you speak to yourself about this?

5) Where do you still feel pressure—internal or external—to become a parent? What happens when you loosen your grip on that pressure?

6) How have you grown through this experience? In what ways might your capacity to nurture be expressed beyond biological parenthood?

7) What new questions—not answers—has this experience invited you to sit with?

Chapter 30

Abortion

Young Soul

The young soul clings tightly to absolutes—life or death, right or wrong, truth or falsehood. Abortion becomes not just a decision but a moral battlefield. There is little room for nuance, because nuance threatens the foundation of your reality: that things must be either good or bad, that identity must be protected at all costs, and that righteousness is the safest shield. Abortion, therefore, is often seen in a harsh light—whether experienced personally or observed in others.

If you are the one undergoing it, you may feel caught in an unbearable storm of shame, fear, and judgment. You imagine how others will see you if they find out—what it says about your worth, your femininity, your value as a partner or parent. You try to justify it, to make it okay in your mind, while also fearing that your body will remember everything. Your thoughts spin between guilt and victimhood, never finding stillness.

You may feel alone, unsupported, abandoned—by a partner, by family, even by God. It's difficult to see anything spiritual in the experience. It feels clinical at best, traumatic at worst. Something in you tightens around the event, trying to seal it away, hoping time will erase it. But the more you suppress it, the more it lingers—in dreams, in your body, in the subtle feeling that you did something wrong and cannot be made whole again.

You might fixate on the life that could have been, playing out timelines in your head, constructing futures that never arrived. The pain becomes a loop, not because of the event itself, but because of the meaning you've wrapped around it. The act has fused with your identity, shaping your sense of self-worth. You keep searching for either punishment or redemption—some storyline that will finally make it all make sense.

If you are on the outside, you may use abortion as a measuring stick. You judge based on inherited beliefs without question. You moralize pain without understanding it. You speak of life as if it is a concept, without ever sitting in the silence of what it actually is. Even when trying to be compassionate, you may still offer explanations or half-truths to bypass your own discomfort. You have not yet learned to hold grief without trying to control or package it.

But life has its way of bringing you back to the places you've judged. Perhaps through a friend, perhaps through your own body. Over time, the rigid certainty begins to soften. You meet someone's experience and—for the first time—you truly listen. Or you return to your own memory years later, realizing how tightly you had shut the door on yourself. The grief is still there, but quieter. Less tangled. More real.

This is when the story starts to fall away, and something deeper arrives. You begin to see that the deeper rhythm of life is messy, never linear, but always guiding you towards the experience you need to have to evolve. Once you can accept this, you soften, because something in you finally understands that this, too, was part of it.

Old Soul

As an old soul, you approach abortion not through the lens of politics or morality, but through presence. You know life is not defined solely by the body, nor is death the end of anything real. You sense the soul's sovereignty. You know it remains untouched by human events, and that beings arrive and depart only when the design calls for it. There are no accidents, only unfolding.

If you've experienced an abortion, you let yourself feel fully—whether grief, relief, emptiness, or silence. You don't cling to these feelings or assign them fixed meaning. They arise, they move, they pass. What remains is a deeper truth: that the soul is never lost, and you are never forsaken.

You may even feel the presence of the one who did not come through. Not as punishment, but as a being who chose, like you, not to cross that threshold. Perhaps there was an agreement before incarnation. Perhaps their appearance was only meant to awaken something in you. Perhaps their path was always meant to be brief. You don't pretend to know. You no longer need to. Mystery is enough.

You no longer make the event part of your identity. You don't bury it, nor do you dramatize it. It becomes another thread in the tapestry of your life—one that stripped away judgment, softened the edges of self, and widened your compassion.

At the spiritual level, abortion is neither right nor wrong. It is an experience. For some, it is grief. For others, sovereignty. For others still, confusion or silence. You don't project meaning—you allow the meaning to reveal itself. Each path is unique, and each soul is intact.

Over lifetimes, you've come to see that some lives are meant to be only a spark. The soul arrives briefly to remind you of your power, your limits, your humanity. And even this passing interaction shapes you—deepening your intuition, expanding your discernment, anchoring your trust in divine timing.

Eventually, the event is no longer something you replay or try to explain. It simply is. In that allowing, there is peace. Not because you made sense of it, but because you no longer need to.

And if you listen closely, if you lean into the silence, you can hear what you could not before: this, too, was love.

Prompts

1) What cultural, religious, or personal stories have you inherited about abortion?

2) If you've experienced an abortion, what emotions have you allowed yourself to feel? What emotions have you avoided?

3) Have you ever judged someone else's decision around pregnancy? What's behind that judgment?

4) In what ways did the experience of abortion, directly or indirectly, change your relationship to choice?

5) What parts of yourself did you lose, or discover, through this experience?

6) How do you relate to the soul of the being that did not arrive? What would you say to them if you knew they were listening?

7) Is there any lingering shame, guilt, or grief that hasn't been given space to be?

8) What would it feel like to hold this experience as sacred, even if painful?

Chapter 31

Parenthood

Young Soul

As a young soul, parenthood often begins as an instinctive duty or expected milestone—something you step into because it's "the next step," not necessarily because you've reflected on what it truly means. You may enter the role hoping to do better than your own parents did, or trying to recreate what they modeled. Either way, your focus tends to be external: *Are they healthy? Well-behaved? Achieving what I consider success? Am I doing a good job?*

At this stage, you often see your child as an extension of yourself. Their behavior feels personal. Their struggles can feel like your failures. You may place subtle or overt expectations on them—to succeed, behave, fulfill your image of them, or even heal parts of your own past. Because your sense of self is still entangled with outcomes, you measure your parenting by milestones or by how others perceive you through your children.

You might also find yourself parenting from reaction, judgment, and control rather than presence. When your child challenges you, the impulse may be to shut it down quickly—not because you lack love, but because their chaos stirs your own discomfort or feelings of inadequacy. You may rely on discipline to shape behavior, rather than recognizing behavior itself as communication—often more honest than words.

A young soul lives so tightly from identification with "me" that it's hard to see outside of yourself. Your need for order may override your child's need for expression. Your desire to be loved may quietly steer how you treat them. The things you didn't receive growing up, you try to provide—whether or not they are aligned for your child. Without realizing it, you enforce compliance and pass on your baggage rather than teaching connection to their inner self.

This leads to pressure and power struggles. Your child pulls away from not feeling seen. They don't want to be raised as a smaller version of you. Parenting isn't about leaving your mark on the world; it's about protecting a space where someone else's truth can emerge. Only when parenthood stops being about doing it "right" can it start focusing on being real—i.e. your willingness to grow alongside your child. Every conflict becomes a doorway into deeper trust, truth, and connection.

And yet, many young souls cling to the idea of parenting as performance. The social media post, the school grades, the praise from relatives—these become proof that you're doing well, when in fact they only reinforce the pressure. You may feel the burden of comparison with other parents, chasing a standard that was never yours to begin with. The more you strive to appear successful, the more disconnected you become from the quiet, real moments where love naturally happens.

Old Soul

As an old soul, you step into parenthood not just for the role, but for the soul who chose to come through you. You don't see your child as someone to mold, but as someone to walk beside—an autonomous being with a blueprint uniquely their own. Your role is not to program them, but to create space where their true being can unfold.

Your presence, more than anything, is what matters. You listen more than you instruct. You set boundaries without harshness. You encourage emotions without judgment. You're not trying to make your child "fit in"; you're helping them stay true to themselves. You're aware of your influence, but your authority doesn't carry superiority.

Of course, the role isn't effortless. Your child mirrors your shadows, and triggers still arise. But instead of reprimanding from defensiveness, you reflect. Your life motto—in all things, not just parenting—becomes: *What does this situation reveal about me?*

So rather than reacting, you pause. You apologize when needed. You adjust without shame. This is how you model the qualities you hope to nurture. You know children don't need a perfect parent; they need a present one.

An old soul parent holds the long view. You're less concerned with obedience, knowing that authenticity is a sturdier compass than compliance. You don't aim to raise someone who fits neatly into the world—you raise someone capable of carving their own way. You want them to know themselves, trust themselves, and express themselves freely, even if it disrupts convention.

Ultimately, parenthood is not about filling your emptiness or rewriting your childhood; it's about loving your child as whole. It's not about clinging to the role of parent for identity, but trusting their soul's path. You know that your greatest gift is not to protect them from life, but to model how to live it fully. By embodying truth, presence, and compassion, you give them permission to do the same. That legacy lasts far beyond any rule or lesson—it becomes the frequency they carry into the world.

Parenthood Chart

Any pre-conceived attitudes and expectations can have a big impact on everyone involved. The following chart highlights how young souls vs old souls experience parenthood.

Young Souls (Parentinig from Ego)	Old Souls (Parenting from Soul)
Sees the child as a reflection of self-image or legacy	Sees the child as a sovereign soul on their own path
Controls the child to avoid embarrassment or failure	Guides the child to develop inner awareness and autonomy
Uses praise or punishment to mold behavior	Uses presence and boundaries to foster self-trust
Projects unresolved wounds onto the child	Clears their own energy to parent from clarity
Fears losing control or being rejected	Honors the child's uniqueness, even when it challenges them
Seeks obedience, performance, achievement	Encourages inquiry, expression, and alignment
Feels threatened by the child's resistance	Stays grounded and curious in moments of conflict
Parents from shoulds, roles, and social comparison	Parents from intuition, respect, and spiritual attunement
Tries to make the child into someone	Helps the child remember who they already are
Equates success with continuation of family values and external results	Equates success with indipendence, connection, growth, and presence

© 2025 Cirak

Prompts

1) What beliefs did you inherit about what a "good parent" should be? Do these still serve you?

2) What part of parenthood feels most intuitive—and what part still feels heavy or confusing?

3) How does your child reflect the parts of yourself you're still learning to love?

4) In moments of tension, do you respond from presence or from unhealed patterns? What helps you return to presence?

5) How do you balance boundaries with freedom in your relationship with your child?

6) What are your greatest fears as a parent—and what do they reveal about your own healing?

7) How do you model emotional awareness for your child?

8) What kind of adult are you helping your child become—and is that vision rooted in soul or society?

9) What do you hope your child remembers most about how you made them feel?

Chapter 32

Breakup

Young Soul

When you go through a breakup as a young soul, it can feel like your entire world collapses. The pain is rarely just about the other person—it's the loss of who you thought you were with them, the imagined future you built, and the emotional safety you believed they gave you. You may incessantly replay moments, question your worth—even resist closure because you're holding onto the hope that they'll return so you can feel whole again.

In hindsight, it's easy to idealize the relationship, even if large parts of it weren't aligned. You focus on the highs, the memories, the potential—not so much the day-to-day reality. You may internalize the ending as personal failure, as proof that you're not lovable enough or worthy enough. It hurts deeply because you gave your heart to the best of your abilities.

In the aftermath, you might rush to fill the void—with distractions, rebound connections, or by trying to "up your game" and become someone more desirable. To show that person what they're missing. But this only perpetuates the energetic cord and keeps you stuck in the past. Furthermore, it prevents you from addressing all the other contributing factors, such as fear of loneliness, judgment, and loss of control.

Breakups at this stage often trigger survival fears—you may cling to routines, stalk their social media, or replay what you "should" have done differently. The mind turns the ending into a puzzle you obsessively try to solve. But there's no solution at that level, only exhaustion.

Eventually, you realize the breakup isn't about losing them—it's an invitation to find yourself. The silence, though unbearable at first, begins to show you the parts of your inner life you've neglected. You see that the real heartbreak isn't that they're gone—it's that you abandoned yourself for so long in the hope of being loved.

Old Soul

As an old soul, breakups still hurt—but the pain is cleaner. Your world doesn't come crashing to a halt. You don't let yourself fall apart. There is just the heartfelt ache that something precious has reached its end. You feel the grief and let it move through you—slowly, honestly, giving your heart the time and space it needs to heal, without rushing to reframe or escape.

You understand that endings are not failures, and certainly that heartaches don't last forever. No matter how brief or long, intense or tame, there is always something to be discerned about yourself from every experience. Nothing deserves to be diminished—everything moves you closer towards recognizing your own divinity. You loved genuinely with your whole heart. And when love is real, nothing is ever wasted.

You also know not to rush back into something new. You hold space for the tenderness, the questions that have no clear answers. You might still revisit the *why*, but you already sense the deepening. And in some strange way, the honesty and purity of it is beautiful.

From here, you begin to see the breakup as a refinement. A chance to shed identities, roles, and expectations that no longer serve you. What remains is clearer, stronger, and more real. Instead of closing your heart, you allow it to expand—to include the pain, but also the wisdom born from it.

Over time, the relationship becomes a chapter that shaped you, not a chain that binds you. And in that freedom, you realize that love never truly leaves. It just changes form.

Prompts

1) If you're going through a breakup right now, what part of you is hurting the most? Your heart, your identity, your future vision? What part of you is afraid to let go, and what is that fear trying to protect?

2) What did this relationship teach you about yourself, both the beautiful parts and the parts that still need healing?

3) In what ways did you show up with love and honesty? In what ways were you not entirely true to yourself?

4) What needs or longings were you hoping this relationship would fulfill? How can you meet those needs now, from within? How can you love yourself better than you ever have before?

5) What story do you carry about what this relationship meant? Can you let that story dissolve into forgiveness and refocus forward?

6) Where have you mistaken love for intensity, validation, or safety?

7) What version of you is emerging from this ending—and what does that version need from you right now?

Chapter 33

Infidelity

Young Soul

Infidelity can feel like a blow from which there is no recovery. It's not just a betrayal of trust—it's the collapse of the very reality you believed in. What once felt safe, mutual, even sacred, suddenly dissolves, leaving you broken and untethered. Your mind spins with questions: *Was I not enough? How did I miss this? How could someone who claimed to love me do this?* The shock doesn't only wound your heart—it rattles your identity, your instincts, your sense of what's real.

Your reactions may swing wildly—from rage to grief to numbness. You might demand answers, seek revenge, or cling desperately to the hope that the old relationship can somehow be restored. Your nervous system reels, looping through memories, hunting for missed signs, imagining alternate timelines. Whether you fight, forgive, or flee, no path feels solid when your sense of safety has been shattered so fundamentally.

To a young soul, the pain feels personal. You may internalize their actions as proof of inadequacy. You obsess over details, searching for closure that never comes. You replay what you could have done differently. You don't yet see that the heartbreak reveals all the ways you made your worth dependent on someone else's approval.

You may also find yourself comparing your body, your attention, your love to the person they turned to. The wound grows deeper the more you engage in these mental battles, because the illusion is that you're in a competition. But infidelity is never about who was better—it's about disconnection, avoidance, or pain inside the one who strayed. Until you recognize this, you keep fighting shadows instead of reclaiming your own light.

Sometimes, young souls try to "win back" the relationship by over-performing—becoming more accommodating, more attractive, more available. Yet this effort only reinforces the original wound: the belief that your worth depends on someone else's choice. Healing begins when you stop bargaining for love and start standing for yourself.

Other times, the wound drives you in the opposite direction—into numbing, distractions, or even your own betrayals. You may think, *If they hurt me, I'll hurt them back.* But vengeance doesn't heal. It only layers more shame and confusion on top of the pain already present. The emptiness remains, because the core wound is untouched: the illusion that your value is fragile.

Eventually, the suffering burns itself out. The energy to chase, compare, or control runs dry. In that silence, new questions arise: *Is this who I am? Is this what I'm worth?* Slowly, the answer emerges—not in words, but in a subtle returning to yourself. Their betrayal does not define you. Your healing begins not with fixing the relationship, but with no longer fixating on it.

With time, your power returns. Trust is rebuilt, but now on a different foundation. You begin to ask: *What kind of love—starting with my own—am I willing to embody now?* Whether you stay, leave, or begin again elsewhere, you carry this vow forward: I will no longer abandon myself in order to be loved by someone else.

Old Soul

For an old soul, infidelity cuts even deeper—not only through the heart, but through the spirit. It's not just the breaking of trust. It's the fracturing of what once felt like a sacred container, a union consecrated by love. What you grieve is not only the person, but the energetic bond, the soul agreement that once felt holy. The pain can feel karmic, archetypal—as though it touches a wound older than this life.

And yet, you don't rush to conclusions. You pause. You feel the contraction in your chest, the ache in your energy field. You sit with the wound without immediately trying to explain it away. You ask not only *what happened*, but *why your soul called this in*. You don't seek revenge, but you also don't bypass accountability. You understand that people act from their own unconsciousness and pain, but you also know truth is sacred. Compassion matters. So does honesty. You can hold both.

Even with all your awareness, it takes time before you can see infidelity as a passage toward transcendence. For the time being, you know not to skip the grief. You let the burning hollow you out, because you understand that every false shelter eventually dissolves. From a spiritual perspective, the safety we place in others is always illusory.

You also see infidelity as a mirror, exposing unspoken fractures in the relationship itself. Sometimes the act is the symptom, not the root. The question becomes: *What in this bond had already gone silent, avoided, unexpressed?* The betrayal forces truth to the surface—not to punish, but to pull what was hidden into the light.

And paradoxically, the pain deepens your compassion. You recognize how easily humans act from fear, loneliness, or lack of consciousness. This doesn't excuse the act, but it broadens your heart's capacity to understand. You learn to hold the paradox: that someone can love you and betray you, that someone can be beautiful and broken at once.

From this vantage point, you are reminded that love is never meant to be owned. You realize that attachment masquerading as devotion creates fragility, while true devotion creates freedom. Infidelity shatters illusions of possession, forcing you back to the deeper truth that love is not a contract, but a frequency.

And so, in the raw silence of loss, you remember: You are your own sanctuary. Your worth was never compromised. Your light was never dimmed. You are not the victim of reality—you are the maker of it.

Whether you choose to stay or to leave, you act from alignment, not reactivity. If you walk away, it is not with bitterness, but with forgiveness to set yourself free. If you rebuild, it is not from fear, but from a willingness to do the deep work. Either way, you no longer see yourself as broken. You see your wholeness more clearly than ever.

Prompts

1) If you've recently felt betrayed, what part of you feels most wounded—your heart, your ego, your spirit?

2) What story did this relationship represent for you, and how has that story shifted?

3) In what ways have you taken responsibility for something that was not your fault?

4) What do you need to forgive—not to excuse, but to release yourself from ongoing harm?

5) What emotions are you avoiding—and what might happen if you allowed yourself to feel them fully? What boundaries are becoming clear to you through this experience?

6) How can you begin rebuilding trust—not just in others, but in your own perception and intuition?

7) What would it look like to stay loyal to *yourself* now, regardless of what happens next?

CHAPTER 34

DIVORCE

YOUNG SOUL

For a young soul, divorce isn't just the end of a relationship—it's the dismantling of an entire life you've built and identified with. It's not just love that ends, but the home, routines, traditions, finances, and the future plans you once assumed were certain. The loss feels multidimensional—a collapse of identity, stability, and belonging all at once.

Then comes the legal reality. The sterile language of settlements and custody agreements collides with the rawness of your emotions. Suddenly you're navigating lawyers, paperwork, and bank accounts in the midst of heartbreak. Each signature feels like a reminder that something sacred has been reduced to a transaction.

Socially, the shift is heavy. The label "divorced" can feel like a brand you never wanted—changing how friends, family, and even strangers perceive you. You may sense pity, judgment, or awkward silences. Relationships with in-laws, mutual friends, and communities may dissolve or force you to choose sides. What once felt like a shared world now feels fractured.

In quiet moments, grief becomes overwhelming. You're not only missing a person, but a role—spouse, partner, half of a pair. You may replay the vows, the promises, the certainty you once believed in. Beneath the anger or sadness may live a private fear: *If this didn't last, what can I trust?*

You may also find yourself clinging to the past, replaying arguments or wishing you could rewrite history. The mind obsesses: *What if I had tried harder? What if I had compromised more?* But this self-blame only prolongs the wound. You haven't yet seen that relationships tend to end—not from failure, but from growth that diverges.

At the same time, the instability can awaken survival fears—about money, housing, even identity. Who are you without the roles and structures that once defined you? At first, the answer feels terrifyingly blank. But this blankness is also the canvas. Divorce strips away what was false, making room for something truer to emerge.

For many young souls, there's an urge to rush into the next relationship as a way to avoid the emptiness. You may want to prove you're still lovable, still desirable, still capable of being chosen. But this often repeats the same patterns that led you here. Until you pause and look inward, the cycle continues.

Eventually, divorce reveals itself not only as a public ending, but as a personal rebirth. Yes, a chapter closes. But you now have the chance to write a new one with more honesty, freedom, and authenticity. The question is no longer *Who was I in the marriage?* but *Who am I willing to become now that it's over?* In time, you see that the very ground you feared losing was never stable to begin with—and that the real foundation must come from within.

Old Soul

As an old soul, you see divorce as a sacred disentanglement, not only from a person, but from the structures, identities, and energetic agreements you held together. You recognize that while love may have been the seed, marriage grows roots that run through homes, finances, families, and subtle energetic fields. Uprooting them takes care, patience, and presence.

You grieve consciously—not only the companionship, but the dissolution of rituals, spaces, and rhythms of daily life. You don't rush to fill the void. Instead, you honor the dismantling as part of the process, knowing that endings of this magnitude deserve reverence.

You also understand the public weight of divorce. The narrative of "success" and "failure" in marriage can tempt you toward shame, but you decline. You know a union can be complete without lasting until death, and that duration says nothing about the authenticity of the love that once was.

Rather than treating legalities as cold or impersonal, you see them as acts of closure and tangible release. Dividing property, signing documents, and releasing obligations become important gestures of return. At the energetic level, you sense the need for clearing, cord cutting, and integration, so that both can move freely. This is forgiveness in action.

There's also gratitude, even amid the grief. You can bless what was given—the laughter, the growth, the companionship—without demanding it remain forever. You hold both truth and tenderness, knowing that love doesn't disappear simply because its form changes. What was real will always live in you, even if the partnership dissolves.

Ultimately, you emerge from divorce not only as a single person, but as a being more whole than before. You no longer see divorce as evidence of failure, but as a form of integrity: the courage to stop living a life that no longer aligns.

DIVORCE CHART

The way you view endings has a big impact on how you move forward. This chart illustrates the differences between how young souls and old souls cope with divorce.

Young Souls (Contractual Marriage)	Old Souls (Soul Partnership)
Sees divorce as ultimate failure	Sees divorce as sacred completion
Feels loss of person, role, and stability	Feels completion of soul contract and shared structures
Overwhelmed by legal and logistical process	Uses legal process as ritual closure
Fears social judgment and stigma	Releases societal labels and stigma
Clings to marriage ideals despite misalignment	Accepts seasons and natural endings
Feels identity collapse without partner	Finds renewed wholeness beyond partnership
Rushes to fill the void or prove worth	Holds space for healing and integration
Views settlement as loss of resources	Views settlement as return of energy
Seeks quick "moving on"	Seeks full "moving through"
Focuses on past promises	Focuses on future alignment

© 2025 Cirak

Prompts

1) What did your marriage teach you about yourself, your needs, your wounds, your patterns?

2) Where in the relationship did you stay silent to keep the peace? What did that cost you?

3) Are you grieving the person, the identity, or the future you imagined together?

4) What do you fear most about life after divorce—and what deeper truth might be hidden beneath that fear?

5) How are you relating to your ex—through blame, compassion, indifference, or unfinished longing?

6) What part of your self-worth is still tied to how the relationship ended?

7) If you saw this divorce as a soul agreement completed, what did both of you come here to learn from each other?

8) What parts of yourself are beginning to return now that the relationship has ended?

9) How can you create emotional closure for yourself, even if you never get it from the other person?

Chapter 35

Empty Nest

Young Soul

The shift into an empty nest can feel like a seismic disruption. The compass that once guided your every day is suddenly gone. For years, even decades, your life revolved around your child's needs, schedules, and growth. Their becoming became your anchor. So when they leave, it's not just their absence you feel—it's the vanishing of a role that defined who you were.

You may find yourself asking, *Who am I now? What do I do with this space?* The silence in the house feels louder than expected. Without the constancy of caregiving, you may feel useless, invisible, or unmoored. The temptation arises to fill the space with new obligations, or to stay overly involved in your child's life, hoping to preserve that sense of being needed.

Much of the pain comes from mistaking the role of parent as purpose. You may have forgotten that you existed before parenting—and you will continue after. But without that role, a fear creeps in that your best years are behind you, that your worth depends on someone needing you. You grieve not only the loss of connection, but the deeper sense of direction.

The mind replays milestones, birthdays, holidays, the laughter and chaos that once filled your days. You can feel like the center of gravity has shifted outside of you. In the absence of constant responsibility, old doubts may surface: *Do I still matter? Is my story complete?*

And yet, as with all endings, a new horizon waits. Over time, the nest no longer feels empty but open. What once seemed like loss begins to reveal itself as possibility. A new beginning, not a final chapter. The invitation beneath the ache is always the same: to return to yourself, to the parts of you that have been patiently waiting for space and time.

Old Soul

As an old soul, you know the empty nest is not an ending but a transition—though one that carries its own ache. You always knew parenting was a chapter, not the whole book. You raised your child not to hold onto them, but to release them. And so when they leave, the grief is tender, but not bitter—an honoring of the depth of love you've poured into them, and the grace of letting go.

You don't resist the sadness. You sit with it as it moves through you, knowing it will pass. You honor the spaciousness it brings—the quiet after years of noise, the stillness after decades of giving. Finally, you return to your own inner world, to the longings set aside, to the whispers that had to wait.

This is not the end of nurturing. It's a redirection. Now it flows inward—into creativity, service, play, solitude, and soul. What once was given outwardly is now free to blossom within you as the wisdom of your presence.

You also trust. You trust their path, even if you don't understand it. You trust your own unfolding, even if it looks unfamiliar. You offer insight only if invited, knowing that the greatest gift you can give your child now is faith in their sovereignty.

And when grief still visits, you let it open you. You no longer mistake absence for loss. You know love only changes form. And in the acceptance of this change, you find peace.

PROMPTS

1) What role has parenting played in shaping your identity—and who are you beyond that role?

2) What emotions are arising in this transition? Which ones are you avoiding or resisting?

3) Are you trying to stay needed—and if so, what deeper need is that fulfilling in you?

4) How would it feel to bless your child's journey, without inserting yourself into it?

5) What parts of yourself have been set aside during your parenting years that now want attention?

6) In what ways are you being called to nurture yourself now, as you once nurtured others?

7) What does this newfound space in your life invite you to explore or create?

MENTAL

Chapter 36

Knowledge

Young Soul

Young souls tend to believe that knowledge is everything. You crave answers, facts, and certainty. And why wouldn't you? Society rewards this kind of mind. You're praised for being articulate and informed. Degrees, promotions, and social status all seem to hinge on what you know. So you naturally equate knowledge with intelligence, and intelligence with self-worth.

The more you know, the more control you feel. And the more control you feel, the safer you believe you are. An entire structure of mental truths is erected through which you interpret life. It feels comforting to think the world can be organized, labeled, and understood—that everything has a name, a reason, a rule. This becomes your shield against uncertainty or change, and against the deeper vulnerability of feeling lost.

But what no one tells you is that most knowledge is simply organized opinion—a temporary consensus shaped by language, culture, and conditioning. You think you're creating stability, when in fact your sense of self becomes as fragile, rigid, and easily threatened as the mental framework it is based on.

Over time, the cracks begin to show. Truths you once defended start to look naive. Ideas you believed absolutely yesterday get revised today. A subtle panic grows as you try to anchor yourself in something that keeps shifting. You double down, get defensive, or seek more and more information, hoping the next insight will bring peace. But the more you consume, the more incomplete you feel. Knowledge becomes a substitute for wisdom, presence, and trust.

Eventually, life delivers situations knowledge can't resolve: a diagnosis, a betrayal, a dark night of the soul. Despite all the information you've gathered, you still feel lost. You realize knowledge can't teach you how to feel, how to heal, or how to trust. And though destabilizing, this is also the beginning of something more powerful—the slow shift from mental certainty to intuitive clarity.

And yet, the young soul still clings. You study harder, read more books, attend more trainings—thinking that if you just "know enough," life will finally cooperate. But the peace you're chasing never comes, because peace doesn't live in the mind. It arises in the spaces the mind cannot touch: presence, silence, surrender. Until you glimpse this, the loop of grasping continues.

Eventually, exhaustion sets in. You can no longer deny that information cannot substitute for inner knowing. You start to see that the most important things in life—love, grief, beauty, truth—can't be captured by concepts at all. That recognition humbles you. And in humility, the old soul begins to awaken.

Old Soul

As an old soul, you've let go of the fantasy that anything can be known in a final way. You've watched facts get rewritten, experts fall from grace, and "truths" dissolve under closer inspection. You see now that knowledge is not solid ground but shifting sand. The moment you think you know something, life surprises you. The moment you hold something too tightly, it slips through your fingers.

You've come to see that most knowledge is a projection—a mental overlay on reality too fluid to be captured in names and numbers. The more aware you become, the more you feel the limits of language and the futility of arguments. You stop confusing information with truth. You stop clinging to certainty and grow comfortable with mystery. Even if you say aloud, *"This is my car,"* inwardly you know, *"This is what I call my car."* By softening the label, you let life remain alive.

This loosening brings lightness. You no longer move through the world trying to prove, persuade, or be right. You no longer confuse intellect with wisdom. You live life from a deeper guidance that is not logical, not linear—but precise, embodied, and unmistakably true.

Old souls typically carry very few opinions and feel little urgency to defend them. They've seen how opinions often mask fear. They wait, they watch, they respond only when truth resonates. Their presence itself becomes a form of knowing that doesn't rely on words.

You now live from an intelligence that doesn't belong to the head but arises from the field of being. You're not generating thoughts anymore; thoughts arise in you. You're not demanding answers; you're willing to let questions unfold until they ripen. Truth becomes something you experience, not something you argue for. And in this surrender, synchronicity, clarity, and grace flow in like air entering an open room.

This is the shift from knowledge to wisdom. From needing to know to being willing not to. You don't reject information, but you no longer worship it. You don't fear uncertainty, but find aliveness in it. True intelligence lives in the willingness to not know, and still be fully present. True wisdom doesn't live in accumulation, but in refinement. You've noticed the less you cling to concepts, the more directly you can perceive reality. A bird song, a breath, a sudden intuition. Every moment offers knowledge beyond anything you could read in a book.

And so, instead of stockpiling ideas, you trust that what you truly need to know will arise when needed, no sooner, no later. This dissolves urgency, and what replaces it is a quiet confidence that no matter what happens, you and life will meet it together.

Knowledge Chart

One of the great challenges of life in the physical dimension is to discern inner wisdom from outer information. Your ability to do so has a significant impact on how you experience everyday life. The following chart highlights the young soul vs old soul relationship with knowledge.

Young Souls	Old Souls
Knowledge is equated with intelligence and worth	Knowledge is seen as provisional and never final
Facts, degrees, and labels define identity	Labels are softened; truth left fluid and alive
Control and safety sought through mental certainty	Humility and mystery embraced over certainty
Clings rigidly to frameworks that keep shifting	Holds beliefs lightly, ready to let them dissolve
Confuses recalling information with true wisdom	Recognizes wisdom as embodied, intuitive, beyond thought
Seeks validation by "being right" and proving others wrong	Has no urgency to defend positions or opinions
Collects more knowledge to soothe insecurity	Lives from presence, trusting the right knowing will arise
Fearful of the unknown and resists uncertainty	Finds aliveness and freedom in not knowing
Identity built on mental scaffolding that collapses under pressure	Identity dissolved into flow, presence, and open awareness
Knowledge as shield against vulnerability	Knowledge as tool, not master—wisdom flows from being

PROMPTS

1) What are some truths you were taught growing up that you no longer believe?

2) Where in your life do you still cling to needing to be "right"? How does this affect your relationships or your ability to stay open?

3) Can you recall a time when what you thought was a failure turned out to be a blessing? Or when something you were proud of became a burden?

4) When you experience choice overload, how do you respond? With frustration, or do you tune into your body?

5) In what ways has your desire for certainty blocked your growth, creativity, or intimacy?

6) How does it feel to admit "I don't know"? What do you associate with not knowing—weakness, relief, shame, freedom?

7) Reflect on a recent situation where you formed a quick opinion. What would change if you held that opinion more lightly—or let it go entirely?

8) How often do you allow intuition to guide your decisions, even when it contradicts logic? What are the outcomes when you do?

CHAPTER 37

Planning

YOUNG SOUL

As a young soul, life is all about The Plan. You're taught that if you don't map it all out—the 1-year, 5-year, 10-year goals—you'll fall behind. There's a plan for school, a plan for career, a plan for marriage and kids, and eventually a plan for retirement and even death. The fact that society has invented neat labels for each of these stages—each carrying a truckload of unspoken expectations—should be a wake-up call that something is too rigid, too prescriptive for life to blossom fully. But for a young soul, it's reassuring. There's comfort in knowing what comes next, and in surrounding yourself with others who are also trying to stay "on track."

Talking to your peers, almost every conversation circles back to *What's your plan? When are you getting married? When are you buying a house?* Beneath it all sits a quiet but terrifying fear of not knowing who you are without a plan to hold on to. Young souls internalize these timelines as truth, then project them onto each other. The pressure is constant and mutual. You push yourself and those around you to keep checking the boxes, believing it's the only way to make life meaningful.

You haven't yet realized that life doesn't care about your plan. Whenever it breaks the script, bends the rules, or throws you a curveball, you feel like you've failed, that you need to plan harder to regain control. But then the plan stops working altogether. A career falls apart, a relationship ends, an illness reroutes your trajectory. The disruption rattles your sense of self.

You start to consider that not everyone is meant to follow the same path. No template, however convincing, can accommodate every soul's design. Maybe no amount of strategy will guarantee meaning, safety, or belonging. Maybe life isn't about following the beaten path, but about carving your own.

You may still plan—old habits don't vanish overnight. But you're no longer trying to impress, prove, or keep up. You speak less and listen more. You allow the unknown a seat at the table. Not begrudgingly, but out of full recognition that your best life can only emerge when it contains a big dose of uncertainty.

And for the first time, you take steps not in someone else's footprints, but in your own.

OLD SOUL

As an old soul, you know better than to over-orchestrate life. You've tasted the illusion of control and seen how fragile it is. Planning doesn't offend you—you'll book the flight, keep a calendar, show up on time—but you've stopped pretending you can predict the future. There's humility in your approach: the recognition that life reveals itself through what you don't yet know about yourself. The future manifests not from your plans, but from your blind spots, shadows, and unexpressed potentials—the parts of you waiting to be met.

That's why planning the whole path is futile. Growth cannot happen in the known. Your path appears only in the steps you take into the unknown. And what unfolds depends on whether you meet it with fear, resistance, and judgement, or with curiosity, openness, and acceptance. Each orientation shapes the terrain ahead.

You may still hold intentions, move toward a vision, or follow a calling, but there's always space for the unexpected. In fact, you expect it—and so it no longer surprises you when the script changes. What's meant for you arrives. What isn't falls away. Life has a rhythm, and you've learned to dance with it rather than enforce your own.

That doesn't mean you're immune to the lure of planning. You still catch yourself imagining how things *should* go. But you've learned to notice the contraction that follows. When plans tighten, you adjust, remembering that the less time you linger in resistance, the quicker you return to alignment.

You also see that the best opportunities in life rarely arrive on schedule. The friendships, the breakthroughs, the moments of grace—they come when they're ready, not when you think you are. By trusting this, you free yourself from the anxiety of constant preparation. You keep your hands open, ready to receive what you couldn't have planned for in a thousand lifetimes.

Where young souls measure their worth by milestones, old souls measure it by resonance. It's no longer *Did I do what I said I would?* but *Did I follow what felt true?* Not *Did life happen as expected?* but *Did I allow it to become even more than I imagined?* By now you know that the most extraordinary moments in life are impossible to plan for, yet always perfect in their timing.

Instead of clinging to a perfect plan, you stay alert but relaxed, intentional but surrendered. You keep your calendar but also keep it open. You catch the signs, you welcome surprise, and you let synchronicity lead the way. You offer your presence to what's here, without rushing toward what's not. In this way, life is about participating in the mystery. And the mystery proves itself endlessly wiser than any plan could be.

Planning Chart

The following chart illustrates how young souls vs old souls make use of planning.

Young Souls	Old Souls
Life feels safe only with a detailed roadmap	Life feels alive when the path is discovered step by step
Future measured by timelines and milestones	Future welcomed as mystery and unfolding
Worth tied to sticking to "the plan"	Worth tied to inner alignment and presence
Disruption seen as failure	Disruption seen as initiation into deeper truth
Rigid schedules used to feel in control	Intentions held lightly, leaving space for flow
Planning driven by fear of falling behind	Planning guided by resonance and intuition
Unknown treated as threat	Unknown embraced as the field of possibility
Focus on what should happen	Focus on what is actually happening
Attachment to outcomes creates stress	Trust in divine timing creates peace
Life organized as a checklist	Life experienced as a dance with the unexpected

© 2025 Cirak

PROMPTS

1) What do you most often try to control through planning, and why?

2) How do you respond when things don't go according to plan?

3) Where in your life are your plans rooted in fear instead of trust?

4) What would it feel like to plan from a place of inspiration, not pressure?

5) Do you make space for spontaneity, intuition, and rest in your plans? Why or why not?

6) What old belief about "being prepared" might be holding you back from being present?

7) How has life surprised you in ways your plans never could have predicted?

8) Can you predict the future? If not, why do you continue to live as if you can?

9) When has surrendering the plan brought you more peace or clarity?

10) What's one area where you can simplify your planning to make more room for flow?

Chapter 38

Procrastination

Young Soul

It starts with a small delay. You tell yourself you'll get to it after lunch, after one more email, after scrolling just a bit longer. But the hours slip by, and the thing you know you should be doing stays untouched—looming like a shadow you're pretending not to see. This isn't laziness. This is avoidance. Not of the task itself, but of the feelings you believe will come with it: fear, pressure, not being enough.

Procrastination is an emotional block in disguise. You avoid the start because starting invites thoughts about the future. *What if I fail? What if it's not perfect? What if others see me stumble?* To compensate, you keep yourself busy with low-stakes distractions. You overthink, overplan, make excuses, and push the start date into a mythical "tomorrow" that you never want to have arrive.

The longer you delay, the heavier it becomes. Guilt creeps in because you keep breaking promises to yourself. Over time, you stop trusting your own word. Your self-esteem dips, making action even harder. Life begins to feel like one long backlog of unfinished intentions, each one quietly draining your energy.

Deep down, this resistance is a kind of self-protection. A younger, more vulnerable part of you is trying to shield you from difficult feelings. But avoidance doesn't spare you from discomfort—it keeps you locked inside it, trapped in the very fear you're trying to escape.

The shift begins when you stop making procrastination the enemy and start listening to what it's telling you. Every delay is an invitation to look closer: *What am I afraid of? What am I protecting?* And when you start to answer honestly, the paralysis begins to loosen. This is the threshold where procrastination changes from an endless cycle into a teacher leading you toward old soul awareness.

OLD SOUL

You've stopped seeing procrastination as proof of weakness. When resistance to doing something shows up, you pause and ask: *Is this aligned? Am I forcing something that doesn't want to be forced?* Sometimes the answer is yes. And in that case, waiting isn't failure—it's wisdom.

You've learned that not all delays are avoidance. Sometimes they're incubation. The soul moves in rhythms the mind can't always plan for. Inspiration is a tide—it comes in, it goes out, and forcing it only muddies the water. You trust the tide.

Then there are times when procrastination is simply a sign that the vision is too big or the path too vague. You've stopped shaming yourself in those moments. Instead, you shrink the task down to one gentle, doable step. You make it smaller so you can meet it, rather than overwhelm yourself out of it.

You've also learned to tell the difference between two kinds of tension: the stretch of growth and the strain of misalignment. One invites you forward. The other warns you to stop. That discernment keeps you from chasing things that don't belong to your path.

You now see that procrastination, when held consciously, is never wasted time. Even in stillness, something is ripening beneath the surface. What looks like delay on the outside can be preparation on the inside—a quiet gestation that ensures when you finally act, it's with clarity, alignment, and power. From that place, the doing feels effortless, because it's not fueled by force. It's carried by flow.

Prompts

1) What task or responsibility are you currently avoiding, and why?

2) What emotions arise when you imagine starting the thing you've been putting off?

3) What are you telling yourself about the importance or pressure of the task?

4) How do you typically respond to your own procrastination—with judgment or curiosity?

5) How would your life change if you trusted your natural rhythm instead of forcing productivity?

6) What does "inspired action" feel like in your body? How is it different from pressure?

7) What's one loving, small step you can take today toward what you've been avoiding?

8) How can you make the first step toward your task less intimidating or more inviting?

9) What would happen if you worked on it for just 10 minutes, without pressure to finish?

CHAPTER 39

EXPECTATIONS

YOUNG SOUL

As a young soul, your life is unconsciously built around expectations. You move through the world assuming it owes you something—love, success, recognition, happiness. And why wouldn't you? Earth dazzles the senses. Beauty is everywhere. Possibilities stretch in every direction. The sheer variety of experiences makes it seem like joy must be just around the corner. So you chase it with confidence, believing that once you reach the right milestones, everything will finally fall into place.

You expect relationships to fulfill you. Careers to validate you. Even spiritual practices carry the hidden agenda that they elevate you. When life falls short—as it inevitably does—frustration takes over and the mind starts spinning: *This isn't fair. This isn't how it was supposed to go. I did everything right.* You cling to imagined outcomes and feel betrayed when life moves in another direction. But the suffering doesn't come from what's happening—it comes from what you thought *should* be happening.

Beneath every expectation is a deeper longing—not just for pleasure or ease, but for permanence. You want the good to last forever. You want guarantees. You want to arrive somewhere and never have to leave. But trying to make life hold still in a constantly shifting world is a battle you cannot win. Every time you get what you thought you wanted, the satisfaction fades quickly. Society may dress it up as ambition or motivation, but energetically and spiritually, it's illusion.

For a while, you keep clinging to the old, while already chasing the next thing, trying to keep the high continuous. Yet there is a quiet desperation in the chase that slowly exhausts you. Eventually, you notice that expectations don't actually help you. All they do is keep you locked in a cycle of craving and disappointment.

And then one day, life lets something fall apart in just the right way. A plan. A relationship. A hope collapses. It's painful, but that's what makes you look up from your comfort zone. And from that moment of disillusionment, a new question arises: *If not through expectations, where does fulfillment come from?* That's the threshold where your old soul begins to stir.

Old Soul

As an old soul, you no longer expect permanence in a world built on change. You don't anchor your peace in things that can be gained or lost. And because of that, your relationship with life becomes quieter, lighter, freer. You suffer less—not because life has grown easier, but because you've stopped insisting it conform to your preferences.

Sometimes you still notice the pull toward certainty and control. After all, it's a deeply conditioned reflex. But you no longer let it drive you. You've discovered that the only real constant is your connection to Source. That's where your trust lives now. Not in outcomes. Not in timing. Not in promises. In the pulse of life itself moving through you.

When you set intentions, you hold them loosely. You let resonance lead the way. You leave space for divine timing and the unexpected. Instead of trying to bend the current of life to your will, you've turned downstream to flow with it.

That doesn't mean all desires vanish. You may still want things, but they're no longer conditions for happiness. You don't bargain with life by saying, *I'll be at peace if this happens.* Peace is now. Joy is now. And into that open space of *now*, life delivers more than you could ever script for yourself.

You've also realized that it's not wrong to want permanence in peace, love, or stillness. That longing is sacred—it's the soul's memory of home. What changes is where you look for it. You stop expecting the world around you to give you what only the world within can provide. When expectations fall away, the higher self rises. Perfection appears not because life is how you wanted it, but because it is exactly as it is.

Ultimately, life is no longer a race you're trying to win. It becomes a continuous dance, each moment inviting you to step in as you are. In unmet hopes, dismantled plans, and disappointments, you feel identity layers falling away—beliefs, demands, illusions. What remains is so simple, yet so profound: a presence that needs nothing, a heart ready for anything, and a soul free to love without conditions.

Oddly enough, life gives you everything you ever longed for when you finally stop expecting it to.

Expectations Chart

It can be challenging to stay out of one's head and keep expectations at bay. Life feels too important not to get involved. The following chart highlights the difference between how young souls and old souls set expectations.

Aspect	Young Souls (Demanding Life)	Old Souls (Dancing with Life)
Core Belief	Life should give me what I want if I do things "right"	Life owes me nothing, but gives everything in its own timing
Source of Peace	Getting desired outcomes	Remaining present regardless of outcomes
Relationship to Permanence	Clings to the good, fears loss	Accepts change as natural, trusts in what endures beyond form
Response to Disappointment	Feels betrayed, spirals into frustration or despair	Feels the sting but adjusts, looking for what's unfolding instead
Approach to Desire	Chases goals with urgency or attachment	Holds intentions lightly, allows them to ripen
View of Control	Believes control ensures safety and success	Sees control as limiting, trusts in flow
Measure of Fulfillment	How closely life matches the plan	How deeply one aligns with truth in the moment
Reaction to the Unknown	Seeks certainty before moving forward	Steps into the unknown as part of the journey
Energy Orientation	Transactional – "If I do this, I'll get that"	Reverent – "I'll give my all and receive what's meant"
Underlying Lesson	External circumstances cannot create lasting peace	Presence itself is the source of lasting peace

© 2025 Cirak

Prompts

1) When have you felt most disappointed by life? What were you expecting to happen?

2) What unspoken expectations do you place on your relationships, and how do they shape your interactions?

3) In what areas of life do you still feel entitled to a particular outcome?

4) What does it feel like in your body when you're clinging to an outcome?

5) What fears lie beneath your strongest expectations?

6) How would your energy shift if you held your goals with more curiosity than attachment?

7) When have your unmet expectations led you to a deeper insight or turning point?

8) What are three expectations you're ready to release today?

Chapter 40

Comparison

Young Soul

As a young soul, comparison is not just a habit—it's the natural result of living in your head. The head operates by sorting, measuring, ranking, and analyzing. It needs reference points. It can't know itself without something to compare against. So your eyes are always scanning: peers, colleagues, friends, even strangers online. Their highlight reels become your mirror, their milestones your scoreboard. You measure yourself not by truth, but by proximity to others.

It's not that you want to be them—you just don't want to feel like you're losing. The head convinces you that life is a race, and unless you're ahead, you're behind. Every achievement you witness is interpreted through this filter: either fuel to drive harder or evidence that you're falling short. And because culture reinforces this through grades, rankings, performance reviews, follower counts—you internalize comparison as reality itself.

The trouble is that comparison flattens your experience. A moment of joy is instantly muted when you notice someone else has gone further. Success dissolves the moment it's measured. Even love and friendship can feel heavy when filtered through the head's constant evaluations. The body may feel content, but the head insists: *You're not enough. Keep going.*

This leaves you restless, anxious, and disconnected from your own truth. You don't notice how deeply comparison alienates you from yourself—because every ounce of energy is projected outward. Only in rare pauses can you glimpse another possibility. You notice that your body doesn't compare. It just feels. And that subtle noticing—that maybe worth doesn't need measurement—marks the first stirrings of your old soul

OLD SOUL

As an old soul, you've stepped out of the tyranny of the head and dropped into the wisdom of the body. You've seen that comparison is not real—it's a mental overlay, a distortion that makes you chase illusions. The body doesn't compare. It senses resonance, truth, and alignment. Where the head says *Am I better or worse?*, the body says *Does this feel right?*

This shift changes everything. You stop using others as your mirror and start listening inward. Self-worth is no longer defined by metrics or milestones—it's felt directly, in the quiet steadiness of your own presence. You can look at another's success and feel genuine joy without it subtracting from your own. Their path is theirs. Yours is yours. No overlap is possible because no two bodies, no two blueprints, no two souls are the same.

Comparison still arises from time to time, but now you can feel the contraction immediately. It's tight, small, restless—an energy that belongs to the head, not to you. Instead of reacting, you observe the sensations in your body: your breath, your chest, the feeling of being here. In that shift, the illusion dissolves. You no longer need to argue with the thought; you simply stop giving your attention to it.

Over time, fulfillment no longer comes from being "ahead." It comes from being present and aligned. Joy no longer comes from winning. It comes from feeling whole, in tune with your own design. In this embodied state, comparison falls away on its own—because truth is no longer measured, it's lived.

Prompts

1) Who do you most often compare yourself to, and why?

2) What sensations arise in your body when you notice yourself comparing?

3) How has comparison shaped your choices in the past?

4) What's one achievement you downplayed because someone else did "better"?

5) When has comparison motivated you in a healthy way?

6) What would your life look like if you measured yourself only by inner alignment?

7) How can you celebrate others' successes without diminishing your own?

8) How can you remind yourself that your body's truth is not dependent on anyone else's?

Chapter 41

People-Pleasing

Young Soul

As a young soul, your sense of self is still primarily based on how others perceive you—how people treat you, what they say, how they react. Approval feels like proof that you're worthy; disapproval feels like rejection. You naturally become skilled at scanning the room, adjusting your tone, and suppressing your truth. You're not being dishonest, you're just not in touch with your true self. And there's nothing more terrifying than showing off a version of yourself that you yourself are unfamiliar with.

This fear of being seen is so ingrained that you can't name it. But somewhere along the way, you learned that being yourself is not enough. As is often the case, the roots trace back to childhood. Perhaps you grew up with emotionally unavailable or overly critical parents. Perhaps the only way to feel loved was to be useful, agreeable, and meet their demands. That early conditioning—*I must earn love*—becomes the lens through which you see yourself and how you engage with the world.

Unless you do the inner work, this dynamic never ends. The child seeking love never really disappears; it just becomes better at pretending. People-pleasing becomes a strategy for safety: *If others are happy with me, maybe I'll finally be safe, loved, and worthy.* You're not consciously saying that to yourself, but that's what's going on underneath, motivating your behaviors. So you walk on eggshells, constantly monitoring yourself, trying to say the right thing, be helpful, be needed. You might even believe you're being kind—not realizing that kindness without truth is just servitude. There's always another scene, another person, another way to lose yourself in pleasing others.

What makes this cycle especially heavy is that it feeds on itself. The more you please others, the more approval you crave. The dependence on others grows stronger, leaving you emptier and more anxious. It becomes a loop of external validation and inner emptiness that never resolves—until the tension forces you to see that no amount of pleasing others can ever give you the love you've been searching for.

This ongoing self-abandonment comes at a tremendous cost. In your relationships, resentment builds on both sides. The clinging energy of people-pleasing makes others take you for granted. When you try harder, you only get treated worse. You overextend and burn out, managing everyone's feelings except your own. The longer you live outside yourself—attending to everyone else's opinions—the harder it becomes to hear your own voice. And without your voice, you have no anchor.

At some point, a quiet knowing arises that you can't keep sacrificing your truth for temporary soothing. The shift toward old soul maturity begins when you turn inward. When you stop seeking approval and start practicing self-acceptance. When you stop meeting everyone else's needs and finally meet your own.

Old Soul

As an old soul, you see clearly that you cannot control how others feel about you—nor is it your responsibility to try. You've outgrown the belief that love must be earned or that worth can be negotiated. You know who you are, and you trust that being true to yourself will resonate with the right people. If your authenticity rubs someone the wrong way, you recognize it as their reaction, not your issue. You no longer confuse people-pleasing with kindness. Real kindness is rooted in truth—because truth honors both you and the other person.

You've walked through fire to get here—through heartbreaks, betrayals, and the exhaustion of carrying masks. You've learned that contorting yourself for harmony only breeds resentment and disconnection. So now, you choose clarity over comfort. You'd rather be known for integrity than likability. Loving yourself first is the only place you feel at home.

When your self-worth no longer depends on circumstances, you free your well-being from external limitations. Whether someone admires you, misunderstands you, or walks away—your inner peace remains intact. You don't pine for approval or shrink to avoid conflict. You trust that your authenticity is both your protection and your gift.

You also extend compassion toward the part of you that once needed to please. You see it as a survival mechanism that once kept you safe, but is no longer necessary. You choose to be seen, regardless of consequences. You choose to be you, even if it means walking alone. And that choice—repeated daily—becomes your superpower.

From this place, you no longer trade your truth for connection. Instead, you bring your truth into every connection. Your intimacy with life deepens—not because you're working to be lovable, but because you are finally, fully, loving yourself.

People-Pleasing Chart

Self-worth runs to the core of who you are and defines how you navigate your world. Treating others better than you treat yourself can drain the life out of you. The following chart illustrates how young vs old souls engage in people-pleasing.

Young Souls	Old Souls
Needs approval to feel worthy	Self-worth independent of others' opinions
Adapts to avoid disapproval	Speaks truth even if it risks disapproval
Seeks love through usefulness or agreeableness	Sees love as natural when authentic
Confuses kindness with compliance	Knows kindness includes honesty
Masks true feelings to keep harmony	Allows genuine expression to guide connection
Fears rejection if authentic	Accepts authenticity may be triggering
Overextends energy to manage others' feelings	Respects own limits and boundaries
Resentment builds from self-abandonment	Peace grows from self-honoring choices
Connection depends on pleasing	Connection deepens through realness
Avoids conflict to stay liked	Allows conflict as part of truthful relating

© 2025 Cirak

PROMPTS

1) When do you feel most tempted to please others, and what are you afraid might happen if you don't?

2) What was your role in your family growing up, and how does it affect your relationships today?

3) Whose approval are you still unconsciously seeking—and why?

4) When was the last time you said "yes" when you really meant "no"? How did it feel?

5) How does your body feel when you're pleasing others versus when you're being yourself?

6) What qualities define the truest version of you, and are you living in alignment with them?

7) Who in your life sees and accepts the real you? How do you know?

8) What boundaries could you set that would honor your energy and truth more deeply?

9) How would your relationships change if you stopped managing others' feelings and started expressing your own?

Chapter 42

Self-Esteem

Young Soul

You've spent your whole life trying to prove you're good enough. To your parents, to your peers, to yourself. Whether it's collecting degrees, chasing admiration, or sculpting the perfect body, your sense of worth hinges on what others reflect back to you. If they're impressed, you feel worthy. If they criticize or ignore you, you plummet. Your self-esteem is only as intact as your most recent win—or as fragile as your latest loss.

It's exhausting to always need validation. You might call it ambition or self-improvement, but underneath is all kinds of fear. Fear of being ignored, invisible, or unlovable. Fear of abandonment or not getting it all done. You measure yourself against others, scanning constantly to see how you rank. You curate your image, manage perceptions, and try to anticipate everything that might happen in response to every step you might take.

To combat the sense of "not enough," you pile on achievements, polish your image, set bigger goals, and push yourself harder. But it's not sustainable. You either feel like a fraud or keep raising the bar. Your identity becomes an accumulation of carefully maintained masks. One unexpected gust of rejection or failure, and it all comes apart.

The story is always the same: as a young soul, you mistake being admired for being whole. But as long as you look for your worth outside of yourself, you'll remain dependent on forces you can't control. You'll resent how brittle your confidence feels, even as you keep feeding the very mindset that makes it so.

It takes burnout, heartbreak, or sheer exhaustion for you to pause and let the question emerge: *Who am I if I stop trying to be somebody and just let myself be?* And that's when your old soul transition begins.

Old Soul

You no longer rely on others to tell you who you are. Your self-esteem isn't inflated by compliments or deflated by criticism—it's rooted in something much deeper. You've touched the peace of knowing your truth. You've experienced yourself as an extension of Source. You no longer need to posture, dominate, or shrink. You stand firmly as you are in the shifting winds of other people's opinions.

Doubt may still visit, but it no longer owns you. Thoughts of inadequacy no longer control your moods. Now that you see that self-worth is inherent to presence, the need for external approval ends. You stop shaping yourself to fit expectations. Instead, you let life shape you, trusting it knows what you're here to become. After all, it created you. Self-esteem, you realize, is not something you build. It arises naturally when you let go of who you're not.

As an old soul, you no longer have a need to be seen. When you act, it is not to prove yourself but to express your truth. Your presence brings clarity to those around you. True alignment is what you now model.

From here, you shine without trying. No external acclaim could add to what you already carry, and no criticism could take it away. The self-esteem born of authenticity is silent, deep, and unshakable.

Prompts

1) What does your current self-esteem depend on? Whose opinions still shape how you see yourself?

2) When do you feel the need to impress, and what emotions are driving that behavior?

3) What achievements or roles do you cling to for identity? What would happen if you let them go?

4) Write about a time you felt truly confident without external validation. What was different?

5) In what ways do you silence or shrink yourself to avoid disapproval?

6) If you no longer needed to maintain an image, what parts of you would emerge?

7) What might it look like to live from the knowing that you have nothing left to prove?

CHAPTER 43

SELF-LOVE

YOUNG SOUL

You didn't get everything you needed growing up—no one does. But instead of recognizing the gap and healing it, you run away from it. You let it direct your actions and choices. You seek love in achievement, praise, beauty, productivity. You try to love others in the hope they'll love you back. Underneath it all, you're motivated by lack. Your drive to be "somebody" is a desperate search for the nurturing you never got.

This fuels patterns you don't even see as wounds: people-pleasing, over-accommodating, You try to earn love by becoming what others want, hoping someone will finally choose you. Yet no amount of outside love fills the void. Compliments don't complete you. Approval fades. Even when others love you, you still don't love yourself more. You might rationalize your loneliness away by proclaiming that self-love is selfish, indulgent, or arrogant. Or you go into the other extreme and over-indulge by buying things, distracting yourself, pampering the surface while ignoring the deeper wound.

And so the cycle continues—over-attaching, over-giving, overthinking—because stopping might reveal the emptiness inside. You don't yet see how you've been conditioned to reject yourself, to minimize your light, to critique your every move. But the more you deny yourself, the more disconnected you become.

You get so used to ignoring your needs that you can't always name them. You numb out, keep busy, or attach to people who mirror your unworthiness back to you. You keep experiencing situations that are "beneath" you and wonder why life keeps repeating itself.

But true love doesn't numb. It doesn't inflate your sense of self. It allows you to finally stop pretending. To stop reinforcing the beliefs that keep you small. To move from judging yourself to freeing yourself. To go from blaming yourself for your wounds to removing their roots.

Ultimately, love is at your core. It comes through as a faint ache for truth, for rest, for love that doesn't have to be earned. That ache is your higher self calling you home. Slowly, you see that the love you've been chasing was always meant to be generated from within.

OLD SOUL

You no longer wait for someone else to love you into wholeness. You've become the parent you needed to your inner child—the one who shows up with warmth, truth, and steady presence. You don't deny the wounds, but you no longer let them decide who you are. Healing is no longer a project—it's an act of ongoing connectedness to self, to flow, to the divine.

The voice of self-criticism no longer runs unchecked. You've become intimately familiar with your inner dialogue, choosing to engage only with what elevates you. You don't live from mentally imposed positivity, but from a felt knowing that your inner state shapes your outer reality. Kindness is not a noble idea anymore—it's the tone of your voice, the way you speak to yourself, the way you move through the day.

You've stopped shrinking to keep others comfortable. You don't downplay your light, your insight, your gifts. You know real love never asks you to dim. On the contrary, it wants you to shine. And when your fullness triggers someone's discomfort, you recognize it's not yours to fix. Self-love is the frequency you bring to the world—and it naturally spills into everything you do.

Now you see that self-love is not just affirmations on your bathroom mirror or nighttime comfort rituals. It's a deep alignment with that which permeates all of life—the passion for creation. The more you love yourself, the more you feel the divine alive within you, the more effortlessly you offer it outward. Your love is no longer conditional—it flows without restraint.

And with that realization comes humility. True self-love doesn't make you feel above others—it dissolves the very need to compare. You recognize the same divine spark in everyone else. Loving yourself becomes inseparable from loving life itself, and in this space, there is no room for arrogance or self-centeredness.

To love yourself is to honor the intelligence that formed you. To affirm the design of life is to walk radiant, rooted, and real. And in being real, you align with the creative force that stirs the oceans and moves the stars. When you love yourself, you become a field where life itself feels loved.

Self-Love Chart

You cannot help others until you help yourself first. You can only love others to the degree you love yourself. The following chat highlights the key differences in how young souls vs old souls approach the topic of self-love.

Young Soul	Old Soul
Seeks love in achievement, appearance, productivity	Generates love from inner presence and alignment
Believes self-love is selfish, indulgent, or arrogant	Understands self-love as humility and reverence for life
Over-attaches, over-gives, overthinks to earn worth	Lives in steady connection with self, not needing external proof
Numbs out, keeps busy, or clings to unworthy situations	Allows all feelings, meets them with compassion and awareness
Critiques self constantly, minimizes own light	Speaks kindly to self, uplifts inner dialogue, honors own gifts
Confuses pampering or over-indulgence for true self-love	Embodies self-love as frequency, radiating through daily presence
Depends on external approval, compliments, or validation	Recognizes wholeness as inherent, not dependent on outcomes
Sees love as conditional, to be earned or lost	Experiences love as unconditional flow, effortless and abundant
Shrinks or adapts to keep others comfortable	Stands rooted in authenticity, even if others feel discomfort
Thinks self-love will make them superior	Realizes self-love dissolves comparison and reveals shared divinity

© 2025 Cirak

Prompts

1) How did your early experiences shape your beliefs about what makes you lovable?

2) In what ways do you still seek validation or love from others to feel complete?

3) What parts of yourself do you hide or shrink in order to be accepted?

4) What's your relationship with your inner voice? Supportive or critical? How would you like it to sound?

5) What does self-love feel like in your body, when it's truly present?

6) How does your self-talk change when you make a mistake? What does that reveal?

7) Write a letter from your highest self to the child within you who didn't feel loved enough.

8) What daily habits would change if you truly believed you were already enough?

9) What are three ways you can express the love within you today, toward yourself and toward life?

Chapter 44

Overthinking

Young Soul

As a young soul, overthinking is the theme of your entire life. And to no surprise. You live inside your head—constantly evaluating, analyzing, defending, reacting. Every thought feels urgent, meaningful, and true. You try to solve overthinking by thinking more. You obsessively plan out your life, all the way to the end. You assume the more you ruminate, the more responsible you are. Your identity fuses with thought until you can't tell the difference between the mental chatter and your inner voice.

Your sense of "me" thrives in this environment. It narrates everything, judges everyone, and places you at the center of every scenario—usually as either the victim or the hero. You compare yourself to others obsessively, worry about how you're being perceived, and defend your beliefs with vigor. You try to think your way through life to stay safe from uncertainty, vulnerability, and from confronting the discomfort of emotional depth.

In that way, overthinking is avoidance masquerading as intelligence. You analyze instead of acting. You replay conversations, fantasizing about different outcomes, instead of feeling the hurt of what you actually experienced. You invent a new story of the past, instead of meeting the present moment. And while your mind is busy running loops, life quietly passes by—unnoticed and unlived.

If you took a closer look, you'd notice that your thoughts are rarely about what's actually in front of you. They are anchored in the past or projections about the future—places where nothing can be changed because nothing is real. This creates an addictive sense of control—one that skews your entire life perspective away from flow and towards constant comparison and re-evaluation. You feel productive only when your mind is busy, even though you're not actually solving anything. You find yourself consumed by *what-ifs, shoulds,* and *coulds,* stuck in indecision, afraid to move for fear it will be the wrong move.

You may even mistake overthinking for a kind of virtue. You tell yourself that worrying is caring, that anticipating every outcome is being responsible, that analyzing every angle means you're thorough. But this is just fear dressed as diligence. You think if you keep circling through all possibilities, it will shield you from discomfort. But all it does is drain your energy and shrink your world to match your mindset. Your thinking becomes the lens through which you perceive reality.

If your lens is fear-based, everything looks threatening. If it's control-oriented, everything seems out of control. Challenges feel like personal attacks, you easily get defensive, and you find more reasons to stay small. Life feels overwhelming because you're trying to manage it all mentally without involving the much fuller spectrum of your heart, body, and spirit. Trying to create from *me* is much harder and more limited than co-creating with Source.

In fact, when the going gets tough, you easily slip into a state of victimhood. Life feels like it's happening *to* you. Other people seem powerful and unpredictable. The future feels scary. You feel unsupported, unloved, and unseen. This becomes so normal, you don't realize you're not seeing life clearly—you're seeing it through the fog of overthinking.

Overthinking also makes you accident-prone. You're not necessarily careless, you're just not here. You bump into things, misplace items, forget details—all because your mind is elsewhere. Even worse, you miss the synchronicities and invitations life keeps placing in your path—the chance meeting, the insight, even the opportunity of a lifetime—simply because you're too distracted to notice.

Even practical tasks suffer. You burn out from perfectionism. You procrastinate out of fear. You start five things and finish none. Imagined scenarios consume your mental bandwidth, so when real life calls for your attention, you've got nothing left to give. Keeping busy overrides being effective, leaving you wondering why your workload never lightens, yet your goals remain out of reach.

But the most damaging consequence is that you lose touch with your intuition. With your inner guidance. With your connection to your higher self. With making decisions that bring joy, that invite spontaneity, and nurture your ability to play and co-create. You stop trusting your instincts because your inner voice has gone faint. You doubt your worth because you've been feeding yourself fear. And perhaps worst of all, you forget that life—in its beauty and divine orchestration—is happening *now*.

Yet even in this darkness, the light of awareness begins to dawn. You start to notice the drain of wrestling with thoughts. In moments of forced downtime, you begin to wonder: *There must be a better way to live life than to be exhausted constantly.* This reflection marks the beginning of your journey out of the mental maze and into awakening as an old soul.

OLD SOUL

As an old soul, you've come to see that most overthinking is about fear, lack, and control. The mind tries to create safety by running ahead, building maps for a future that hasn't arrived, or reworking a past that cannot be changed. But you no longer mistake this for progress. You recognize it as the nervous system's attempt to predict what can't be predicted.

You've learned that the mind will happily spin in circles, manufacturing complexity when life is actually really simple. The difference now is that you don't need to follow your thoughts. You notice the sensations of being caught in a mental loop—tightening in the body, the heaviness of mental fog, and instead of pushing harder for clarity, you let your awareness clear the air, and without frustration or self-criticism, you smoothly return your attention to the task at hand.

Overthinking is no longer an enemy to be conquered. Instead, it is simply another form of feedback. It's a signal that you're grasping for control again. Or that it's time to take a break, eat, go for a walk, or otherwise change the energy of the space. And so your awareness of overthinking becomes yet another tool in your arsenal to notice when you're out of alignment, and remind you to re-center and come back into it.

You've also realized that clarity is rarely the result of forcing an answer. It comes when you've created enough inner stillness for insights to surface on their own. Old patterns may still try to pull you back into analysis, but you know now that forcing the mind only makes the water muddier. Your job is to ask the question as precisely as possible, and then step back and let the answer reveal itself.

All of this is possible because there's a deeper trust now—in yourself, in life, in Source. You've realized that certainty doesn't come before action—it comes after. That thinking you can know anything is futile. That not knowing is not the same as being lost; it is living at the cusp of co-creation, where life reveals itself.

Even in complex situations, you see how the mind's imagined scenarios are never accurate enough to replace the power of just showing up and responding to what's there. That's why you save your energy for what's real—the conversation in front of you, the choice you can make today. This shift from mental rehearsal to present engagement frees vast reserves of energy you didn't know you had.

You've also noticed that the less you believe your thoughts, the more your intuition sharpens. It guides you—not through the desperate energy of planning and predicting—but through a quiet knowing, through subtle nudges that feel both obvious and effortless. And with practice, you trust that feeling more than the most elaborate mental argument.

Sometimes you even laugh at your own mind now. You catch it spinning elaborate stories, trying to map every possible outcome. Instead of getting tangled, you see the absurdity. Overthinking has become transparent—it's just noise the nervous system makes. This humor lightens the load. Instead of fearing the mind's chatter, you meet it with compassion, even amusement, and it dissolves as fast as it appeared.

You also discover that in the space once occupied by mental loops there arises joy. You notice colors more vividly, hear music more deeply, taste food with greater detail. You find yourself laughing more easily, speaking more sincerely, and feeling more connected to others because you're actually with them, not half-lost in a mental commentary. You're no longer just managing life, you get to savor it.

With time, you've come to see that overthinking was never about solving problems—it was a symptom of trying to live life from the head alone. Now, you live from the whole of you—mind, body, and heart in concert, engaged in soulful conversation. And when the mind does begin to overreach—perhaps as the urge to anticipate, or to solve every possible problem—you can smile, knowing they are remnants of an old survival strategy. You no longer have to live in those loops. You can notice them without entering them, and return to the present, where life is never as complicated as the mind makes it out to be.

And eventually, you see that the dissolution of overthinking is not just about peace of mind—it's about opening to synchronicity itself. Life begins moving toward you with more grace, aligning events, people, and opportunities in ways no amount of thought could ever orchestrate.

Overthinking Chart

Overthinking is such a universal "condition", it's not a question of whether or not you overthink, but how soon can you catch yourself when you do and how do you process the experience. The following chart contrasts how young souls vs old souls deal with overthinking.

Young Soul (Mental Control)	Old Soul (Mental Clarity)
Constantly analyzes, plans, and rehashes	Observes thoughts without identifying with them
Believes every thought must be resolved	Understands most thoughts are noise
Uses thinking to avoid feeling	Allows feelings to arise and pass without judgment
Tries to predict and control outcomes	Trusts the unfolding of life moment by moment
Seeks certainty through overprocessing	Finds peace in not knowing
Mistakes worry for responsibility	Practices presence as the highest responsibility
Feels mentally exhausted and stuck	Feels mentally spacious and light
Attaches identity to thoughts and beliefs	Sees thoughts as temporary mental activity
Over-prepares and second-guesses	Intuits and acts from inner knowing
Thinks more to feel safe	Thinks less to feel free

© 2025 Cirak

Prompts

1) What situations trigger your overthinking most often, and what underlying fear is fueling it?

2) How does overthinking affect your ability to notice beauty, enjoy rest, or connect deeply with others?

3) What signals does your body give you when your mind is racing, and what signals show you've returned to ease?

4) In what areas of your life are you still trying to manage outcomes instead of allowing them to unfold?

5) How would it feel to act without having every detail figured out first?

6) Where in your life could you rely more on intuition and less on mental rehearsal?

7) What would it look like to use overthinking as a signal to come back to your body?

8) How might you create enough stillness in your life for clarity to arise on its own?

Chapter 45

Creative Block

Young Soul

You've got something to say. Something to make, to build, to put out into the world. But every time you try, it's like hitting a wall. You sit down—and nothing. Or maybe something comes, but it feels clumsy. Or maybe there was flow at first, and now it's gone. You second-guess every idea, edit before you begin, and quietly retreat from your own potential. You blame your environment, your schedule, your so-called lack of talent. You might even decide it's just not "meant to be." But beneath all of that is a quieter truth: you're scared.

Scared to be seen. Scared you're not good enough. That you'll be judged, dismissed, or worse—ignored entirely. That your big launch will be met with silence. So you freeze. The stakes feel too high. You've tied your worth to the outcome, and the weight of that pressure crushes your ability to create. This is the real source of creative block:

a resistance to vulnerability, camouflaged as a lack of ideas or motivation.

You wait for the perfect conditions—the mood, the inspiration, the sudden clarity. But they never arrive, because you've turned creativity into a showcase rather than a co-creative process. You see it as something to prove, not something to explore. And the more you wait for perfection, the more distant the act of creating feels.

The good news is, experiencing creative block doesn't mean you're broken. It simply means you're in your head, trying to create from the *little me* that attaches itself to *my* talent, *my* reputation, *my* worth. But creation isn't born from identity. You can't make something new using only what you already know.

When nothing flows, don't think of it as punishment. See it as feedback. It's asking: Are you aligned? Are you connected? Are you forcing this? Are you trying to prove something? Until you answer honestly, the block stays in place.

But the moment you shift from *How do I make this perfect?* to *How do I meet this moment?*—something moves, motivated by forces beyond yourself. But no need to put words on it. Just feel how the pressure lightens, and the light begins to returns.

Old Soul

You no longer fear the empty page. You've stopped confusing output with self-worth. You know creativity doesn't answer to pressure—it answers to presence. So when flow feels distant, you pause, you breathe, you listen. You remember that creativity is a dance, not a life-or-death duel. Your job isn't to force the formless into a particular form, but to create space for it to express itself however it choses to arrive.

You've also stopped waiting for lightning to strike or for the ideal time to arrive. You show up, again and again, even when it's uncomfortable. You understand that creativity is a rhythm, not just a single spark. Resistance isn't the enemy. It's another signal. Some of your best work has come from staying with that tension long enough for it to soften and reveal what wants to come through.

You don't create to get somewhere anymore. You create from here. To channel something honest. To let life speak through you. The outcome is still fascinating as a frame of expression. But paramount is the integrity of the process. You're not here to impress anyone—you're here to move with the greater current.

You've learned to treat every pause as sacred. The silence before the note. The stillness before the brushstroke. The empty page isn't a threat—it's an offering for Source to take shape. What comes through you isn't yours to own or control—it's yours to welcome.

Prompts

1) How do you typically respond to creative resistance? Do you push through, avoid, self-criticize, or distract?

2) What fears might be hiding beneath your resistance to creating? Failure, success, or being truly seen?

3) When was the last time you felt effortless creative flow? What supported it?

4) Are you trying to do too much at once? How could you scale it down to one clear next step?

5) What thoughts or emotions arise the moment you begin? Can you witness them without reacting?

6) How might your creative process change if it became playful, imperfect, and exploratory instead of controlled?

7) Where in your life do you feel most connected to inspiration, even outside of "creating"?

8) What would it mean to create without any need for recognition or validation?

CHAPTER 46

PERFECTIONISM

YOUNG SOUL

You think perfection will keep you safe. If you can just get everything right—your words, your choices, your appearance, your timing—maybe no one will criticize you. Maybe no one will reject you. Maybe, finally, you'll be enough. So you push harder, plan tighter, and hold your breath while trying to control every detail of life.

You think external excellence translates into internal worthiness. You've been conditioned to believe that mistakes are unacceptable and that love must be earned, not received. So you work yourself into the ground to feel like you deserve rest, approval, or peace. But even when you get it, it never lasts—because it's not rooted in truth.

Perfectionism pretends to be ambition, but it's really fear. Fear of being ordinary. Fear of falling behind. Fear of losing control. And all this fear, in turn, is just a distraction from the deeper layers of your essence, of who you truly are.

The irony is, the harder you try to perfect everything, the more disconnected you become—from joy, from creativity, from your own aliveness. You leave no space for the unknown, for the spontaneous, for grace. Everything becomes a task to optimize. Your body may protest—through fatigue, burnout, tension, anxiety. But you try to push through even that, because honest self-reflection is just too scary and even rest feels suspiciously like failure.

Then a quiet moment arrives—always unexpectedly, but usually because you've run yourself into the ground. You see the flash that perfectionism isn't keeping you safe. It's keeping you small. That no amount of control can shield you from life's messiness. And that maybe, just maybe, imperfection isn't a shortcoming, but an opening to something more real.

Old Soul

You've seen through the illusion of perfection. In fact, you've learned that wholeness includes the cracks. Striving to do everything "right" is the surest way to not just to become disappointed, but to lose your soul. Life is meant to be much simpler. You trust the process.

Before getting caught up in details and overthinking, you recognize the early signs: shallow breath, constricted thinking, the feeling that you have to do it all or everything will fall apart. When those symptoms appear, you pause, observe sensations, and reflect: *Am I forcing, or am I flowing?*

You remember that all symptoms are here to remind you to return to presence. They're not here to shame you or make you feel like a problem—but to tell you when you've drifted from Source. When it's time to return to trust. To the deeper intelligence that moves through you when you stop trying so hard.

That doesn't mean you should not make any effort, but it comes from a different place. You're not focused on outcomes or worshipping so-called success. You're executing on behalf of Source—being a conduit for the formless to take shape. You know true creativity requires surrender and that beauty arises from what *wasn't* planned. You know when you give space for the unknown to guide you, it delivers more elegance than anything the mind could engineer.

So now you live with more flow. You create with more ease. You show up with confidence. You speak with less fear. You love yourself and you love living life. Not because everything is perfect—but because you no longer need it to be.

Prompts

1) What are you afraid would happen if you stopped striving to be perfect?

2) In what areas of life do you feel the strongest pressure to be flawless?

3) Whose approval are you still working for, even unconsciously?

4) What does your body feel like when you're caught in perfectionism?

5) What do you sacrifice in your pursuit of perfection? Joy, rest, creativity?

6) When was the last time you let something be imperfect—and it turned out just fine?

7) How do you distinguish between healthy effort and fear-driven control?

8) What might it feel like to create from a place of inspiration instead of pressure?

9) What is one area of your life where you can practice deliberate imperfection this week?

Chapter 47

Reactivity

Young Soul

As a young soul, life feels like a constant battle—one where you must be hyper-alert, ready to prove, defend, or retreat. You believe you're reacting to what's happening around you, but what you're really reacting to is the story your mind has created about it. It feels like the intensity is coming from "out there," but most of your energy is actually consumed by your reaction to your own internal state.

This creates a loop where you interpret events through a lens of threat or lack. A traffic jam isn't just a delay—it's an attack on your time. A comment from a coworker isn't just feedback—it's a blow to your self-worth. The body becomes habituated to constant contraction, and the mind to ongoing defensiveness. Peace feels impossible when you're always bracing for the next disappointment.

These triggers don't come from nowhere. They are conditioned responses—either shaped by your own experience or inherited from your lineage. As long as you don't see that life is happening independently of you—that you're upset because of how you interpret things—the pattern repeats. You stay stuck in defensive mode, in limiting beliefs, in blaming life for a state you unknowingly keep creating.

That's why young souls tend to believe everything must be controlled. If you don't seize every opportunity, outperform others, or avoid emotional pain, life will abandon you. But when you make your environment responsible for how you feel, it's no wonder you feel overwhelmed. Instead of relaxing, you grip even tighter. This shows up as overplanning, overworking, emotional volatility, or depression—all attempts to manage a world that you've made to feel dangerous.

Living this way is not only exhausting—it's deeply alienating. When you're always on the defensive, you miss the chance to collaborate with life. You react instead of respond. You overcompensate with strategy, appearance, or avoidance. The idea of surrender sounds illogical and feels weak. The unknown feels threatening. Life gets more and more complicated, and you wonder where it all went wrong.

What you don't yet realize is that feelings—when not judged—are just sensations. A flutter in the stomach. A tightness in the chest. A quickening of the breath.

If you stay in witness mode, these sensations will arise and pass. What could grow into a drama can dissolve in seconds. But you haven't yet developed that awareness. Every uncomfortable feeling is treated like something to fix, suppress, or escape.

Reactivity also distorts time. It pulls you into the past, which is full of regret. Or the future, which is full of anxiety. Rarely do you allow yourself to be in the present moment. This mental time-travel robs you of the simplicity of the here and now. Tasks take longer. Joy feels out of reach. Your energy is scattered across imagined timelines, none of which are real.

You wind up not seeing open doors. You overlook synchronicities. You miss cues in conversation that could spark real connection. The mental noise makes you clumsy, distracted, numb. Life feels unkind when you're absent from it.

Every human has been conditioned into reactivity. But for young souls, it's still the default setting. It governs your tone, your posture, your decisions, your relationships. You lack the ability to listen deeply, to see clearly, to hold a higher perspective when things get hard. Your inner commentary is your reality—full of judgment, fear, comparison, blame. You completely miss the simplicity of *just being*.

Victimhood follows. When you're lost in mental noise, detached from stillness, the world feels like it's doing something *to* you. Challenges are threats, not teachers. Uncertainty is chaos, not an invitation to co-create. Invariably, this resistance to the design of life leads to suffering. Young souls often stay trapped in the very cycles they long to escape, not realizing their reactivity is keeping them there.

But even this has a purpose. When the exhaustion becomes too much, the illusion of control collapses, and in that moment when you stop trying to fix your existence—the transition to life as an old soul begins.

Old Soul

As an old soul, you've spent years—or lifetimes—learning to temper your reactivity. You've discovered that most of what happens in the world isn't personal, even if it touches you deeply. This shift in perception changes everything. Life isn't trying to hurt, judge, or block you. On the contrary, it wants you to be whole. You begin to see it as a mirror—reflecting where you're still entangled, still holding limiting beliefs, and where you're already free.

The difference is greater awareness. You're no longer fused with your thoughts. You've cultivated space between stimulus and response—space to breathe, to pause, to feel, to observe. Triggers still arise, but now they serve a purpose. They point to something unhealed. They lead you inward. You witness the sensation without attaching a story. Pleasant or unpleasant, you let the energy move through you without suppressing or indulging it.

This gives you clarity in chaos. You no longer need to control every detail or defend every opinion—if you even still have any. You feel the heaviness of being opinionated. You feel the weight of attaching yourself to drama, projection, urgency. Reactivity doesn't just rob you of energy—it takes away your presence. It disconnects you from Source, from now, from peace.

Over time, your nervous system has recalibrated itself to move with more intention. You no longer brace for life to happen. You invite it. You no longer resist what has already happened. You accept it. There is more pause in your speech, more spaciousness in your being. Your decisions become more intuitive. You follow what resonates and leave what doesn't alone. You respond to what *is*, not to the mental story about it.

You become less interested in being right and more devoted to being real. Truth is no longer about facts, but about the *felt sense* of truth in your body. You listen for it and follow it. You discern what's worth your attention and what's just noise. You no longer abandon yourself to prove a point or protect an image.

When it comes to others, you sense the pain behind their behavior. You see how they're just projecting themselves. You don't take their criticism or urgency personally. You don't escalate. You hold space, or you walk away, depending on what's aligned. Your boundaries are clear and uncompromising. When someone forcefully trespasses, you act—again, not from reactivity, but from embodiment. Your aura becomes unmistakable.

More and more, you listen to the timing of life. You don't force decisions. You don't demand answers. You're comfortable in the mystery of not knowing. You wait for the full-body "yes"—should it choose to come. You bring questions into silence and let answers arrive. That's why old souls feel so grounded—they're not reacting. They're tuning in.

And in this attunement, this receiving mode, you invite life force to enter your being. What was once scattered by mental noise becomes fuel for co-creation, love, insight. This is when your whole being comes online. This is when the angels rejoice. You let life move through you. You trust it. Even the hard parts. Especially the hard parts.

Reactivity Chart

Learning to respond to a situation as it shows up, instead of reacting to what you think it should be, has a significant impact on your life. The following chart illustrates the difference between young soul reactivity and old soul responsiveness.

Young Soul	**Old Soul**
Sees life as constant battle, always on defense	Sees life as mirror, reflecting inner state without threat
Reacts to stories in the mind, not reality itself	Responds to what is, with awareness and embodiment
Feels everything as personal attack or judgment	Recognizes most events as impersonal, not about them
Clings to control, overplans, overworks	Releases control, trusts timing, allows flow
Suppresses or explodes feelings, fueling drama	Feels sensations directly, lets them pass without story
Lives in past regrets or future anxieties	Anchors in present moment, listens for intuitive guidance
Blames others or life for their suffering	Uses triggers as teachers, opportunities for growth
Seeks validation through being "right"	Seeks authenticity, truth felt in body and presence
Easily destabilized by others' criticism or chaos	Holds boundaries with clarity, doesn't absorb projections
Misses synchronicities, doors, and joy due to noise	Notices subtle cues, synchronicities, lives as co-creator

© 2025 Cirak

Prompts

1) What situations tend to trigger your reactivity the most? What story do you tell yourself in those moments?

2) Think of a recent conflict. Did you react to what was happening—or to what you *felt* about what was happening?

3) What physical sensations accompany your emotional reactivity? How do they shift when you stop resisting them?

4) When was the last time you truly felt peaceful? What was different in your mindset or environment?

5) How do you typically react to uncertainty or not having control? What would it look like to meet uncertainty with trust?

6) Write about a time when you overreacted. In hindsight, what belief or fear was driving that reaction?

7) What part of your life feels the most reactive right now? What would it mean to engage that area from stillness instead?

Chapter 48

Anxiety

Young Soul

Anxiety is the baseline hum of the young soul's life. Even when the surface looks calm, there's a low-grade tension under everything, a constant scan for what could go wrong. It's not just situational worry, but a nervous system wired for survival, shaped by the belief that life must go a certain way for you to feel safe. You try to control outcomes, people, even your own feelings. The unpredictable nature of reality feels like a threat, so your body stays on high alert all the time.

In this state, the mind feels like the ultimate authority. A negative thought arrives, and you believe it. A low feeling arises, and you assume something must be wrong. You react by thinking more, planning more, doing more. You try to regain control through mental overdrive. But that only makes it worse. The mind that generates the anxiety can't also dissolve it.

All your planning, steering, and expecting results is resistance to what's happening. All your thoughts about what should be happening, or what might happen, only add more fuel. Your head is full of replayed conversations, worst-case scenarios, and "what ifs"—ironically, believing they protect you. But all they do is pull you out of the only place life is actually happening—here and now. Anxiety feeds on that distance from presence.

Soon the fear starts to feel personal—like it's part of your identity. You explain it, justify it, avoid it, or hide it. You try to manage it with distraction, overwork, substances, or relentless self-improvement. But these offer only short-term relief while reinforcing the belief that something is wrong with you.

Of course, there's nothing wrong with you. You're not broken—you're just disconnected. Anxiety is—yet again—just another type of feedback. It's not there to be ignored. It's meant to be taken into full consideration. Life is so simple when you stop organizing your day around avoiding fear. And it becomes so nourishing when you and start experimenting with discomfort, presence, and trust.

Just don't think that you need to make it happen overnight. Otherwise, you stress yourself in trying to feel better. Just know there is a place where all that you long for awaits. For now, and until you get there, just let yourself be.

OLD SOUL

Anxiety may still arise for an old soul—but it no longer runs the show. You don't automatically identify with every thought that crosses your mind. Instead, you observe it, notice its associated sensations, and from your awareness of it decide whether to engage. You bring curiosity rather than judgment. You understand that fear is often just energy that hasn't been welcomed yet—so even if it's a fear-based thought, you welcome it. Not to amplify it, but to transmute it into wisdom.

You've also seen how overthinking is a strategy to avoid feeling, and you know it doesn't work. Only presence dissolves tension. So you stop letting anxiety steer your choices. Instead, you let it point you toward what needs attention: a misalignment, a forgotten truth, a call for stillness, or even just one conscious breath. You don't try to fix yourself—you ground through your body, the one place that always exists in the now.

This doesn't mean you never worry or feel unsettled. But you don't get lost in it. You're tethered to something deeper—a felt trust in life's design. When you think you're in control, there's only the anxiety of losing control. But when you surrender to the greater intelligence moving through all things, there's beauty, flow, and ease. You understand that suffering comes from clinging to your version of reality. So you loosen your grip. You let life surprise you. You expect the unexpected.

Anxiety becomes a messenger. Sometimes it reveals old trauma that's ready to be released. Other times, it signals that your outer life is out of sync with your inner truth. The only time it truly becomes suffering is when you resist it. But when you welcome it—not because it's pleasant, but because it's useful—it becomes an opportunity to access even greater depths and truth within yourself.

Ultimately, the old soul lives with less anxiety—not because life got easier, but because you stopped making it harder than it is. You discovered that peace doesn't come from fixing problems, but from releasing the belief that something is wrong.

Let your body be your guide, not your mind. Let your heart show the way, not your plans. And when anxiety comes knocking, as it occasionally will, you welcome it as a reminder to return to presence, to drop back into flow, and re-align with Source.

Anxiety Chart

That which can dominate and even ruin one person's life, can be a helpful tool for others to maintain balance and deepen. Anxiety is one of those things. The following chart contrasts how young souls and olds souls deal with it.

Young Souls	**Old Souls**
Constant low-grade tension under everything	Inner calm with occasional passing waves of tension
Believes safety comes from controlling outcomes	Trusts that safety comes from alignment with presence
Negative thoughts believed as truth	Negativity observed as passing energy
Mind tries to fix what the mind created	Awareness dissolves what the mind generated
Anxiety feels like personal identity	Anxiety seen as a messenger, not self
Distracts, overworks, or self-medicates to cope	Grounds through body, breath, and presence
Life organized around avoiding fear	Life organized around welcoming and transmuting fear
Suffers by resisting discomfort	Frees energy by allowing discomfort
Peace sought in control & certainty	Peace found in surrender and trust
Sees anxiety as proof something is wrong	Sees anxiety as guidance toward deeper truth

© 2025 Cirak

PROMPTS

1) What situations trigger the most anxiety in your life? What beliefs are you holding about them?

2) When anxiety arises, do you try to fix it, run from it, or ignore it? What would it feel like to sit with it instead?

3) How often do your anxious thoughts turn out to be true? What does this say about the reliability of your fears?

4) What physical sensations accompany your anxiety? Where do they show up in your body? Can you observe them without labeling them as bad?

5) What is one daily practice you can adopt to anchor yourself when you start to spiral into overthinking?

6) What would it mean to trust life, even just a little bit more? How might that change how you relate to anxiety?

7) Are there any stories about yourself you've attached to your anxiety (e.g., "I'm a worrier," "I'm weak")? Can you begin to let them go?

8) How does your environment or the people around you affect your level of calm or stress? Where can you make shifts?

CHAPTER 49

STRESS

YOUNG SOUL

For a young soul, stress feels almost inevitable—not because life is inherently stressful, but because of the mental load you place on it. You carry a constant list of *shoulds*: how people should act, how your plans should unfold, how you should feel. Every time reality fails to match these mental expectations, friction builds. The deepest layer of stress comes from the belief that what's happening *shouldn't* be happening.

Your whole worldview is dense with judgments, labels, and imagined outcomes. You're rarely present because your attention is consumed by mental commentary about what's wrong, what needs fixing, and who's to blame. Life becomes an endless chain of problems to solve and potential disasters to avoid. Stress stops being an occasional state and becomes part of your identity. Being stressed is proof—to yourself and others—that you're working hard, being responsible, and "on top of things."

You push yourself to know the right answer, predict the safest route, and avoid failure. This creates rigidity, over-caution, and a constant state of hyper-vigilance. You live under the illusion that if you think harder, plan longer, or try more, you can control the uncontrollable.

Naturally, the body can't sustain this dynamic. Eventually, the tension seeps into your relationships, work, sleep, and health, causing real damage. That's when you might pause and realize: *I can't keep going like this.* But to slow down, you must confront the fear that's secretly running the show—that if you stop grinding and gripping, life will collapse. What you don't yet see is that it's the gripping that creates most of the pain.

When the system crashes it may feel like failure, but it's actually an opening. A chance to shift from steering life to flowing with it. From constantly fearing the future to meeting moments with genuine curiosity. From clinging to glimpsing a freedom that lives in letting go. This is where the old soul begins to awaken.

Old Soul

As an old soul, stress is no longer a constant backdrop. When it appears, you recognize it as a sign of some level of resistance in you. Perhaps to what is happening. Or to the thoughts running through your head. Whatever it is, you pause. You tune into the sensations. You release. You return to the simplicity of this moment and let presence show the way.

You no longer compare reality to an idealized version in your head. You see life as it is. This creates space inside you—space to see the bigger picture, to respond rather than react, and to move without the weight of false urgency. You're no longer chasing an imaginary finish line or protecting a fragile image. You trust that what's meant to unfold will do so, and that you'll meet it with clarity in real time.

There is a deep calm that comes from surrendering to the unknown. Instead of judging the moment, you facilitate its unfolding. This cooperation frees your energy and makes you more receptive to guidance from your higher self. You understand that stress doesn't come from events themselves, but from the demands you place on them.

You treat stress as information. It might be pointing to a truth you've avoided, a boundary you've neglected, or an inner misalignment. You explore it with curiosity, feeling it in the body, listening to what it wants to tell you, so you can make changes and realign before the cost grows too high.

Ultimately, you no longer try to anticipate every possibility in a bid for safety. You know that awareness is enough—and that the deepest clarity comes not from strain, but from making stillness your anchor.

STRESS CHART

This chart shows how young vs old souls deal with stress.

Young Souls	Old Souls
Stress seen as constant, unavoidable	Stress seen as occasional, purposeful
Driven by "shoulds" and unmet expectations	Guided by presence and acceptance of what is
Hypervigilance mistaken for responsibility	Awareness used as guidance, not control
Life experienced as problems to solve	Life experienced as unfolding to meet with curiosity
Control clung to as safety	Control released in favor of trust
Stress signals threat and failure	Stress signals misalignment to address
Body overridden to meet demands	Body listened to and honored as ally
Urgency and judgment added to every task	Calm and clarity maintained even in challenge
Fear of unknown fuels over-preparation	Trust in unknown allows real-time response
Effort equated with tension	Effort aligned with flow and ease

PROMPTS

1) What is one recurring situation in your life that consistently causes stress? What beliefs do you hold about that situation that might be amplifying it?

2) When you feel stressed, where in your body do you feel it first? Can you locate and observe those sensations without trying to change or fix them?

3) How much of your daily stress comes from resisting what is, rather than responding to it?

4) What are some "shoulds" you impose on yourself or others that create internal pressure?

5) Do you believe stress is necessary in order to be successful, responsible, or worthy? Where did that belief come from?

6) Describe a time you let go of control and something beautiful still unfolded. What can that memory teach you about stress?

7) What role does your inner critic play in your stress levels? What does that voice sound like, and is it actually helping you?

8) How would your life feel if you trusted your ability to handle things as they come rather than trying to manage everything preemptively?

9) What practices—spiritual, physical, or creative—help you transmute stress into presence?

10) If you're currently stressed, what might it be trying to tell you?

Chapter 50

Depression

Young Soul

As a young soul, depression feels like something has gone terribly wrong—with your mind, your body, your whole life. You don't yet know how to hold heavy energy, so you assume you're deficient or failing as a human being. The idea that this mood could be meaningful hasn't entered your awareness. You believe you are the problem—and that the solution must be external: a pill, a distraction, a surface-level reinvention.

You may try to keep going—numbing, escaping, pushing through—but when your energy is already low, even basic tasks feel burdensome. The disconnection from your inner truth, which may have been building for years, suddenly envelopes you like a fog you can't lift. You don't understand why life feels flat, why what used to excite you feels so distant. But the more you try to "fix" your feelings, the more entangled you become in them, and the more they pull you down.

At this stage of your evolution, you're still identified with your thoughts, which is what depression essentially is: the continuous belief in detrimental or demeaning thoughts about yourself or life. When you take every thought that comes along as truth, it's hard to pull yourself up. If your mind says you're worthless, you believe it. If it says life is meaningless, you assume it's true. You haven't yet learned that thoughts are not facts—just passing interpretations that shift with your energy, hormones, and environment.

You're also still deeply concerned with how others see you. You mask your pain to avoid looking weak or unstable. You smile, function, perform—further deepening the inner split. The more you disconnect from how you actually feel, the more lost you become. No one told you your feelings are supposed to be a compass, not a curse.

Surrounded by other young souls who avoid depth or complain about life, victimhood can pin you down and prevent you from letting in some light. You absorb the idea that life is unfair and that your only options are to medicate or give up. You will stay in that dark place until you can somehow recognize that depression is a signal that points to the chronic misalignment between how you're living and who you really are. If you treat it as a wake-up call rather than a flaw, it can become one of your greatest teachers.

You may even romanticize your depression, wearing it like an identity or badge that sets you apart. It becomes part of how you define yourself: the one who struggles, the one who hurts, the one who can't catch a break. This mistaken belonging keeps you tethered to the very energy that weighs you down. Only when you realize you are not your suffering—that depression is an experience, not your essence—can you begin to step beyond it.

Old Soul

As an old soul, you fundamentally understand that you are not a problem that needs to be fixed, and that depression is only a messenger. It's your inner system alerting you that something is out of tune. You're being called to meet the heaviness with compassion, awareness, and stillness—to allow your energy field to realign.

You don't say, *I am depressed.* You say, *Depression is moving through me.* You no longer believe how you feel has anything to do with who you are. Your awareness muscle is so developed, you can witness and release even the lowest energetic states without giving yourself over to them. You observe your sensations, let the energies pass, and listen for what wisdom wants to surface.

You know the last thing you should do is rush to fix or suppress your emotions. It's all about making space for them, letting them come and go. Sometimes the message is simple: more rest, cleaner food, less noise. Other times, it's deeper—an identity to release, a misaligned relationship to end, a return to creativity. You no longer resist your intuition. You live by it.

You know you're not your thoughts. So, instead of reacting to them, you tune in to your body, your breath, and your subtle inner movements. You return to what nourishes your frequency—time in nature, solitude, a kind conversation, rest. You know that a high vibration is your natural state. Healing can't help but arise when the ground is prepared.

Above all, you know depression is not shameful. It's part of the human curriculum—especially for deep-feeling souls who cannot pretend life is fine when it isn't. Depression is not weakness—it's an opportunity for greater self-mastery and calibration. Every time you meet it with presence, something old dissolves and something more truthful emerges.

Lastly, you've seen that depression often signals collective heaviness, not just personal imbalance. Old souls are especially porous to the grief, fear, and confusion moving through the collective field. You've learned to ask, *What part of this is truly mine?* That discernment lets you release what isn't yours while transmuting what is. In this way, depression becomes a portal—one that deepens your compassion, strengthens your sovereignty, and expands your capacity to hold the light.

Depression Chart

The following chart contrasts how young souls vs old souls deal with depression.

Young Souls	Old Souls
Believes something is wrong with self	Sees depression as a messenger, not identity
Thinks the solution must be external	Looks inward for alignment & guidance
Identifies fully with negative thoughts	Observes thoughts as passing interpretations
Masks pain to avoid judgment	Honors emotions fully without shame
Feels worthless, flawed, or broken	Knows worth is inherent & untouched
Distracts or numbs to cope	Slows down and makes space to feel
Treats depression as failure	Treats depression as curriculum
Absorbs victimhood from others	Uses awareness to clear collective heaviness
Waits for circumstances to change	Depression as a call to recalibrate life
Defines self by suffering	Remembers self as awareness beyond all states

© 2025 Cirak

PROMPTS

1) What recent events or inner shifts might be contributing to how you're feeling right now?

2) Are you honoring your body's needs for rest, nourishment, movement, and quiet?

3) Where in your life do you feel disconnected or out of alignment with your truth?

4) How do you typically respond to emotional heaviness? With judgment, distraction, or compassion?

5) What parts of your identity or lifestyle might no longer be serving your evolution?

6) In what ways could you create a life that is more supportive of your inner peace and aliveness?

7) What relationships, habits, or environments drain your energy?

8) What simple daily practices could help you reconnect to presence and inner steadiness?

9) If you trusted that this low period had purpose, how might you move through it differently?

Chapter 51

Failure

Young Soul

Failure is a threat to your identity. When things don't go your way, you take it personally. If you lose the job, get rejected, or fall short of a goal, it feels like you're falling apart inside. There's no buffer between the event and your self-worth. You treat mistakes like moral verdicts, forgetting that falling down and getting back up is how growth actually works.

But that's not what the world taught you. You learned that success equals safety, and failure equals punishment—not just temporary punishment, but lifelong shame. Once a loser, always a loser. No wonder you panic about what people will think if they find out you dared to try and didn't succeed. Instead of honoring your courage, you blame yourself—that you should've known better than to reach beyond your current limits.

So you play and stay small. You second-guess your instincts, afraid of stepping out of line. You stick to the rules while denying your wisdom. A part of you longs to explore, to risk, to create—but fear speaks louder than curiosity. You want to grow, but only if you can guarantee a flawless performance. And so you never start to begin with. You secretly admire the bold ones who do—the contrarians, the adventurers—but you don't know how to join them.

The day will come when you fail anyway, despite your careful caution. And in the mess, something surprising happens: you're still here. The world didn't end. You're not ruined. Tomorrow's another day. The people you thought would judge you are preoccupied with their own fear of being judged. And so you're wiser now—because you tried. And trying matters more than getting it "right."

Slowly, you start to stretch again. You let yourself dream bigger. You take a few risks. Failure is no longer something to avoid. It's part of growing. And something in you begins to move—away from perfection and toward freedom. The old soul in you begins to stir.

OLD SOUL

You no longer believe in failure the way the world defines it. When things don't go as planned, you don't get frustrated—you get curious. *What does this say about me?*

FAILURE

You've learned that what appears to be failure is life asking you to re-assess, or redirecting you to somewhere better. You stop labeling experiences as good or bad, success or failure, because you know how often blessings come disguised as disappointments, and when one door closes, another one opens.

Instead of trying to "win" at life, you prefer to experience it. To flow with it. To be your private detective and figure out how this so-called failure is an invitation to deepen, refine, realign. The dead ends are never dead—they're just limiting beliefs in your head. You've learned to say, *Thank you—let's see what happens next*, whenever something falls away.

Because you don't cling to outcomes, you don't suffer in the same way. You're not obsessed with doing everything "the right way," because you understand there is no right way. There is only *your* way, which is the way of resonance, not rules. There's no final exam—only this living moment, full of mystery and grace. Long ago, you let go of the fantasy of controlling every outcome, predicting every timeline, and rehearsing every appearance. In doing so, you discovered something much more powerful: trust.

You try things. You mess up. You try again. You stay curious. You let what feels alive guide you to the highest frequencies of co-creation. Every loss, every unraveling, expands your view. You no longer fear letting go, because you know letting go clears space. Every detour, every obstacle, every misstep is a teacher. The ride is unpredictable—but you wouldn't have it any other way.

Failure Chart

When things don't go according to plan, it can be an invitation to reflect or a reason to plummet. The following chart shows how young souls vs old souls deal with failure.

Young Soul (Failure as Defeat)	Old Soul (Failure as Growth)
Sees failure as proof of inadequacy	Sees failure as feedback for alignment
Feels shame and personal worthlessness after failing	Feels humility and openness to learning lessons
Avoids risks to preserve self-image	Welcomes challenge as part of growth
Clings to success as identity and validation	Releases attachment to outcome, trusts the process
Judges the self harshly for falling short and disappointing others	Uses failure to deepen self-compassion and discernment of outside voices
Fears being seen as wrong or weak	Accepts mistakes as essential to life mastery
Believes failure sets them back or ruins chances	Understands failure refines direction and deepens wisdom
Tries to fix or hide failure quickly	Allows failure to be fully felt, digested, and integrated

© 2025 Cirak

PROMPTS

1) What does "failure" mean to you, and where did that definition come from?

2) How does your body respond when you feel like you've failed? What do you do with that feeling?

3) Recall an incident when you felt like you failed—what did it teach you that success couldn't?

4) What is more pronounced in you, failure or fear of failure?

5) What is one area of your life where fear of failure keeps you from trying something new?

6) How would you live differently if you didn't see failure as a bad thing?

7) In what ways have "mistakes" redirected you to something better?

8) Can you think of a past even where a failure later turned out to be a blessing? How does that change your attitude towards all the other times you thought you failed? How about the times you experienced success, do you still see them the same way?

9) Write a letter to yourself from the version of you who's no longer afraid to fail.

Chapter 52

Purpose

Young Soul

As a young soul, you grow up believing that purpose must be something tangible, measurable, and outward-facing. You feel an invisible pressure to justify your existence by what you accomplish—a career path, a passion project, a legacy. Something to prove you mattered. The idea of simply existing without striving feels not only unfamiliar but deeply alienating and uncomfortable. If you're not moving toward something, are you even living?

You attach your sense of purpose to job titles, relationships, or socially approved visions of success. Without realizing it, your life becomes a lengthy checklist of milestones: degrees, promotions, marriage, children. But each one offers only a fleeting sense of arrival, quickly followed by *What's next?* It's a race with no finish line, designed to keep you feeling like you're never enough.

This is the deeper confusion: you've equated purpose with self-worth. You believe that unless you achieve something "big," your life won't mean anything. That's a crushing burden to carry. No wonder there's anxiety, urgency, and burnout. No wonder it feels like time is running out. You don't see that behind all the striving is a simmering fear that, if you stop to reflect, you might have to feel how empty and disconnected you've become.

And so, you keep moving. You call it ambition, but it's really just avoidance. Always looking "out there" spares you from facing what's unresolved inside. Rarely do you pause to ask: *Who am I without the goals?* Only when life interrupts the chase—through loss, exhaustion, illness, or forced stillness—does something in you listen up. The first whisper of putting *How do I want to feel?* over *What should I do?* makes itself known. If you continue to listen, purpose stops being a destination you chase and becomes the way you meet the moment you're already in.

Old Soul

As an old soul, you've released the myth that purpose is something you have to find or create or achieve. You no longer live under the weight of having to prove your value to your environment. You deeply grasp that life doesn't need to be justified. It only needs to be lived—consciously, fully, with reverence. Your very being is purposeful.

You no longer create to be validated or to be remembered. You create because life stirs within you and longs to be expressed through you. True purpose doesn't arise from mental strategy—it is found in the resonance with the unfolding, in co-creation with Source. There's a certain frequency you embody when life is able to move through you without effort.

This way of living is not passive. It's deeply engaged. No more half-hearted yeses. No more hesitating nos. You act only when the moment calls with clarity. The more still you are, the clearer it gets. The more surrendered you are, the more life brings what's needed. Your path doesn't require a map. It reveals itself as you walk trustingly into the unknowable.

And when others ask, *What's your purpose?*, you may simply smile. You don't need to explain. You've made peace with being misunderstood by those who haven't yet glimpsed the emptiness of striving. When you don't seek prominence, you radiate presence. That's what makes you magnetic.

As an old soul, your purpose lies less in *doing* and more in *being available*—to truth, to beauty, to service, to love. You no longer ask, *What should I build?* You ask, *What does life want to build through me?* In this way, purpose becomes inseparable from your essence, which is part of the greater consciousness. Purpose is not something you achieve. It's something you are.

Purpose Chart

The question of purpose can elevate you or depress you. This chart shows how young souls vs old souls find purpose.

Young Soul (Performance)	Old Soul (Co-Creation)
Seeks external validation through achievement	Seeks internal alignment through authenticity
Defines worth by success, status, and productivity	Sees purpose as the expression of soul truth, regardless of outcome
Chases clarity through planning and goals	Discovers clarity through presence and surrender
Attaches identity to career, roles, or missions	Sees identity as fluid, co-creation as purpose
Needs to "make an impact" to feel valuable	Knows presence and being of service are the deepest form of contribution
Uses purpose to escape discomfort or emptiness	Allows purpose to emerge from stillness and connection to Source
Views purpose as a destination to reach	Experiences purpose as a state of continuous presence
Driven by fear of wasting time or missing out	Moved by love, trust, and moment-by-moment awareness

Prompts

1) What is your current definition of "purpose"? Where did that definition come from?

2) Have you ever reached a goal and still felt empty afterward? What did that teach you?

3) What part of you feels uncomfortable without a clear direction or plan?

4) If you had no pressure to prove your worth, what would you spend your time doing? What activities make you feel most connected to life, regardless of outcome?

5) How much of your identity is wrapped up in doing versus being?

6) If purpose were a feeling instead of a title, what would it feel like for you?

7) What does it mean to you to co-create with Source rather than force outcomes?

EMOTIONAL

CHAPTER 53

HEARTBREAK

YOUNG SOUL

When something you've built your life around shatters, it can feel like the air has been sucked out of your world. The pain is raw, heavy, and inescapable. It might be the end of a relationship, the loss of someone you love, the collapse of a dream, or the moment you realize something you trusted wasn't what it seemed. Whatever the cause, it leaves you disoriented—like you've been torn from the life you thought you were living.

In these moments, you often cling to the past, replaying every scene, wondering what you could have done differently. The anguish consumes you because your sense of self was fused with what you lost. Without it, you feel incomplete, unseen, unworthy. The idea that you could be whole again seems impossible.

You might try to outrun the pain—filling your days with distraction, reaching for numbing comforts, or desperately seeking reassurance. Or you might drown in it, letting the loss define you. Heartbreak feels like proof that you weren't enough, that life can't be trusted, that love only leads to ruin.

But beneath the devastation, there's something else: a pointer towards truth. Heartbreak is showing you where you gave your power away, where your safety depended on something fragile, where your worth was borrowed from outside yourself. You can't see it clearly yet, but the same pain that's breaking you is also clearing the space for a deeper, truer foundation.

Eventually, light begins to return. You notice moments of presence, glimpses of yourself apart from the loss. The healing is slow, uneven—but it is real and it is inevitable. With each step, you begin to learn that your whole self was never truly gone. It was only waiting for you to come back home to it.

Old Soul

As an old soul, you're by no means immune to heartbreak. But you process it differently. You've learned that heartbreak arrives with its own intelligence. When it happens, you allow yourself to feel it fully, without rushing, without taking it as a sign that you're broken. The grief is still sharp, but it doesn't make you unravel.

You understand now that all forms are temporary: relationships, dreams, identities. You can love them deeply while you have them, and still release them when life asks you to. This isn't detachment born of apathy—it's the freedom that comes from connecting to your higher power, entrusting your worth to that which cannot be taken.

Heartbreak is one of life's great mirrors. It reflects the places where love was tangled with fear, where connection rested on expectation, where meaning depended on a particular form. In seeing this, you get the opportunity to refine yourself and reclaim the parts of yourself that were fragmented and scattered in the illusions of longing and belonging.

You know that nothing true is ever lost. The look of love may change, but its essence is unchanging. The beauty, the connection, the expansion you shared—all of it still exists in the vast field of everything possible. Knowing this, you can grieve without closing up, and you can let go without erasing what was sacred.

And when the wave of heartbreak passes, you emerge with a quieter kind of strength. Not the kind that needs to be invincible, but the kind that can bend without breaking in the face of endings. You carry the knowing that even here, in heartbreak and loss, life is happening for your highest good.

PROMPTS

1) Recall a heartbreak in your life. What exactly was lost, and what did it mean to you?

2) How did that loss shape your beliefs about love, trust, or safety?

3) What coping patterns did you use, and how did they serve or limit your healing?

4) Where do you still feel remnants of that heartbreak in your body or mind?

5) If the loss was also a loss of identity, what part of you did it strip away?

6) What has heartbreak taught you about attachment and impermanence?

7) How might you love or dream again without attaching your self-worth to the outcome?

8) In what ways has heartbreak clarified your values or boundaries?

9) What would it mean to see your heartbreak as a teacher rather than a punishment?

10) How can you honor what was lost while also stepping fully into what is here now?

Chapter 54

Forgiveness

Young Soul

Forgiveness feels impossible when the wound is still raw. Not only would forgiving seem like letting the other person "off the hook", it would also feel like you're betraying your own hurt. So, you hold on to the story, the pain, the injustice—believing that holding on will not only punish the perpetrator, but also protect you from ever being hurt that way again.

But the longer you carry the energy of feeling wronged, the heavier it gets. You replay the moment endlessly, hoping for clarity, vindication, or a different ending. You keep waiting for an apology or for some kind of cosmic justice, thinking only then peace will come. You don't see that by waiting for the other party to change, you've placed your healing in the very hands that hurt you.

Energetically speaking, forgiveness has nothing to do with the other party. It's about releasing yourself from the grip of the past. But the young soul believes freedom is conditional—that unless the other person apologizes, suffers, or sees what they did was wrong, healing is out of reach.

So the pain is kept alive through resentment. Your nervous system stays wired to an old moment. You live in reaction to something that's no longer happening. You may even get upset at the thought that they have moved on, and the only person still carrying the hurt is you.

You may even begin to use your pain as part of your identity. The story of betrayal or mistreatment becomes something you tell again and again, as if keeping it alive proves it was real and unjust. But in doing so, you unknowingly tether yourself to the very person or event you wish to escape. Your past becomes a lens that colors every future interaction, making trust and openness nearly impossible.

And because you don't yet realize that forgiveness is for you, not for them, you resist it fiercely. To the young soul, forgiveness feels like defeat. It feels like weakness. But in truth, it is strength—strength you don't yet know you possess. Only when the exhaustion of carrying the resentment finally outweighs the illusion of control will you begin to consider that letting go is not betrayal of your pain, but liberation from it.

OLD SOUL

You understand that forgiveness is not the same as excusing harm. It's not about erasing the past or pretending it didn't matter. Forgiveness is an energetic release—a choice to cleanse yourself of what no longer serves you and free up inner space to invite something new.

When pain arrives, you feel it. You observe it. You allow it to move through you without wrapping your identity around it. You've seen how blame keeps you energetically bound to the person or event you wish to free yourself from. With this wisdom, you ask: *What wound in me is this touching? What message is it revealing?*

You see that most harm is born of unawareness—people acting from their own fear, shame, or pain. *Hurt people hurt people,* as the saying goes. While that doesn't make it acceptable, it does make it understandable. And when you've done enough inner work, you no longer get pulled into blind reactivity to your emotions. You're able to feel your feelings without judging them. This enables you to respond with clear boundaries instead of revenge. You stay grounded and connected to your true self, able to protect your peace without closing up your heart.

Forgiveness is no longer some lofty moral gesture. It's part of daily energetic hygiene. Caring for your body means clearing your energy field. You let go of grudges because you've chosen to live unburdened. You've tasted the lightness and spaciousness that comes from release, and nothing is worth giving that up.

You've learned that forgiveness is rarely a one-time event. Sometimes, it's a practice repeated again and again, whenever a new layer of pain surfaces. Rather than seeing this as failure, you honor it as deep healing. You trust that every cycle of release carves out more space for compassion, clarity, and freedom. Forgiveness becomes less of a finish line and more of a rhythm woven into your life.

And perhaps the most profound realization is this: forgiving yourself is paramount—for all the times you abandoned your intuition, stayed too long, lashed out in pain, or couldn't yet see clearly. Self-forgiveness dissolves the last chains of shame and self-blame, allowing you to stand fully in the present. In this way, forgiveness becomes not just a tool of healing, but an act of love that restores you to yourself.

Forgiveness Chart

Carrying old energy is one of the primary factors in repeating the past. Learning to let go of it clears the path towards a new, more aligned future. The following chart illustrates how young souls vs old souls approach forgiveness.

Young Soul Orientation	Old Soul Orientation
Holds grudges as a form of justice	Releases others to reclaim inner peace
Sees forgiveness as condoning harmful acts	Understands forgiveness is freedom, not approval
Waits for apology or change before forgiving	Forgives to liberate their own energy
Identifies as the victim of someone else's actions	Sees every wound as part of soul curriculum
Replays the story to stay in control	Stops feeding the story, allows healing
Blames to maintain identity & power	Takes responsibility for their response
Equates forgiveness with weakness or passivity	Recognizes it as an act of strength and clarity
Thinks forgiveness is about the other person	Knows it's about releasing inner burden and negative charge
Tries to forgive mentally but still carries resentment	Processes feelings by observing sensations until they dissolve naturally
Forgives to be good or spiritual	Forgives from truth, not pretend

© 2025 Cirak

Prompts

1) What past situation or person do you still feel tension around?

2) What story do you keep telling yourself about that event, and how is it shaping your inner state?

3) What need—validation, apology, justice—feels unmet within you, and how can you offer it to yourself now?

4) What would it feel like to let the emotional charge go, even if the memory remains?

5) What patterns or habits keep the pain alive?

6) How might your energy shift if you forgave for your own sake, not theirs?

7) What boundaries would you still hold, even after forgiving?

8) What's the difference between excusing harm and releasing its hold on you?

9) How has holding onto pain affected other areas of your life?

10) What might open up if you released this weight today?

Chapter 55

Conflict

Young Soul

Conflict seems to follow you everywhere, though you can't always see why. Sometimes it erupts in dramatic arguments, but often it simmers under the surface—as a constant readiness to defend, critique, or judge. Even when you stay silent, your mind keeps rehearsing what you'd say if provoked. You replay conversations, imagine confrontations, and anticipate betrayal. You're always bracing for the worst-case scenario. Even when you think you're calm, you're never really at peace.

Through this lens of antagonism, every person or situation feels like a battleground—friend or foe, right or wrong, for you or against you. You measure yourself against others, tallying who's better, smarter, more deserving. When someone challenges you, your defenses kick in immediately. Being "right" feels more important than being real—which is still something of an enigma for you, anyway.

When conflict arises, your energy matches it instantly. You raise your voice, talk over people, retreat into icy silence, or weaponize your words. Pride, hurt, and fear flare up quickly, turning what would otherwise be small bumps into volcanic eruptions. Relationships fracture over minor misunderstandings. You hold grudges for years, even decades, convinced you were wronged, unable to let go until they see it your way and apologize.

You don't yet see how much of this turmoil comes from unexamined patterns. You react automatically, thinking control is a show of strength and surrender a sign of weakness. The irony is, your need to win ensures everyone loses—especially you.

But there's no reason to feel bad about yourself. This is all part of your learning curve. Eventually, a new desire emerges—that maybe not every disagreement needs to be a threat, and not every challenge needs to result in a victory. You start catching yourself mid-trigger, rather than after the meltdown has occurred, as it used to be.

You begin to see that peace isn't something others give you—it's something that naturally sets in when you stop needing to win. And in those moments of clarity, the path to your old soul opens up.

You'll likely still resist surrender at first, mistaking it for passivity. But eventually you'll see that surrender doesn't mean giving up—it means you've stepped out of the game entirely. When you no longer make your identity dependent on being right, the fire of conflict loses its fuel. You realize you don't need to dominate or retreat—you can simply let things be.

And slowly, through trial and error, you discover that what you were chasing in conflict—validation, superiority, safety—never comes from winning an argument, anyway. True strength doesn't come from how loudly you speak, but from how silent you are inside.

Old Soul

You no longer see conflict as something to avoid or conquer. Like everything in life, what tends to irk the outward-focused mind is actually an invitation to look inward. *What does this say about me? What patterns or wounds is it pointing to?* You recognize that most conflict stems not from simple malice, but from complex emotions of confusion, pain, or projection. Even when hostility is directed at you, you see it as someone's unprocessed suffering. Instead of counter-attacking, you meet it with presence.

You're not here to win at life—you're here to see it clearly so you can co-create and be part of the unfolding. Defending some mental opinion or position is far too petty to garner your attention. You're much more interested in uncovering your inner truth. When engaging with others, you listen not to the surface meaning of their words, but to the energy behind them. You know silence is more powerful than the noise of rebuttal, and that your calm speaks louder than logic. You trust your intuition to guide when and how to respond.

Rooted in stillness, you avoid getting pulled into other people's chaos. You can hold space without needing to fix, knowing that your acceptance of them is the fast track for them to move through whatever it is they're caught up on. You're also able to set boundaries without anger whenever necessary. You know who you are, and that self-anchored clarity becomes a calm center as the storm rages around you.

Should your own buttons get pushed, as might still happen from time to time, you pause, breathe, and feel the sensations in your body. You let the energy arise and pass. You no longer fuel a story because there's no story you maintain. You let any charge move through you instead of acting it out. You walk away clean—not suppressing, not retaliating—just free.

As an old soul, you actively use life as a mirror. Conflict is another opportunity to deepen your discernment through inner body awareness. You know when to engage, when to step back, and when to let silence do the work.

You've become fluent in the space between words—able to hear the grief beneath anger, the fear behind control, the longing at the root of hostility. Sometimes you answer with a phrase. Sometimes with a pause. Sometimes with nothing but the quiet clarity of your awareness. It's the mark of a soul no longer at war with life, but in harmony with it.

You also see that conflict, when met with presence, can be profoundly creative. It doesn't have to end in fracture; it can lead to breakthrough. Sometimes, the tension of differing perspectives births a third way neither party could see alone. Because you don't cling to outcomes, you stay open to these surprises and life keeps delivering adventure.

Ultimately, you recognize that the end of conflict is not agreement, but freedom. The freedom to let others have their experience while you get to have yours.

Prompts

1) What patterns show up in your conflicts? Defensiveness, avoidance, blame?

2) What childhood experiences might have shaped how you handle conflict now?

3) When you feel the urge to "win" an argument, what are you really seeking?

4) How do you react when someone challenges your opinion or corrects you?

5) What would it look like to respond to tension without needing to be right?

6) How does your body and breath change when you're in the middle of a conflict?

7) Think of a conflict you regret—what would you do differently today?

8) How might conflict serve as an invitation to grow closer to someone instead of further apart?

9) What would change if you saw every conflict as an opportunity to deepen your self-knowledge?

Chapter 56

Trauma

Young Soul

You carry your trauma like an open wound. Whether or not you speak of it, it shapes your choices, your reactions, your self-image. You don't see it as something that happened to you—much worse, you see it as who you are. You might even advocate for others with similar pain, hoping to help. But if you haven't truly healed, you're just keeping it alive for yourself by keeping it central.

If you're still looping through the story, it means there's pain you haven't fully faced. You may have buried emotions because they once felt too overwhelming to meet. To survive, you learned to disconnect from your body, your feelings, your past—not realizing that distance doesn't dissolve trauma. It only buries it, where it festers and resurfaces in your triggers and unhealthy patterns.

When you're identified with your trauma, the very thing you try to avoid is what keeps replaying. You blame the past for who you've become—as if the damage is permanent, as if the script is already written. You might even cling to your suffering as proof that life is unfair, that healing is impossible. You don't yet see that reliving your pain doesn't make it virtuous. It just deepens the grooves of resentment and reactivity.

To heal, you have to be willing to stop running. To feel what you once had to suppress. To face what you've spent years avoiding. Waiting won't help. Time alone won't fix it. The only thing that unwinds trauma is presence—presence in the body, in the breath, in the now. And that's what life keeps inviting you back to. That is the purpose of your trauma. You can't erase the past, but you can change your relationship to it.

Slowly, the old soul in you whispers not to escape your pain, but to hold it with kindness and compassion. To stop seeking identity in your wounds, and start remembering the deeper self that never needed fixing in the first place.

Old Soul

You remember your trauma, but you no longer live inside it. The memory remains, but it no longer defines you or dictates your choices. The wound has closed—not from time or avoidance, but because you allowed yourself to meet it fully, to feel it without resistance until the charge dissolved. You know now that healing isn't the erasure or denial of what happened. It's the release of your attachment to it.

Once the charge is gone, you can remember it without reigniting the pain. You can speak about it without falling apart. The emotions that once overwhelmed you now move through you—felt, acknowledged, no longer resisted or clung to. In this space, compassion arises naturally—not only for yourself, but for those still caught in destructive patterns.

Some remnants may persist. Your body remains your ally—a compass. You notice subtle cues, tension, contraction, and you meet them immediately with the light of your awareness. You no longer need to avoid certain memories or people. Avoidance is no longer a strategy you entertain. You respond with discernment, choosing where to focus your attention instead of recycling the past.

The greatest shift is that you no longer see your trauma as a personal flaw or cosmic mistake. You see it as part of your soul's journey—how life carved depth, resilience, and understanding into you. The pain you endured has widened your capacity to hold space for others in theirs. You no longer speak from the wound, but from the wisdom it gave you.

Prompts

1) What beliefs about your identity have formed as a result of your trauma?

2) How do you cope when old emotional wounds are triggered?

3) What would it feel like to approach your trauma with curiosity instead of judgment?

4) Where in your body do you feel unresolved pain, and how do you respond to it?

5) What stories about your past are you still repeating? Are they helping or holding you back?

6) Write a letter to your younger self who went through a traumatic experience. What would you want them to know?

7) How might your trauma contain an invitation to uncover deeper strength or wisdom?

Chapter 57

Feeling Lost

Young Soul

You wander through life wondering who you are, what you're supposed to be doing, and where you're meant to go. You feel perpetually behind—uncertain, untethered. Your comparison-obsessed mind makes it seem like everyone else got the map of life and you didn't.

You search for clarity in titles, relationships, accomplishments, and social identity, hoping something external will finally reflect your true self back to you. But the more you seek outwardly, the more confusing it becomes. One path feels promising for a while, then dissolves. Another excites you briefly, then leaves you empty. Every time you feel close, it turns out to be a dead end. You keep changing directions, thinking the problem is your career, your city, your relationship—when really, it's that you're looking for your permanence self in impermanent things.

No doubt, the world is captivating. It sparkles with experiences, temptations, and the thrill of sensory delight. As a young soul, it's easy to believe that this is your playground and that somewhere among all the toys, your enduring happiness must exist. Without the memory of who you've been before, or the awareness of your inner world, it's natural to lose yourself in the illusions of form and forget your formless essence.

But as always, the design of life leads you down the path of self-discovery. Forgetting plants the seed of remembering. The doubts about your worth, your intuition, give rise to certainty. The constant comparison, the fear of being left behind, opens you up to surrender. The exhaustion from chasing what doesn't last makes you finally pause.

That pause is the turning point—the quiet admission that you've looked everywhere but within. And from that humility, a door opens—not to instant clarity, but to remembering who you really are.

Old Soul

You no longer fear feeling lost, because you've let go of the idea that there's a single, fixed path you're supposed to be on. You understand that life isn't meant to feel linear, clear, or certain all the time—in fact, uncertainty is a key ingredient of the creative unfolding of things. What appears to be "off track" is often the most fertile ground for transformation.

The path isn't something you find—it's something that reveals itself by being present with each moment. You've dropped the need to figure everything out and instead let your awareness rest in what is.

When you can see things as they are, life is very simple. That's when objective reality—the one without your personal narrative—becomes the centerpiece of your life experience. That's when answers don't need to be forced, they come to you because you're constantly connected. And when things seemingly don't go your way, rather than resisting what's happening, you stay open and curious. You work with it. And in that cooperation, direction arises naturally.

Days of feeling rudderless may still come, but they no longer scare you. You don't rush to fix them or escape them. You trust that if you stay tuned in, the next step will present itself. Clarity arrives on its own when you're still enough to receive it.

The deepest shift is that you now feel at home, regardless of circumstances. You remember you're not here to "become" someone; you're here to express that which wants to become form through you. You walk through life as a conscious co-creator, fully trusting the flow. And should a flicker of "off track" arise, you recognize it as a gentle nudge to turn inward again.

Prompts

1) In what areas of your life do you feel the most lost right now?

2) What have you been chasing in hopes that it would make you feel whole?

3) How do you define "being on the right path"? Where did that definition come from?

4) What fears arise when you don't know what's next?

5) When was the last time you truly felt at home in yourself, regardless of your external situation?

6) In what ways has feeling lost deepened your self-awareness?

7) What parts of yourself have you neglected while trying to "figure it all out"?

8) What if feeling lost was actually your soul's way of guiding you inward?

Chapter 58

Hopelessness

Young Soul

Hopelessness rarely strikes all at once—it builds slowly, layer by layer, after years of chasing peace in all the wrong places. You run after success, relationships, status, stimulation, and control, convinced each one will finally deliver lasting happiness. Sometimes they do—briefly. But the feeling always fades and your emptiness and confusion only grow deeper.

What you can't yet see is that it's not bad luck—it's the framework you're living from. You've been taught to believe fulfillment exists somewhere out there, just a few upgrades or accomplishments away. So you keep pushing, grasping for the next milestone, the next fix. But all that effort only makes the gap between "here" and "where you should be" feel wider. It's why it feels like you'll never arrive—because in this mindset, you won't.

It doesn't help that the culture cheers you on in this chase. The world runs on ambition, image, and performance.

No one teaches you to pause, to be still, to rest in the present. So when things fall apart—or never quite come together—it tells you to double down: try harder, plan better, focus more. But the more you push, the more exhausted and disillusioned you become.

For many, the illusion only becomes apparent when you hit rock bottom. Even if you brush against mindfulness or spiritual teachings before then, they rarely take root until the inner tension becomes undeniable. It's not enough to hear wisdom; it must be lived, felt in the body, met in experience.

The guidance you need is all around you—but when you're still identified with the race, you can't hear it. Messages about slowing down or sitting in stillness sound naive, impractical, or even threatening. Only when a deeper voice in you starts to question the whole game will you step away from the scoreboard—just long enough to see there's more to life than trying to win.

Old Soul

You've walked through hopelessness before—more than once, and not just in this lifetime. You've felt the short-lived ring of achievement, the sting of loss, the futility of trying to control what cannot be controlled.

Over time, you've stopped trying to outsmart suffering. Instead, you've let it teach you.

By developing a practice—whether meditation, breathwork, nature walks, or quiet reckonings in your journal—you've found the still point within. Far from cold detachment, it's a living clarity. You've seen how every form is temporary, how desperately you once clung to things that could never complete you, and how suffering ensued when you made your peace dependent on them.

Looking back, you see the strange beauty in your own unraveling. Every heartbreak, disappointment, and dead end turned out to be a lesson that deepened you. Your wisdom is no longer just mental knowing—it's something your body feels in an ongoing manner. This doesn't make you superior—you don't think you're "above it all". But you're no longer fooled by flash words or appearances. Your entire being is now oriented to go straight to the heart of the matter, in every situation that presents itself.

So, when you meet others still caught in the chase, you don't rush to pull them out. You see their station in life and remember the necessity of their path, the way pain ripens into readiness. That doesn't mean you don't offer compassion or a helping hand. But you don't rush them out of their experience. You hold space until they are ready to move beyond it on their own.

Most significantly, hope is no longer an element in your energy field. You're not waiting for someone to save you. You live instead from acceptance—not passive resignation, but the steady, full-bodied presence with what is. This is the soil in which fulfillment grows naturally. You don't need to believe things will get better to feel whole. You now live in the quiet, unshakable freedom you once thought you'd never find.

Prompts

1) When in your life have you felt hopeless, and what brought you back?

2) What beliefs do you hold about what needs to happen before you can feel at peace?

3) How do you define success, and is that definition helping or harming you?

4) In what ways have you tried to "fix" your suffering instead of listening to it?

5) What parts of you still resist accepting what is?

6) How would your life feel if you no longer needed hope to be at peace?

Chapter 59

Trust

Young Soul

Growing up is tough. It's not that you don't want to trust, but it happens: promises are broken, life throws curveballs, and even *you* let yourself down. Trust becomes a tricky thing in a world where most things are a moving target. You might become guarded, skeptical, and wary. With enough instability around you, you might even begin to expect betrayal. You stop opening fully, and before long, being closed off becomes your default state. You protect yourself so fiercely that connection becomes difficult. And this guardedness becomes the way you know yourself to be.

You keep searching for something out there to lean on. But nothing ever feels solid enough, good enough, forever enough. You keep learning the lesson that if you lean too heavily on others, no matter how much integrity they may have, eventually you will find yourself disappointed. That doesn't mean they're bad people. Everyone is on their own journey, going through their own things. It just means you're placing a weight on others that they were never meant to carry. You've been asking people to be the reason you trust life—when that's never been their job.

No doubt, it's hard to see the bigger picture when you're young and vying for your caregivers' attention. They are your first mirrors for love, truth, and stability. While some family systems offer more nurturing in certain ways, they often lack in others. Whatever your circumstances, eventually, you must find a way to forgive your parents for their limitations and accept that they did the best they could—otherwise, they would have done it differently. They were portals for your arrival, not the final authorities on your worth. Real trust in life derives from a place far beyond what people, places, or circumstances can provide.

Real trust is found in stillness, in encountering the part of you that doesn't change. The part that can observe the chaos and remain balanced. This awareness is who you really are—and it's the space in which you no longer need the outer world to prove itself safe, because you've found the quiet that cannot be shaken.

Still, it takes time to realize that. You'll likely keep projecting your unmet needs onto lovers, teachers, leaders, and institutions, hoping someone will finally show up exactly how you need them to and never change. But they will change—because they're not here to complete you.

They're here to reflect where you're still shifting within yourself. Until you see that, trust will feel like a gamble. But once you do, it becomes unshakeable.

Old Soul

You no longer think trust requires permanence. You've come to see that everything in life moves, grows, and shifts—including the people you love. You've stopped expecting others to remain constant in order to feel secure. Instead, you trust with an open energy field, allowing people to be who they are, without needing them to stay who they were.

You hold others with reverence, not ownership. You trust them not because they're perfect, but because you recognize their humanness. And in that recognition, your expectations soften. You read the world in a more fluid way. You rely on people up to a point—gratefully, humbly—but your deepest reliance is no longer placed on shifting forms. You've rooted your faith in something far more enduring.

You've developed a living link to your higher self, your inner wisdom, and a greater intelligence that orchestrates life with precision. This is the trust between Creator and creation. It's a connection that doesn't depend on circumstances, that cannot be broken, and that has always been there—even when you weren't aware of it. It's a surrender into the now, an ongoing relationship with the unfolding. A place of such intense clarity and calm, you can't help but feel safe.

The love, trust, and stability you once sought from your parents—or anyone else—were never meant to be complete. All humans are limited. And yet, through their imperfection, you were being shown a deeper calling: to reach through them to the infinite canvas upon which it all happens.

You walk differently now. Grounded. In receiving mode. Trusting change for what it teaches. But most of all, you trust the part of you that stays centered through it all. Where peace lives, love belongs.

And because you've built that trust within, you extend it without clinging. You don't fear letting others in—you simply meet them where they are, without needing them to be different. You let people ebb and flow in their own time, knowing their path isn't yours to control. You trust life's intelligence to handle the choreography. Your only job is to enjoy the dance.

Trust Chart

How much you trust yourself and the world plays a fundamental role in your ability to engage with it effectively and fruitfully. The following chart highlights the difference in how young souls vs old souls perceive and generate trust.

Young Soul	**Old Soul**
Sees trust as fragile, easily broken	Sees trust as natural, not dependent on permanence
Leans heavily on others for stability	Roots trust in higher self and Source, not shifting forms
Closes off after betrayal, defaults to guardedness	Opens with reverence, allows others to change and grow
Expects caregivers, partners, or institutions to be perfect	Recognizes human imperfection as a mirror, not a failure
Confuses outer constancy with safety	Finds safety in inner stillness that does not change
Trust feels like a gamble, often projected onto others	Trust becomes surrender to life's unfolding intelligence
Searches for unshakable ground in circumstances	Discovers unshakable ground in awareness itself
Carries fear of abandonment and disappointment	Holds others lightly, without ownership or control
Protects self through skepticism and defensiveness	Walks with openness, grounded in inner clarity
Waits for the world to prove it's safe	Lives as if life is already safe, trusting its choreography

Prompts

1) What people, outcomes, or systems have you placed your trust in? How has that worked out for you?

2) How do you react when someone you trust changes or pulls away?

3) What does trust mean to you, and where did that definition come from?

4) In what ways have trust issues shaped your relationships or sense of safety?

5) What deeper longing hides beneath your need for people to be reliable or unchanging?

6) How might you develop a relationship with your inner self as a source of steadiness?

7) What would it look like to trust life, even when things aren't going your way?

Chapter 60

Anger

Young Soul

Anger often feels like it comes out of nowhere. One moment you're fine, the next you're on fire—tense, loud, reactive. But in truth, anger doesn't arrive suddenly. It builds. Slowly. Silently. It simmers beneath your surface through every unmet expectation, every past hurt you've buried, every moment you felt dismissed and didn't know how to speak it.

Anger isn't really about what's happening right now—it's about what has been happening for a long time. It's rarely about the dishes, the traffic, the delay, or the offhand comment. It's about the underlying story: the disrespect, the betrayal, the chronic invalidation. You react strongly because your identity feels threatened. And to relieve the pressure, you explode—at the expense of those around you.

If you look closely, you can spot the moment the raw sensation in your body gets hijacked by your mind. The sensations themselves—tightness in the chest, heat in the face, clenched fists—are temporary and manageable. But the mental story of "how dare they" or "I shouldn't have to feel this" turns a ripple into a tidal wave. The mind fans the flame.

Without awareness of that split, you get swept up in the reaction every time. You believe your anger is justified, even righteous. You think others should behave differently, life should be fairer, and you should never be disrespected. These mental positions prolong your pain. You mistake intensity for strength. You think you're regaining control by lashing out, when you're actually reinforcing your own helplessness.

The real cost comes afterward. You may apologize, or you may dig in your heels—but deep down, you sense the energy didn't actually resolve anything. The original wound remains untouched, waiting for the next trigger. And so the cycle repeats, leaving you exhausted and ashamed, even as you cling to the belief that your rage is protecting you.

After the storm passes, you're left in the rubble—hurt feelings, damaged connections, shame. And quietly, you begin to wonder if there's a better way to meet this fire. A way to feel it without letting it own you. A way to show strength without destruction. That's the moment your old soul starts to emerge.

Old Soul

You no longer fear your anger—you respect it. You've learned to recognize the first signs in the body: the contraction in your chest, the flash of heat, the quickening breath. You don't suppress it, but you also don't act on it. You pause. You observe sensations. You let them be until they go.

You've come to understand that anger is not a problem to fix or a weapon to wield—it's energy with a message. When met with presence, it reveals your boundaries, your wounds, your unmet needs. Only when left unconscious, it becomes volatile. So you've trained yourself to allow the fire without pouring gasoline on it. You've discovered the gap between sensations and your reaction to them—and that's where clarity begins.

You've watched so much of your old anger stem from identification: needing to be right, needing to be respected, needing others to behave a certain way. As those attachments have dissolved, so has the charge. You no longer react from wounded pride or fear of losing control. You've stopped taking things personally. You stand in your power.

Your nervous system, once reactive, is now rewired through years of embodiment practice, silence, and self-inquiry. You've cultivated enough inner spaciousness to hold any heat. In fact, you're no longer afraid of any emotions—it's just energy. It comes, it goes. It teaches.

In this space, anger transforms from a force of destruction into a force of clarity. It doesn't demand retaliation—it directs you to where alignment is missing. It helps you see what matters, set boundaries cleanly, and speak your truth.

Over time, anger loses its intensity. What remains may still be unpleasant, but rather than consuming you, it refines you. And should anger rise, you meet it with reverence. You let it sharpen your discernment without clouding your heart. You let it move through, speak what needs to be said with love, and dissolve. And when it's gone, you're still here—present, grounded, whole. You no longer use anger to fight the world. You use it to come back to yourself.

ANGER CHART

Anger can be one of the most challenging emotions because of its intensity. Reactivity happens so quickly, you might find yourself struggling with how to harness it, because by the time you calm down your chance to do something constructive with it is over. The following chart highlights how young souls vs old souls deal with anger.

Young Soul Orientation	**Old Soul Orientation**
Reacts instantly to offense	Pauses to feel what's underneath
Blames others for triggering anger	Sees anger as a signal for unmet needs
Acts from wounded pride or control	Listens for the deeper hurt and message beneath the fire
Uses anger to assert dominance or protect ego	Uses anger to uncover buried truth or boundaries
Feels justified and righteous	Feels compassion for all sides, including self
Suppresses or explodes unpredictably	Observes sensations for anger to move without harm
Seeks revenge or validation	Seeks clarity, integration, and release
Identifies with being "an angry person"	Sees anger as energy—not identity

© 2025 Cirak

Prompts

1) What triggers your anger most often, and what deeper needs or fears might lie beneath?

2) What does anger feel like in your body right before it becomes explosive?

3) How have your past reactions to anger shaped your relationships or self-image?

4) What beliefs do you hold about fairness, control, or respect that fuel your anger?

5) How might your anger change if you allowed yourself to feel it without judgment?

6) Recall a time you handled anger with grace. What made that moment different?

7) What would it look like to express anger without harming yourself or others?

Chapter 61

Abandonment

Young Soul

To a young soul, abandonment cuts deep—whether it's real or imagined, big or small. It might have been something as simple as your mother stepping into the next aisle at the supermarket when you were a scared toddler, or your best friend moving schools without warning. Or a romantic partner disappearing just when you let your guard down. No matter the details, the moment it happens, something primal is activated: panic, confusion, and a deep, aching sense that you've been left behind.

You believe it's your wound—your personal defect. That you're unlovable, forgettable, too needy, or too much to handle. So you compensate. You try to be more agreeable, more helpful, more entertaining. Anything to keep others from leaving. And yet, even when people stay, the fear lingers. It lives in your nervous system. It haunts you in quiet moments.

The pain is amplified because you look to others to make you feel whole, and your trust is tied to them staying close, behaving predictably, and meeting your needs. When they don't, it doesn't just disappoint you—it destabilizes your entire sense of safety. You become reactive, clingy, avoidant, or numb. You blame them. You blame yourself. Either way, you feel powerless.

And this wound bleeds into every connection. You demand proof of loyalty. You test people's love. You withhold your affection out of fear. Even when people are kind and consistent, you doubt it will last. You brace for the drop—the ghosting, the betrayal, the disappearance. And when it happens, you say, *See? I knew it.* You never realize how expectations create a self-fulfilling prophecy and that relating to people through the lens of fear, suspicion, or past hurt, prevents trust from taking hold.

There's no way out other than to do the inner work. Once the question *Why do people keep leaving me?* is replaced with *What am I still looking for in them?* the old soul shift begins.

Old Soul

You've come to see that abandonment is not just a personal wound—it's a universal one. Every human carries the imprint. It's the symbolic fall from oneness into form, from unity into the illusion of separation. Knowing this, you no longer take it quite so personally. Even when pain arises, you greet it as part of the journey.

When people leave, change, forget, or disappoint you, you stay present with the ache. You don't repress it or dramatize it. You feel and listen. Often, the pain reminds you that this life is yours to live—and no one else is responsible for your sense of home. You've stopped looking for others to bring what only your connection to Source can provide.

You've outgrown the need to control who stays and how they show up. You see that relationships are fluid, impermanent, and sacred all the same. When there is loss, you grieve consciously, without clinging or blame. You don't force people to play roles they never signed up for. You let life take its natural course.

What you once called abandonment, you now recognize as redirection—away from dependence, toward a deeper devotion to your truth. The stability, belonging, and unconditional presence you once demanded from parents, lovers, or friends—you've traced that longing back to Source. You've remembered that the only true abandonment was you forgetting who you are. And you've stopped forgetting.

That doesn't mean you never feel pain. It means you trust it when it comes. You let it humble you, bring you closer to the part of you that has never left, that is unshakeable. You are no longer lost. You are at home with yourself.

PROMPTS

1) What early memories stand out as moments of feeling abandoned or left behind?

2) How do you react when someone pulls away from you emotionally or physically?

3) In what ways have you tried to prevent abandonment through control or self-sacrifice?

4) What beliefs about yourself formed as a result of feeling abandoned?

5) How does the fear of abandonment shape your current relationships or attachment style?

6) In what ways have people left your life that, in hindsight, made space for your growth?

7) How would it feel to hold space for your own emotions instead of needing someone else to rescue you?

Chapter 62

Boundaries

Young Soul

Boundaries are confusing when you don't yet know who you are. You're still early in your soul journey, trying on identities and emotional reactions like outfits in a dressing room. You overextend one day and regret it the next. Then you pull back and go quiet, only to wonder if you've vanished completely. Without a stable inner center, your boundaries remain just as unstable.

This confusion spills into every area of life. When you say no, you worry it means you're selfish. When you say yes, you fear you're being used. You try to gauge what others want, adjust yourself accordingly, and maintain harmony—but in doing so, you often betray your own needs. You think being compliant makes you compassionate and that self-sacrifice is a show of strength.

You haven't yet learned that boundaries are not just something you say—they're something you are. Your energy speaks long before your words do. When you don't fully inhabit yourself, others can feel it. It's not always that they mean harm; it's that your field lacks clarity. You send mixed signals without realizing it, because you're still developing the inner alignment that makes truth unmistakable.

So you experiment. You set a limit too firmly, or too late. You shrink when you should've spoken. You erupt when you could've calmly exited. Every misstep teaches you. Every twinge of resentment becomes data. You are not failing—you're learning how to define yourself from the inside out.

And as that inner self becomes clearer, you start to realize: boundaries aren't about keeping people out. They're about keeping yourself in.

Old Soul

You no longer treat boundaries as rigid lines or sharp defenses. You understand them as acts of clarity and reverence—ways of staying rooted in who you are, even as life changes around you. Through lived experience, you've come to discover your inner landscape and that knowing yourself is the pre-requisite of every boundary you hold.

You don't need to announce your limits or explain them at length. Your energy does the talking. There is a stable frequency in your presence, and others feel it. The way you treat yourself becomes the invisible template for how others relate to you. That's not just surface confidence—it's vibrational truth.

When you say no, it's clean. It doesn't come with guilt or tension. You don't flinch when people push back, and you no longer see their disappointment as your responsibility. You've let go of the illusion that boundaries are meant to control others. You know now—they're how you stay in integrity with yourself.

Gone are the days of using boundaries to punish, to prove a point, or to manage fear. That was a surface-level concept of self-protection. You've since learned that true boundaries are clear, kind, and energetically stable. They don't shout or plead. They simply declare what's true and invite others to meet you there.

Of course, this clarity didn't arrive overnight. It came through years of learning to listen, through embracing what elevates you and gently releasing what doesn't. As a result, you've become uncompromising in your alignment—not because you're rigid, but because you've stopped negotiating with your intuition.

Paradoxically, your boundaries don't separate you from love—they make love possible. Because you are no longer split within, you are no longer split without.

Prompts

1) When have you felt your boundaries were crossed, and how did you respond?

2) What fears arise in you when you think about setting or enforcing a boundary?

3) In what situations do you tend to overextend yourself to avoid conflict or rejection?

4) What is one area of your life where your boundaries feel unclear or inconsistent?

5) What would it feel like to protect your energy without guilt or explanation?

6) Who in your life respects your boundaries naturally, and what feels different in their presence?

7) How do your physical sensations change when you're about to violate your own limits?

8) How might you begin to set boundaries not from defensiveness, but from self-love?

Chapter 63

Grief

Young Soul

Grief often strikes like a storm. Even when you see it coming—a breakup, a death, a shattered dream—it still rattles you. Suddenly, you're not just mourning what was lost. You're mourning who you were when it was still part of your life. That's why grief can feel so existential: it's not only the person or dream that's gone—it's the identity you wrapped around it.

When your sense of self is built on roles, relationships, and outcomes, loss doesn't just hurt—it unravels you. And when you cling to form, you may mistake this unraveling for your own destruction. You think the pain means something has gone terribly wrong. You don't yet see that what's dying isn't you—it's your story about yourself. Your imagined control. Your illusion of permanence. And while that doesn't erase the sorrow, it begins to hint at its deeper purpose.

But for now, your relationship to emotion is still developing. You instinctively push away what hurts and cling to what soothes. So when grief comes, your system may shut down. You might avoid it altogether or drown in it for years. You blame yourself, others, or life itself. You decide it shouldn't be this painful—and in that resistance, the pain deepens. You start guarding your heart, believing that to love is to risk devastation.

But unprocessed grief doesn't go away. It becomes bitterness, numbness, or chronic fear of attachment. So the task—however unwanted—is to feel it. Not to fix it, not to explain it, but to let it break you open. Because only in that vulnerability can something truer begin to take root. The old self falls away, and your old soul awakens.

Old Soul

Grief no longer frightens you. You've walked with it. Sat with it. Let it split you open in the dark. You've learned it's not a feeling to avoid, but an opportunity to wash away what is no longer serving you. When grief comes, you don't push it away. You make space for it to stay—for as long as it needs to express itself fully.

You understand that attachment is not a mistake—it's part of the human growth experience. You love fully, knowing all form is temporary. And when someone departs, or something ends, you grieve deeply—but not blindly. You can feel how the soul continues, that love remains, and that even in pain, something gracious is unfolding.

Awareness has made you more sensitive, not less. Sometimes that feels unfair, but, actually, you're just on an accelerated track of learning to feel your feelings fully. That's why the ache goes deeper now, touching subtle places in the psyche and heart that younger versions of you couldn't access.

At the same time, it's only happening because you're ready for it and able to handle it. That's how life is the perfect mirror. You let the sadness move through you as a necessary rite of passage. You allow yourself to dissolve and don't rush to return to normal. You don't distract with activity. You go still. You observe. You listen. You know that grief carries its own intelligence, and that every ending delivers a hidden teaching—if you're quiet enough to receive it.

So when grief arrives, you let it refine you. You let it strip away what's untrue and reveal what matters. You don't cling to who you were before the loss. You bow to who you are becoming because of it.

Prompts

1) What loss in your life has shaped you the most, and how do you carry that story?

2) What beliefs about life, love, or permanence have been challenged through grief?

3) How do you usually respond to grief—by resisting, collapsing, distracting, or surrendering?

4) In what ways has your identity been attached to the things or people you've lost?

5) What part of you is asking to be witnessed in this current or past season of loss?

6) What would it mean to allow yourself to grieve without identifying with it?

7) When you feel the heaviness of grief, what does your body need most?

8) If the person or thing you've lost could speak to you now, what might it say?

Chapter 64

Guilt

Young Soul

Guilt feels like your conscience speaking—and in some ways, it is. But when you're still early in your journey, it tends to arrive not as clarity, but as confusion. It shows up in the body as a dense, contracting energy: tightness in the chest, clenching in the stomach, a lump in the throat, heat in the face. You feel small, tangled, inwardly spiraling. You don't yet realize that guilt is meant to guide—not punish—you.

Your mind reacts to the discomfort with endless chatter: *I shouldn't have said that. I should've known better. What's wrong with me?* You believe that if you think hard enough, regret deeply enough, or punish yourself long enough, you'll make things right. But that looping only traps you. It clouds your discernment and keeps you bound to a version of yourself that's already gone.

Guilt can be a helpful signal, but it becomes toxic when turned against the self. Instead of supporting reflection, it feeds control. You replay the past, trying to rewrite it. You bargain with life. You shrink from new opportunities, afraid to repeat old mistakes. But living from guilt doesn't make you wiser—it makes you hesitant, tight, and disconnected from your deeper knowing.

Often, the guilt you carry isn't even yours. It's inherited from childhood, from culture, from outdated ideas of right and wrong. You've internalized voices that told you what a "good person" should be, and when you deviate—even in pursuit of truth—you feel ashamed. But shame is not the teacher. Presence is.

You are not your mistakes. You are the wisdom they've created in you. Life doesn't go wrong—it unfolds with perfect intelligence to help you awaken. The moment you stop judging the past and start listening to it, guilt loses its grip. You begin to transform through acceptance and understanding. And that's how an old soul is born.

Old Soul

You see guilt clearly now—not as a moral verdict, but as a vibrational cue. When it arises, you don't flinch. You feel it. You observe and breathe into it. You ask gently: *What part of me feels misaligned? Is there something I need to see, to own, to forgive?* You don't rush to conclusions. You listen.

Sometimes guilt points to an unhealed wound. Sometimes it reveals old programming still present in the nervous system. And sometimes, it's just your control freak mind panicking that you didn't meet someone's expectations. You've learned to distinguish what's true from what's inherited.

You don't expect your younger self to have known what you know now. That would be unfair. Growth happens through experience, not foresight. You see that everyone, including yourself, is always doing their best from their current level of awareness. And when you really get that—not just mentally, but energetically—your judgments begin to dissolve.

You've also learned the difference between regret and responsibility. You don't pretend every choice was wise—but you don't carry them like a burden, either. If repair is needed, you offer it. If change is called for, you act. But you do so from presence, not because you feel bad or sorry.

When you come into deeper alignment, your conscience becomes your compass. Guilt no longer controls you. It guides you—briefly, wisely, and then it moves on. You are not trying to be good. You are simply becoming whole.

PROMPTS

1) What do you currently feel guilty about, and how long have you been carrying it?

2) If your guilt could speak, what would it say it's trying to protect or preserve?

3) What are you still trying to control by feeling guilty about the past?

4) What lesson did that mistake teach you, and how has it helped you grow?

5) Where did your ideas of "being good" come from? Do they still serve you?

6) When do you mix up guilt with love, obligation, or morality?

7) How would it feel to forgive yourself, not in words, but in energy?

8) Who would you be without this guilt story? What would open up in your life?

Chapter 65

Shame

Young Soul

Shame is like a shadow you carry without realizing it. You think you're just trying to be more productive, more attractive, more lovable—but what you're really doing is hiding the belief that something is fundamentally wrong with you. You live with the silent fear that if people saw the *real* you, they'd leave, reject you, or confirm your worst suspicion: that you're not enough.

This fear doesn't announce itself as shame. It shows up as perfectionism, overachieving, people-pleasing, social anxiety, or control. You smile when you're unhappy. You give more than you have. You stay busy, so you never have to feel that creeping sense of unworthiness. Beneath it all, shame is what's driving the behavior—but you don't realize it. You just feel like you're always behind, never successful or attractive enough, and constantly at risk of being found out.

Shame tells you that *you* are the problem. Not your actions—which you can always change—but you. And because you're still heavily identified with your form self, you believe every critical thought must be true. You replay your worst moments, dwell on all the ways you've disappointed others, and turn that discomfort inward. You don't recognize yet that shame isn't who you are—it's your conditioning.

Like most things that reveal themselves later in life, most of it began in childhood. You were shamed for expressing needs, instincts, emotions, creativity—for simply being too much or not enough. Instead of being guided, you were punished by those who were imposing their own unresolved baggage on you. Now, as an adult, when life doesn't go your way or someone rejects you, you don't just feel hurt—you collapse inward and armor up. You believe that being "good enough" means hiding your real self. But the more you hide, the more disconnected you become.

Eventually, the strain of pretending becomes too much. You long to feel safe just being you. And that longing begins to override the shame. When you catch yourself in the act of self-rejection—when you hear the inner voice saying you're not worthy—you pause and question it. That's the beginning of old soul style healing.

OLD SOUL

You no longer strive to be flawless, because the need to appear perfect is just shame in disguise. You've seen through it. You've done the work and made peace with your imperfections. You understand now that all judgment is arbitrary, born from fear, pain, or control.

Shame is rarely taught through words—it's absorbed energetically. As a child, you were likely shamed for being too sensitive, too loud, too emotional, too curious. The message wasn't always spoken, but it was clear: you're not okay as you are. That felt sense of wrongness entered your nervous system before you had language for it. And so you adapted. You shaped yourself for love. You learned to self-abandon. The shame didn't start with you—but for a while, it lived in you.

When shame arises now, you meet it with presence. You no longer believe the voice. You see it as a ghost from the past—an inherited vibration, not a reflection of truth. You feel it, stay with it, and let it dissolve. No fixing. No explaining. Just awareness. Because you've learned: shame cannot survive the light of loving attention.

That's why you speak your truth. You show up real. Not because you crave validation, but because authenticity is the most healing vibration. You've discovered that to feel yourself fully is the most divine thing there is. So, when others share their shame with you, you offer the same compassion you learned to give yourself. You become the space where healing happens.

Shame no longer keeps you small. It reminds you that every soul is walking home through confusion and distortion. And still—every soul carries the spark of the divine. You no longer interpret shame as evidence of brokenness. You recognize it as a doorway into your original perfection, a portal back into your inherent wholeness.

You're not here to be approved of. You're here to be *true*. And when you're true, you're free. That's what makes you luminous. That's what makes you a safe place for others. And that's when nothing—not even your past—holds power over you anymore.

Shame Chart

Shame can sit so deeply, and surface so sneakily, you might wonder how you can ever come out of it. But with the light of your awareness, there is always a way. The following chart illustrates how young souls vs old souls deal with shame.

Young Soul Orientation	Old Soul Orientation
Believes shame means something is wrong with them	Recognizes shame as a learned emotional pattern
Hides flaws to gain love or approval	Reveals truth to experience authentic connection
Internalizes judgment from others	Questions the source of all judgment
Feels broken, unworthy, or unlovable	Remembers innate worth is never lost
Avoids vulnerability to avoid exposure	Embraces vulnerability as the path to freedom
Tries to fix, improve, or overperform	Stops striving and begins allowing
Fears being seen for who they really are	Trusts that being seen is the medicine
Identifies with the voice of shame	Sees shame as a signal—not a sentence

© 2025 Cirak

PROMPTS

1) What parts of yourself do you feel ashamed of? Where did those beliefs originate?

2) What are some things you hide or edit about yourself in social settings?

3) What does the voice of shame sound like in your inner dialogue?

4) If you imagined that voice coming from someone else, how would you respond to it?

5) How has shame shaped your personality, relationships, or career choices?

6) What would it feel like to show up without trying to prove anything?

7) In what ways have you already begun to break free from shame-based patterns?

8) What memories need your compassion and understanding—not your judgment?

9) How might your story change if you chose self-acceptance over self-correction?

10) Who could benefit from your authentic presence today, exactly as you are?

Chapter 66

Jealousy

Young Soul

Jealousy tends to hit like a sudden drop in temperature. One moment you're fine, the next you're filled with discomfort, judgment, and comparison. You see someone with something you want—a partner, a job, a lifestyle—and suddenly your mind spins with resentment, lack, and self-doubt. Even if you try to brush it off, the energy lingers. Instead of appreciating your life, you spiral into everything you think you're missing.

You see their joy as your failure. Their success as your loss. Their beauty as your deficiency. You don't yet see life from a higher perspective—that what's meant for you will never pass you by, and what isn't meant for you would never satisfy you anyway. So for now, the world feels like a competition, and someone else's rise seems to lower your value. It's not just painful—it's exhausting.

Jealousy is especially great at tainting your relationships. Even when you're trying to act normal, something bitter simmers beneath the surface. Without realizing it, you may pull away, undermine others, or subtly manipulate your surroundings to feel more in control. But what you're really doing is avoiding the truth: that your own sense of worth feels unstable.

You might double down on ambition or appearance, trying to "catch up." But nothing ever fulfills you. That's because the core wound isn't about others—it's about the belief that you're not enough as you are. The more you seek validation outside yourself, the more you suffer. Jealousy becomes a loop of controlling, proving, and failing to self-reflect.

Conversely, healing only begins when you pause and bring awareness to the sensations. What does jealousy feel like in your body? What story is your mind telling? What fear is being triggered? Jealousy is never really about the other person. It's a call to return inward. A mirror reflecting where love and alignment are still missing within you.

Old Soul

As an old soul, you've encountered jealousy many times—and outgrown it. Not because you're immune to envy, but because you've learned to meet it with presence. You don't judge the feeling or repress it. You observe it, feel its charge, and trace it inward. You ask gently: *Where do I still feel small? What fear or belief is ready to be released?*

You know that life is a mirror and each soul walks a perfectly tailored path. Someone else's success doesn't diminish yours—it can only expand for you what's possible. Their joy, beauty, or brilliance becomes a shared frequency to celebrate, not a threat to defend against. In your old soul wisdom, you've shifted from comparison to inspiration, from scarcity to abundance. The weight you used to put on yourself through others is no longer there.

And because your identity is no longer tied to image or status, you're free. You don't need others to have less for you to feel more. You don't take their win as a sign of your loss. You take it as proof that life is infinitely abundant and generous and that what is aligned for you will come in its time. And even if a flicker of jealousy arises, you recognize it as a momentary dip, not a reality.

You're also attuned to the frequency of jealousy in others. It's unmistakable—tight, covert, slightly distorted. You don't judge them for it, but you no longer stay entangled in those dynamics. You protect your field by removing yourself from frequencies that feel misaligned. Sovereignty means choosing what energies you let in.

And so you walk through life celebrating what's blooming—yours and others'—knowing there is no scarcity in Source. When you're free of jealousy and rooted in enoughness, everybody wins.

Prompts

1) What people trigger jealousy in you and why?

2) How does jealousy show up in your body? What are the physical sensations?

3) What does jealousy reveal about what you truly want or need to heal?

4) What would it look like to celebrate others without feeling less of yourself?

5) How does jealousy affect your relationships?

6) Who do you admire deeply, and what part of you wants to be expressed more as a result?

7) When was the last time jealousy motivated you to grow in a healthy way?

8) How do you behave differently when you feel abundant versus when you feel lack?

Chapter 67

Loneliness

Young Soul

Loneliness haunts you. It's not just the absence of people—it's the ache of not being seen, not being understood, not being known. And it stings. Because you haven't yet developed the capacity to sit with yourself and enjoy your own company, being alone feels like punishment. Silence becomes unbearable. Empty space becomes threatening. That's why, for most humans, solitary confinement is the most severe form of punishment—without someone reflecting you back to yourself, you feel nonexistent.

As a young soul, you're still fully identified with your personality, your needs, your story. You think you *are* your body and mind, rather than the awareness behind them. So when you're alone, it feels like no one is there—not even you. You don't yet recognize the living presence behind your thoughts. You haven't yet made contact with the being beneath the doing. So your refuge becomes seeking stimulation and company—thinking it's connection, when really it's distraction.

Most of your socializing is unconscious. It's not rooted in intimacy—it's driven by fear of insulation. Work, friendships, dating, even personal goals—if you look closely, you'll see that the driving force of filling your calendar is so you never have to face the one person who's always with you: yourself. And ironically, the more you run from yourself, the more disconnected you feel—even when surrounded by people.

But don't fret. The world never taught you how to be with yourself. No school, religion, or culture explained how to sit in stillness without reaching for escape. So when isolation arrives—through heartbreak, loss, illness, or simply life's natural rhythm—it feels like punishment. But it's not. It's an invitation to return to the only place true connection begins: within.

The first time you start to enjoy your own company, something profound shifts. You taste the essence of self-reliance—not as rugged independence, but as spiritual rootedness. You stop seeking yourself in others and begin to dwell in yourself. And in that movement from loneliness to *aloneness*, your old soul begins to rise.

OLD SOUL

You no longer think solitude is suffering. In fact, stillness, silence, space—these are no longer voids to be filled, but sanctuaries. You've realized that the world is noisy, and much of what passes for connection is just mutual distraction. You've lived long enough to know that true intimacy begins within—and that depth with yourself is what allows for depth with others.

When you're alone, you don't feel empty. You feel full. You commune with your higher self, with Source, with the deep stillness at the core of all things. You feel the hum of existence holding you. You know you are never truly alone—not when you're in the presence of your own being, and certainly not when you're tuned into the field of consciousness that connects all life. Solitude is where you receive the next step. It's where the channel opens.

That doesn't mean you've become aloof. Quite the opposite. Because you are anchored in yourself, you're more available to others than ever before—but without attachment. You no longer need others to fill a hole within you. And so your presence becomes clean, clear, and trustworthy. Relationships deepen because your being naturally resonates with truth—theirs and your own.

You see now that loneliness was never the problem. In fact, there are no problems in the world, other than the ones you create for yourself. Everything just is what it is until you come along and assign it meaning, primarily based on your conditioning and past experiences.

As such, every experience, every conversation, every sensation, is just a pointer to the switchboard that is your body. Here, the energy from your feelings either gets stuck—as a result of clinging or resisting—or it is allowed to flow through you freely, leaving behind imprints of wisdom in the form of resonance with your higher self.

For old souls, alone time is high and holy time. You no longer feel the need to be mirrored—you've found the mirror within. From that still, unshakable center, love overflows—not as a need to be met, but as a frequency you *are*. Should you ever do feel lonely, it's because you're disconnected, facing outward, and life is calling you inward. And once you answer the call, the suffering dissolves.

When you walk through life with Source as your closest ally, you are never alone again.

Loneliness Chart

Few emotions can provide as much contrast as those that rise while being alone. It can be heaven for one and hell for another. The following chart illustrates how young souls vs old souls experience loneliness.

Young Soul Orientation	Old Soul Orientation
Feels abandoned, unwanted, or unloved	Recognizes loneliness as a call to turn inward and self-reflect
Seeks constant connection to avoid discomfort	Finds peace and richness in solitude and silence
Believes others should fill their emptiness	Understands no one else can complete them
Equates aloneness with failure or rejection	Treats aloneness as sacred opportunity
Blames others for not being present	Releases attachment, honors what is
Distracts with noise, media, or socializing	Observes sensations until they dissolve
Fears their feelings mean something is wrong	Knows all feelings are visitors, not verdicts
Romanticizes companionship as the answer	Realizes connection must arise from self-realization
Feels isolated in their uniqueness	Finds unity in the shared human experience
Yearns outward without anchoring inward	Meets the longing with presence, not pursuit

© 2025 Cirak

Prompts

1) When do you feel most alone? What are you believing about yourself in those moments?

2) Do you find it difficult to sit in silence without distractions? What comes up for you when you try?

3) In what ways do you seek company or connection to avoid being with yourself?

4) What practices could help you deepen into stillness and enjoy your own presence?

5) What is your relationship to solitude? Is it fearful, peaceful, or something in between?

6) What does your inner child believe about being alone? Is that belief still true?

7) When have you felt the most connected to yourself? What allowed that to happen?

8) What part of your soul might be trying to emerge through this time of aloneness?

9) What could shift in your life if you felt truly at home within yourself?

CHAPTER 68

BOREDOM

YOUNG SOUL

You crave stimulation. New places, new people, new stuff, new goals—anything to keep you engaged and moving. But no matter how exciting something seems at first, it eventually fades. The shine wears off, the novelty dulls, and you're left with a restlessness you don't know how to sit with.

That's boredom. It's what arises when you're not in touch with Source energy, relying on the outer world to keep you entertained. You hop from one activity to the next, trying to squeeze meaning out of your circumstances. You scroll, you binge, you plan trips, you fantasize about the future. But nothing truly satisfies you for long. That's because when you're operating purely from the self, you're limited to creating reality from the known—your past experiences, fears, desires, and mental constructs. And so everything starts to feel repetitive. Even imagination can barely stretch beyond the constraints of your current identity.

Your own thoughts become a trap. They're loud, relentless, always strategizing how to maximize pleasure and avoid pain. Inevitably, you find yourself cycling through the same fears, same cravings, same projections. Life begins to feel small. Boredom eventually devolves into burnout, apathy, or even despair.

The issue isn't that life is boring—it's that your perception is blocked. You've been conditioned to fear the unknown, to see it as chaotic and unsafe rather than engaging and alive. You've been taught that fulfillment comes from doing, not being. And so you chase stimulation to avoid confronting the inner void.

But distraction is only a short-term fix, until finally a quiet suspicion begins to arise: *Maybe the world isn't the problem. Maybe it's my disconnection from myself.* That subtle reorientation—from outer to inner—is the first glimpse of the old soul awakening.

Old Soul

You don't get bored—not because life is always exciting, but because you're connected. You're tapped into an ever-flowing stream of creative, spiritual energy that makes even the simplest moments feel alive. Washing the dishes, sitting in traffic, watching the wind move through trees—these aren't empty stretches of time. They are invitations to just *be* with life. And in that being, there is always richness.

You've realized that boredom is just a surface-level symptom of inner disconnection. So if it arises, you don't run from it—you notice it, drop into your body, and observe. And what seemed like dullness begins to hum with subtle energy again. The boredom dissolves—not because you distracted yourself, but because your presence returned.

You no longer crave stimulation. You crave depth. And when you cultivate inner spaciousness, even the ordinary becomes extraordinary. You don't just pass time—you merge with it. Whether journaling, walking, sipping tea, or doing absolutely nothing, you're awake to life unfolding in real time. Boredom once pointed to emptiness—now it reminds you to go inward, toward the infinite.

When everything is alive, you no longer need every moment to be productive or entertaining. You can sit for hours in stillness, letting the formless speak. That doesn't make you passive—it makes you a vessel in receiving mode. In that spacious state, divine guidance flows freely. The next step arrives not through effort, but because you're in alignment.

You've learned to live with intention, without forcing. To create from fullness, not lack. To trust the unknown, because it knows no limits. Your life becomes a container for Source to move through. And just like that, boredom becomes obsolete.

Prompts

1) When was the last time you felt truly bored? What were you resisting at that moment?

2) How do you respond to boredom? With distraction, productivity, escape?

3) How do you relate to stillness and silence? Are they uncomfortable or nourishing?

4) How often do you slow down enough to listen for inspiration rather than chase it?

5) Have you ever felt deeply present while doing something simple?

6) How would your life change if you lived from inner fullness rather than outer seeking?

Chapter 69

Feeling Stuck

Young Soul

When you feel stuck, your first instinct is to push harder, think more, plan better. When that doesn't work, you assume you must be doing something wrong—that you've gone off-course, or worse, that you're simply not good enough. You cycle through endless options, replay past decisions, and stress about what it all means for your future. You're trapped in your head, and it only deepens the sense of paralysis.

Stuckness is what happens when you try to navigate life using only thoughts, fears, and inherited beliefs. You're attempting to solve a spiritual disconnect with logic and willpower—the very tools that created the problem in the first place. No wonder it feels impossible. When you're cut off from inner guidance, you lose access to the place from which inspired action arises. Life is reduced to a loop of mental conditioning.

This isn't your fault. You were taught to strategize your way through life. To calculate, plan, and predict. You feel like you can't move unless you know what's coming. But life is not a formula that you know ahead of time—it's a mystery. You can't think your way into alignment. You can only learn to show up with presence and respond from within.

And that's the hidden wisdom inside your stuckness: it's calling you to stop forcing, start surrendering, and to open yourself up to the unknown. To stop trying to make something happen, and allow it to happen. To stop fearing the future and start returning to the now. When you stop resisting where you are, flow begins to return.

Old Soul

When you feel stuck, you don't rush to fix it or judge yourself as broken. Instead, you pause, turn inward, and observe your sensations. You listen for what your soul is trying to communicate.

You understand that stuckness is often the result of mental over-efforting. When you're in your head—wrestling with beliefs, seeking certainty—you disconnect from your body's wisdom and presence. And when that connection is lost, flow ceases, and you wind up feeling stuck.

Furthermore, the more you judge your experience, the more frozen it becomes. But with awareness, you can catch yourself early and return to center, with barely a hiccup.

You've learned that feeling stuck is not a failure—it's a time for stillness. A threshold moment. When nothing is moving on the outside, something deeper is realigning within. So you use the pause to restore clarity by dropping beneath the story and letting life reset your internal compass.

If you feel stuck because you've taken on too much or pushed too far, you gently scale back. You make the next step smaller, lighter, truer. You replace pressure with even more presence. You trust that real momentum comes from staying in sync with life, not imposing your version of it.

Above all, you've stopped living as if you alone have to make everything happen. You're a co-creator now. You listen for the intuitive nudge before acting. You recognize the voice of your higher self and can distinguish it from the noise from outside.

And if no guidance comes today, you don't panic. You're no longer interested in forcing the *doing*. You rest in the knowing that not moving is sometimes the most aligned action of all. Because nothing is ever truly stuck. It's just not ready yet.

Prompts

1) In what areas of life do you feel most stuck right now?

2) What thoughts or fears are contributing to your sense of paralysis?

3) Are you trying to force movement in an area where rest or reflection might be wiser?

4) What belief systems might be outdated but still influence your decisions?

5) How does your body respond when you feel stuck? Can you observe it without judgment?

6) What would it feel like to not need an immediate solution?

7) Where might you be trying to skip steps, or biting off more than you can chew?

8) What small, inspired action could you take today to shift the energy?

9) Can you recall a past experience where being stuck led to deep insight or redirection?

10) What does your higher self want you to know about this time of stillness?

PHYSICAL

Chapter 70

Body

YOUNG SOUL

You have a strained relationship with your body, but you don't realize it. You move through life like a disembodied head, rarely tuning in to the rest of you. You see your body as the thing that carries your mind around—and you only really notice it when something hurts or fails. Even then, you're inclined to suppress it or distract yourself—pushing through pain, popping pills, numbing out.

There's little to no connection between your mind and your body. You don't see how your thought patterns affect your digestion, sleep, posture, and immune system. You override your needs or try to chemically manipulate your state with caffeine, sugar, alcohol, or drugs. Sometimes it's to escape. Other times, it's to feel something, or to feel nothing. Either way, it's a refusal to sit with what's going on inside: a world of stuck energy, repressed emotion, and inherited trauma.

You chase altered states, confusing stimulation for aliveness. You try to hack your nervous system or induce breakthroughs through substances or extreme activities. But you skip the most important step: listening. True transformation doesn't come from what you put in or on your body—it comes from presence. From acceptance. From honoring what your body is already saying.

Usually, it takes a breakdown to make you pay attention. A diagnosis, a chronic condition, an injury, a moment when your body refuses to be ignored. You might disavow it at first, resent its limits. But if you relent, these moments become invitations to come home to your body, reflect, and admit: maybe what you think in your head isn't the wisest guide. Maybe truth is felt, not figured out. That's when something shifts and you step onto the old soul path.

Old Soul

You've come to see your body not as separate from your soul, but as its most delicate, intimate instrument. That's why you treat it with deep reverence. No longer a machine to dominate, it's now a sacred vessel to care for. The more closely you listen, the more clearly you hear the wisdom emanating from within.

With awareness comes sensitivity. You feel when food dulls your light. You sense dense or distorted energy in a room. You pick up on the tension in someone's voice, the pull in your gut before a shift, the tingling down your spine when receiving a download. You don't just notice these things—you live by them. Your body has become your compass, your barometer, your place of co-creation with Source.

Health is now paramount. Not for longevity, but to ensure your vessel's spiritual alignment. You eat cleanly, rest deeply, move intuitively. It's no longer an act of discipline, but one of devotion. You understand that a clear body allows for the transmission of truth to come through with ease.

Instead of seeking to escape your body, you now go deeper into it. You track sensations in meditation. You locate where energy is stuck. You let instinct lead instead of intellect. You honor when your body wants stillness, when it craves expression, when it says no, when it lights up with yes. You follow its rhythm instead of mental deadlines.

Most importantly, you've stopped trying to transcend the body to reach the divine. You've found the divine here—in the quiet miracle of who you are, as you are. It's in every heartbeat, in every pore of your skin. You live your spirituality, not by leaving your body, but by loving it. And in that love, your body becomes what it always was: a living temple of the soul.

Body Chart

This chart shows how young vs old souls see their bodies.

Young Soul (Disembodiment)	Old Soul (Embodiment)
Views body as separate from self or as a tool	Sees body as an expression of soul and Source
Treats symptoms but ignores underlying energy	Listens to body's signals as messages from within
Seeks control through diet, exercise, appearance	Cultivates reverence through presence and intuition
Uses body for achievement or validation	Honors body as a sacred vessel for awareness
Distrusts bodily sensations, suppresses discomfort	Welcomes sensations as teachers and guides
Feels trapped in form or disconnected from it	Feels rooted in form without being limited by it
Identifies with youth, beauty, or performance	Identifies with aliveness, vitality, and energy
Overrides bodily needs with mental agendas	Responds to body's needs with care and rhythm
Views illness as failure or weakness	Sees illness as a call to slow down and listen
Fears aging, death, and physical limitation	Accepts impermanence as part of divine intelligence

Prompts

1) What is your current relationship with your body? Do you feel connected? Or do you ignore or override its signals?

2) What messages has your body been trying to communicate that you haven't fully heard?

3) When do you tend to disconnect from your body? What are the patterns or triggers?

4) In what ways have you used substances or stimulation to feel better in your body?

5) What would it look like to treat your body as a sacred vessel?

6) Can you identify moments when your intuition came through physically rather than mentally?

7) What does your body need more of right now—rest, movement, nourishment, or something else?

8) How can you better honor your body's natural rhythms in your daily routine?

Chapter 71

Sleep

Young Soul

Sleep feels like an obstacle—a necessary inconvenience that gets in the way of "doing." You push it off, fight against it, override it with stimulants, and resent the hours it "steals" from your productivity. You treat rest as something to be earned after everything else is done. But you don't let that finish line happen. Instead, you live chronically sleep-deprived, burned out, and emotionally fragile—without realizing that much of your anxiety, impatience, and low motivation is rooted in your fractured relationship with sleep.

As a young soul, you haven't yet made the connection between how you live during the day and the quality of your sleep at night. You don't see how the speed of your thoughts, the quality of your attention, and the emotions you suppress all impact your rest—and vice versa. So your nights are restless, and your mornings are groggy. You wake up with resistance and dread, instead of renewal.

You rely on substances—caffeine to wake up, alcohol or sedatives to fall asleep. You force your body to obey your schedule, ignoring its innate rhythms. You fill your days with stress and stimulation, then wonder why you suffer from insomnia, shallow sleep, or chronic fatigue. Instead of listening, you blame the mattress, your to-do list, even your genetics.

You think you need more discipline to achieve your goals. But what you really need is deeper restoration. Sleep isn't just biological—it's energetic. It's when the soul does its most important work.

True rest begins when you stop resisting the body's wisdom, when you stop seeing sleep as an interruption, and start honoring it as medicine.

Old Soul

To you, sleep is a ceremony. You don't just collapse into bed—you approach it with reverence, like entering the temple of self, where silence and renewal await. You understand that how you transition from waking to sleep shapes the quality of your restoration. So you wind down gently. You let the world go. You treat your bed as an altar and your dreams as messengers. You are not escaping life through sleep—you are entering another dimension of it.

You know that deep rest is integration. Every emotion, every insight, every energetic shift needs space to settle. Sleep is where healing completes its cycle. You trust the body's wisdom, honoring its signals that say, "Now is the time to close your eyes and receive."

Old souls understand that the nervous system must be soothed for spiritual clarity to arise. That's why you treat your sleep hygiene with the same care as your meditation practice or creative flow. You don't fill your evenings with noise or distraction. You don't consume dark or violent media. You don't take your phone to bed. You create stillness that opens the gates to the subtle realms.

Your dreams are not random. They're full of symbolism and nocturnal guidance. You know when a vision is offering you something, and you make space for its message in your waking life. You're not just sleeping to recover—you're sleeping to receive.

And when you wake up, you do so slowly. You don't rush into the noise. You protect your mornings. And so, the rest you receive at night becomes a sacred offering that infuses every action of your day. Sleep is part of your spiritual path. Source speaks loudest when you are quietest.

PROMPTS

1) Is sleep a gift or do you view it more as a chore?

2) Do you often ignore your body's signals for rest?

3) What tends to interfere with going to bed on time?

4) How does your relationship with sleep reflect your values or priorities?

5) Do you allow yourself to rest truly, or do you feel guilty when you do?

6) Have you ever received insights through dreams?

7) How does the energy you carry into sleep affect your mornings?

8) What unresolved emotions tend to surface when your head hits the pillow?

9) What rituals or choices help you transition into deep, restorative rest?

10) How do your dreams reflect your current emotional or spiritual state?

CHAPTER 72

PAIN

YOUNG SOUL

A young soul sees pain as a problem. It's a sign that something is wrong and needs to be fixed immediately. Whether it's physical, emotional, or existential, the instinct is the same: push it away, shut it down, numb it out. You pop pills, distract yourself, run faster, talk louder—anything to avoid the discomfort.

This is understandable. You've been raised in a world that sees pain as something negative, not just physically, but personally. Hurt in your body becomes "poor you." Advertisements promote quick fixes. Doctors tend to offer diagnoses without deeper inquiry. Pain is treated as an enemy, not a messenger. And so, not knowing any better, you do what you've been told and try to silence it with logic, substances, or denial.

But the more you resist it, the more it persists. The more you fight it, the more it surfaces in other ways. It starts to become part of your personal narrative. *This always happens to me. I'm just an anxious person. I'll never be the same again.*

You forget to consider that pain can be a sign that something is waking up. That something inside you needs your attention, instead of your judgment. It doesn't always mean something is wrong. It often means something is changing.

That said, it's hard when you haven't yet learned to be with pain. How to listen to it. How to see it as feedback. How to feel it without dramatizing it or spiraling into fear. Pain only becomes part of your identity when you refuse to let it move through. And ironically, the less you resist it, the less it stays.

Always consider the possibility that pain isn't here to hurt you, but to help you grow.

Old Soul

You know pain is not your enemy. It's your ally. A wise teacher. An alert system that shows you where energy is stuck, where healing is needed, and where awareness has not yet reached. You've developed the sensitivity to distinguish between real harm—like injury or illness—and natural pain— like growth, purification, or emotional release.

Whenever pain arises, you know how to scan your body, locate the sensation, and witness it without drama, denial, or judgment. And in that witnessing, something miraculous happens: the pain becomes bearable. It even starts to speak. Not in words, but in insight. In felt knowing.

You understand that every initiation, every awakening, every expansion, is preceded by discomfort. Life isn't punishing you—you're just being stretched beyond your old self. And that's always uncomfortable.

You've also learned how much the body knows. You respect its messages. Knowing pain is never random, you treat it with reverence. You trust it arises in response to choices, environments, beliefs, and energies. That's why you no longer override your system with stimulants or suppressants. You much more prefer to keep it clean, so you can hear it clearly.

Most of all, you've stopped making pain personal. You no longer ask *why me?* or use it to reinforce a wounded identity. You let it come, and you let it go. Without clinging. Without resistance. Just pure, gentle acceptance. As an old soul, you've learned that by loving your pain, you transcend it.

Prompts

1) How do you typically react to pain—physically, emotionally, and mentally? What patterns do you notice?

2) Reflect on a time when pain led to personal growth. What did it teach you?

3) What substances, habits, or distractions do you use to avoid feeling pain?

4) If pain were a messenger instead of a threat, what might it be trying to tell you right now?

5) In what areas of your life are you resisting pain that might be necessary for change?

6) How does your body respond when you finally allow yourself to feel pain fully?

7) What would it look like for you to develop a more conscious, compassionate relationship with pain?

Chapter 73

Injury

Young Soul

One moment you're charging ahead, the next—you're grounded. Stopped in your tracks. The frustration is instant and intense. Your plans are on hold. You can't do what you wanted to do, and it feels like punishment. As a young soul, your priorities are tied to activity, achievement, and being seen. So when you're injured, you feel like everything's been taken from you.

Your body becomes an obstacle. Pain feels like a malfunction. You reach for quick fixes—painkillers, distractions, ways to bypass what's happened and get back to "normal." You don't stop to ask why the injury occurred in the first place—energetically, emotionally, or karmically. You just want to resume what you were doing.

You lack the awareness that your body might be trying to help you—by slowing you down, by signaling imbalance, by inviting you to reflect on the life you're currently living. It's easy to drift out of alignment. Days blur. You go through the motions. And then something stops you. But instead of treating the pause as a teacher, you feel betrayed. The idea that this interruption might serve a higher purpose hasn't occurred to you yet. So you resist. You feel victimized, unlucky, even angry at your own body. It's inconvenient. It's in the way.

You equate your worth with your output, so being sidelined stirs deeper fears: *Will I fall behind? Will I lose momentum? Who am I if I'm not productive?* In that way, the injury becomes a spiritual crossroads—though you may not see it that way. You focus on recovery with one goal: to return to life as it was.

But somewhere deep down, a different kind of seed is planted. A hint of stillness, a slowing of time. It may not bloom right away, but it will. Eventually, you'll come to see that what looks like a detour is often the path itself. That which feels like a limitation may be a course correction. And in that realization, you'll begin to trust the deeper unfolding of life's design.

OLD SOUL

You no longer see injury as an interruption. You see it as divine intervention. A sacred pause for realignment. Something in you needed to stop, reflect, or receive—and the body, in its wisdom, made that decision for you, often in harmony with the environment around you. As an old soul, you've cultivated enough trust to know that nothing is random, and everything is here to help you grow.

When injury arises, you don't assume it's bad. You've lived long enough to know that what seems like a setback often is a blessing in disguise. You've learned not to label too quickly—or at all. Because you know you can't truly know what anything means in the moment. All you can do is listen, trust, and stay present with what life is asking of you now.

You recognize that this slowing down is an invitation to release control. To sink into being. To recalibrate on every level. And in that sacred stillness, clarity arises. Inspiration emerges. Healing accelerates—not just physically, but energetically. You already knew this. Sometimes you just forget, and life reminds you the only way it can: by making you stand still.

So you meet the injury not just as something to heal, but as something to learn from. You don't just recover—you attune more finely to your own inner rhythm. You come out the other side more aligned than you were before.

This is how life sculpts the soul. Not through constant motion, but through holy interruptions. Through trust in what you cannot yet understand. Through quiet surrender to what is.

PROMPTS

1) What was your initial reaction the last time you were injured? What story did you tell yourself?

2) How do you typically relate to your body—do you push it, ignore it, or listen to it?

3) What emotions come up when you're forced to slow down or rest? Do you feel safe being still, or does stillness trigger anxiety or restlessness?

4) Can you think of a time an injury or limitation led to unexpected growth or insight?

5) What beliefs do you hold about productivity, achievement, and rest?

6) How would it feel to trust that your body's signals are on your side?

7) What might this current or past injury be teaching you spiritually?

8) What can you begin doing now to treat your body as a divine partner in your evolution?

Chapter 74

Illness

Young Soul

When you get sick, your first instinct is to suppress the symptoms, override the fatigue, numb the discomfort—do whatever it takes to get back to "normal." Illness is seen as an unwelcome intruder, something that interrupts your plans, delays your productivity, threatens your lifestyle. You treat it as a random misfortune, or bad luck, or even a betrayal by your body. It never occurs to you that it might be mirroring something much more profound.

As a young soul, you're still living primarily in your head. You haven't yet developed a relationship with the energetic layers of your being, so the idea that your illness could be trying to teach you something feels abstract at best, far-flung at worst. You want a diagnosis, a fix, a solution. You rarely pause to ask why the illness might be showing up right now, or what patterns or beliefs may have contributed to it.

Even if you dabble in holistic remedies, you still tend to treat the body like a machine—when it breaks, you call a mechanic. But your body is not a machine. It's a reflection of your internal state: your relationship with your thoughts, your connection to purpose, your lifestyle choices, your dominant view of the world. When there's an imbalance that you keep repressing, illness is what finally gets your attention.

And when it does, all you can think of is returning to the old life, even if that version of life contributed to your breakdown in the first place. You haven't yet shifted from control to collaboration. You don't trust your body. You don't trust life. And so illness, which could be an initiation into deeper connection, instead becomes fertile ground for fear, resistance, and denial.

One day, you will see illness is a gift. A disruptor of your usual programming. It stirs questions you didn't know you had. And for some young souls, this marks the beginning of the path to becoming an old soul.

Old Soul

Illness no longer frustrates you. If anything, it focuses you by bringing you deeper into yourself. You've lived enough lives to know that the body is not just biology—it's energy.

ILLNESS

And when your energy is off, it shows up in the physical. That's why you don't view illness as punishment or failure, but as cherished feedback. A wake-up call to re-examine how you've been living, thinking, and moving through the world.

You know that every ailment is multifaceted. There's the physical layer, yes—but also the emotional, the mental, the karmic. Illness has energetic roots. It speaks the language of unprocessed grief, suppressed truth, chronic stress, spiritual misalignment. And so, when something arises in your body, you slow down, observe, and listen. What has been neglected? What needs to be felt? What part of you is asking for more authenticity?

You've cultivated a different kind of intelligence—one that senses imbalance long before it surfaces. You feel heaviness where there should be lightness. You notice tension building up or healthy patterns starting to slip. And you respond clearly and with self-compassion. You adjust your lifestyle, shift your thoughts, move energy, and clean up your environment. You treat healing as inseparable from growing your self-awareness.

You don't place blind faith in external medicine, nor do you reject it. You integrate it when it serves. But you know the real work happens within. You've learned to trust your body as a living oracle—its messages may not be convenient, but they are always wise. This is how old souls move through life.

Prompts

1) When was the last time you were sick, and how did you respond emotionally?

2) What beliefs do you hold about illness—do you see it as random, as punishment, or as purposeful?

3) What might your body be trying to communicate to you through its symptoms?

4) Do you treat rest and recovery as valuable, or as a setback to productivity?

5) What parts of your lifestyle feel energetically unsustainable or imbalanced?

6) Are there unprocessed emotions you might be storing in your body?

7) How connected do you feel to your body's needs on a daily basis?

8) What would it look like to treat your body as a sacred partner in healing?

Chapter 75

Diagnosis

Young Soul

Getting a diagnosis feels like receiving a sentence. You take the doctor's words as absolute truth—etched in stone and unchangeable—and internalize them into your identity. You begin saying things like "I have this condition" or "I'm the kind of person who gets sick easily," not realizing that each repetition reinforces the illness energetically. From that moment on, you begin to see yourself through the lens of limitation, giving your power away to external authority.

You turn the diagnosis into a narrative—an explanation for your fatigue, your fear, your failures. You research endlessly, talk about it with others, and mentally rehearse worst-case scenarios. You may even begin to expect further decline as if it's inevitable—which, of course, gives that outcome more momentum. The more attention you give the condition, the more space it occupies. It's not that you want to be sick—it's just that you've woven it into how you see yourself. And because most societies teach compassion toward illness, few around you challenge the story or your ongoing embellishment of it.

Every ache or symptom becomes a reason to catastrophize, worry, and plan your life around what might go wrong. You say things like "This is what happens when you turn 40," not realizing you're echoing collective conditioning, not personal truth. Statistics are merely averages, not verdicts—and outliers are far more common than most people believe.

The first shift is to recognize that your body is not your enemy—and your diagnosis is not your destiny. What you resist persists, and what you identify with, you reinforce. Healing begins when you stop turning medical terms into a life sentence, and instead begin treating them as invitations to go inward to where your old soul lives.

Old Soul

When you receive a medical diagnosis, you listen without fear. You take in the information with discernment but refuse to let it define you. You inquire, reflect, and seek aligned support—but you do not hand over your power, no matter how respected the source. If it doesn't feel right, you may even seek multiple perspectives until something truly resonates with your inner knowing.

To you, a diagnosis is a snapshot, not a prophecy. It can offer insight, but it's never the whole story. Your energy, mindset, lifestyle, and alignment with Source all shape the unfolding of your health. So you speak about it only when needed. You don't make it your identity or feed it with your story. If anything, you infuse it with your highest vibration. You hold a deep reverence for the body's regenerative intelligence.

There's no room for self-pity or doom, only trust. You anchor in faith, not fear. You speak life into your cells. You follow the guidance that arises within—whether it points to rest, nourishment, detoxification, energy healing, or a conversation with a trusted practitioner. You move in partnership with your body, not in opposition to it.

Old souls don't just try to fix illness—they learn from it. You examine the root patterns, the emotional residue, the spiritual cause. You treat every diagnosis as an invitation to realign. And when healing happens—whether partial or complete—you don't call it a miracle. You call it the natural restoration of harmony. No dramatization. Just presence, gratitude, and unwavering surrender to the intelligence that made you.

Prompts

1) In what ways have you allowed a diagnosis to become part of your identity?

2) What beliefs about aging or health have you unconsciously absorbed from society?

3) How do you typically respond to physical discomfort: with fear or curiosity?

4) Do you find yourself over-researching or obsessing about your condition?

5) Can you think of a time when your body was trying to get your attention before something became a full-blown issue?

6) How does your body respond when you speak to it with compassion versus criticism?

7) What does your inner wisdom say about your healing path right now?

Chapter 76

Food

Young Soul

To you, hunger isn't just physical—it's mental and emotional, too. But you haven't yet learned to distinguish between these signals. Whenever the urge arises, you reach for whatever's available—fast, salty, sweet, distracting. You eat to fill a hole. Food becomes a coping mechanism, a reward system, or simply background noise for your overstimulated life. You shovel it in while scrolling, talking, driving—barely tasting, barely noticing what you're putting into your body.

Stress eating. Emotional eating. Boredom eating. These aren't random behaviors—they're symptoms of imbalance. When you're disconnected from your inner world, food becomes one of the easiest ways to self-soothe. The pleasure is short-lived, the crash inevitable. But the pattern persists because your awareness hasn't dropped deep enough to treat the body as more than an afterthought.

You don't listen to its cues. You eat past fullness, eat when you're tired, eat what your mind craves—not what your cells need. And because you're not present in your body, you miss the signs: inflammation, fogginess, fatigue. You normalize it. You see food as fuel, but only in the most superficial sense. The idea of food as medicine still feels foreign. And when digestion is off, your skin breaks out, or your mood crashes—you blame your metabolism or genetics, unaware that energy—not calories—is the true measure of nourishment.

A healthy attitude towards food isn't about discipline. It's about presence—about sensing how food actually feels in your body. Until you develop that awareness, your consumption of food will remain reactive, driven by mind, emotion, or environment. Only once you start listening to your body does the compulsion begin to soften and harmony returns—not because you control your eating, but because you're finally in relationship with it.

Old Soul

To you, food is energy in physical form—vibrational information offered by the Earth to sustain your vessel. You no longer eat out of habit. You feel into what your body truly wants, not what the mind demands.

You bless your food—sometimes with words, always with presence. You're aware that your state of consciousness while eating is just as important as what's on your plate. You sit down. You express gratitude. You chew slowly. You taste. You receive. You're not just consuming nutrients—you're absorbing frequency. You choose high-vibration foods: clean, alive, close to the Earth. You gravitate toward nourishment, not stimulation.

If this sounds like a more elaborate process than you're used to—it is. But it's not because it's more complicated. It's more intentional and conscious. You're no longer rushing. You're moving with the rhythm of the moment.

Instead of moralizing food as good or bad—you feel its impact. You notice what energizes you, what dulls you, what grounds or inflames you. There's no dogma, no need to project your choices onto others—just a quiet honoring of your body's intelligence. And when your body asks for something specific, you comply. You know that intuition includes appetite—as long as the signal is clear.

As an old soul, you no longer eat to escape. You eat to honor and replenish your vessel. When you prepare food, you infuse it with care. You know that everything carries a vibration—how it's grown, cooked, handled. So you choose ingredients and environments that uplift your meals, and you avoid eating around stress, screens, or heavy energy. You eat not just to live—but to elevate your state of being.

FOOD CHART

This chart shows how young and old souls relate to food.

Young Soul (Emotional Eating)	Old Soul (Energetic Nourishment)
Eats to escape feelings or fill internal void	Eats to support energy, clarity, and alignment
Driven by cravings, habits, or emotional triggers	Guided by intuition and body-based awareness
Seeks stimulation, comfort, or distraction	Seeks balance, vitality, and inner coherence
Ignores hunger and fullness cues	Listens closely to hunger, satiety, and energy shifts
Associates food with guilt, reward, or punishment	Relates to food with presence and neutrality
Eats while multitasking, dissociating	Eats slowly, gratefully, with attention
Labels food as good/bad, healthy/unhealthy	Chooses food based on energetic resonance
Follows rigid diets or fads to gain control	Allows natural rhythm and self-trust to guide choices
Treats the body as a machine to be optimized	Treats the body as a sacred vessel to be nourished
Feels foggy, heavy, numb after meals	Feels clear, alive, connected afterward

© 2025 Cirak

PROMPTS

1) What is your emotional relationship to food—do you eat for comfort, distraction, or nourishment?

2) How often do you eat while multitasking?

3) What patterns do you notice between your stress levels and your food choices?

4) Do you pay attention to how different foods make you feel, physically and emotionally?

5) When was the last time you truly savored a meal without distraction?

6) What would shift if you saw food as medicine?

7) In what ways do you override your body's cues for hunger, fullness, or craving?

8) What kinds of environments do you usually eat in—and how do they affect your digestion?

9) What would it mean to eat with presence and gratitude?

Chapter 77

Meat

Young Soul

You think of it as food, fuel, or flavor. You grew up eating it, maybe craving it, maybe even celebrating it. The story around it is simple: it tastes good, it's part of your culture, it builds strength. It fills your stomach and satisfies a craving. That's enough. There's no reason to look deeper. To question it would be to question your traditions, your family, your habits—and for most young souls, that level of disruption feels unnecessary, even threatening.

You eat according to your mind's logic or your body's cravings, but rarely from embodied awareness. A high-protein diet makes sense to you because the culture says it does. You follow fitness trends, diet advice, family traditions, and emotional impulses, without really observing how you feel afterward. Bloating, mood swings, inflammation, lethargy—these are blamed on something else. You rarely stop to consider that the food you eat may be affecting not only your physical health, but your emotional and mental state as well.

Even if you become aware of suffering in the meat industry, you may choose to tune it out. It feels too far removed from your life, too painful or too inconvenient to change. You rationalize. You say everything dies. You say plants have consciousness too. You say moderation is key. You say humans have always eaten meat. And you're not wrong—but none of this reflects a vibrational inquiry. It's mental noise used to keep your current habits in place.

You don't yet perceive food as a transfer of energy. You don't realize that the emotional state of the animal—its fear, confinement, trauma—can become part of your system. You ingest the vibration of its death, and then wonder why you feel anxious, heavy, or numb. But because the cause isn't obvious, you don't link it to the meal. You think something's wrong with you, or with life. You miss the body's messages because you've never been taught to hear them.

Eventually, you begin to feel the dissonance. It may be subtle at first—less enjoyment, harder digestion, emotional fog. You may resist the realization, even mock those who make different choices. But the seed is planted. Something inside you begins to question: *Is this still right for me? Is there a deeper reason my body is pushing back?* Before judgment, a new layer of awareness begins to open—not about rules or morality, but about resonance.

Old Soul

As an old soul, your awareness of food moves beyond nutrition, beyond ethics, beyond ideology. You eat based on energy. You ask how something feels in your body—not just during digestion, but in your field, your clarity, your capacity to stay present. And over time, you begin to notice that meat carries a certain density. It may cloud your intuition, constrict your energy, or subtly dull your inner light. This isn't a belief—it's a felt reality.

You no longer choose based on habit or groupthink. You've stopped eating to regulate your emotions or to prove your worth. Your relationship with food becomes sacred, intuitive, reverent. You feel the difference between something that feeds your soul and something that feeds your attachments. And if meat no longer serves your path, you release it—not from guilt or superiority, but from the quiet intelligence of alignment.

You don't try to convert others. You understand that every soul is walking a unique path, and for some, meat may still serve a purpose. The difference is in the frequency, the consciousness, the intention. You also know that eating something out of fear of judgment—whether spiritual or societal—is just another distortion. It's not about purity. It's always about presence. You've seen how both shame and pride contaminate the act of eating.

You sense that true nourishment is energetic, not moral. If for any reason meat re-enters your life, it is with full awareness, deep gratitude, energetic attunement, and spiritual permission. You don't engage in unconscious consumption, nor do you create identity around abstinence. The body may guide you differently at different times. But your decisions arise from stillness, not programming.

This reverence extends to all of life. You begin to see the entire food chain as sacred—whether plant or animal. You give thanks. You bless the exchange. You listen inward, each day anew. There are no formulas here, only refinement. As your frequency rises, your discernment sharpens. You become a vessel that only resonates with clarity.

And in that clarity, your relationship with meat—like everything else—becomes simple. There is no right or wrong. No good or bad. Mental judgment is not part of the decision. It's all energetic. It either aligns or it doesn't.

Prompts

1) When you eat meat, what sensations arise in your body before, during, and after?

2) Are your food choices based on tradition, convenience, emotion, or energy?

3) Can you recall a time when your body gave you a clear message about what to eat or avoid?

4) How has your relationship with food changed as your consciousness has evolved?

5) What beliefs do you carry about meat for strength, health, or identity?

6) Have you experienced a change in your social circle or lifestyle as your food choices shifted?

7) If meat no longer resonates for you, can you release it without resistance?

Chapter 78

Addiction

Young Soul

As a young soul, addiction doesn't look like a crisis at first. It looks like comfort. Like control. Like something small you turn to when life feels too much—or not enough. The substance, behavior, or distraction becomes a way to manage what you don't yet know how to feel. It helps you bypass your pain, your emptiness, your unmet needs. But the more you rely on it, the more disconnected you become.

At first, it's subtle. You don't call it addiction. You say you're just blowing off steam, just relaxing, just getting through the day. But underneath the ritual, a deep avoidance is brewing. You haven't yet learned how to sit with grief, how to be with longing, how to meet the unknown without reaching for something to tone down the edges. So you numb. You control. You escape.

And that escape becomes familiar. Predictable. Safer than the rawness of what you haven't processed. You build your days around it. You think about it when it's not there. You feel anxious without it. Slowly, it becomes less about the substance and more about the dependency—the way it helps you avoid feeling lost or unworthy or alone. You may still function outwardly, but inside, you've begun to split.

There comes a point when the cost of avoidance becomes too high. The craving that once promised relief now costs you your clarity, your confidence, your relationships, your vitality, your peace. You've broken promises, lost trust, betrayed your own body. Your creativity dulls, your energy fades, your future shrinks. You can't focus. You can't sleep. You feel disconnected from yourself, from others, from life. You've been living in survival mode, chasing highs while your soul withers in the background.

But in the middle of it all—one quiet, inconvenient truth begins to stir: *This isn't who I really am.* You start to see that the real addiction is not to the thing itself—but to the relief it gives you from facing your deeper pain. From feeling powerless. This becomes your turning point. The beginning of healing. Not by waging war on your addiction, but by no longer fighting with yourself. Not by numbing the pain, but by finally learning how to feel it—and survive it.

The real change begins when you stop defining yourself by the addiction. You stop making it your story. You begin rebuilding your life from presence, not avoidance. You choose self-respect over self-soothing. Clarity over craving. Not because someone told you to—but because you're ready to come home to yourself.

Old Soul

As an old soul, you understand that addiction is never about the surface behavior—it's about a wound that hasn't been witnessed, a need that hasn't been met, a truth that's been buried. And so you don't judge the addiction. You listen to it.

It's a familiar pattern—chasing pleasure, validation, control, even transcendence. You've experienced the highs and endured the crashes. You've seen what closes your heart and what opens it. Now, your discernment is refined.

Every addictive tendency is a frequency. And you've become sensitive to them. You feel how alcohol fogs your clarity. How certain habits fragment your energy. How even the subtlest distractions weaken your aura. And so, you make your life about purification. Not out of rigid dogma or to seek external validation—but out of sheer self-respect.

You've tasted what it means to live clean, free, and whole. You know the detox happens from the inside out—not just from substances, but from the self-neglect, shame, and thought loops that once made the addiction feel necessary. Now, you've reclaimed your nervous system by learning to sit in stillness again. You speak to your cravings with compassion: *What are you really trying to tell me?*

You hold space for others with that same kind of compassion—one that doesn't enable, but doesn't shame either. You've met your own shadows and came out on the other side. And that makes you trustworthy. That makes you genuine. You guide not by preaching, but by embodying. Not by teaching sobriety, but by transmitting the energetic clarity that comes from healthy detachment. That which you've overcome has become your superpower.

You no longer need altered states to feel something profound. You've become the open channel through which life moves—unfiltered, undistracted, undiluted. Now, the ordinary feels sacred. Silence has become symphonic. You've stopped reaching outward and started resting inward. And you've remembered what the substances made you forget: that your body is wise, your soul is whole, and presence is the most powerful place there is.

PROMPTS

1) What emotions or situations trigger your desire to reach for substances or distractions?

2) How have you historically dealt with pain, anxiety, or discomfort—by feeling it, or escaping it?

3) What story do you tell yourself about your use of alcohol, drugs, or other mind-altering agents?

4) What does your body feel like *before*, *during*, and *after* using a substance?

5) What would it mean to meet your cravings with compassion instead of shame?

6) Are there places in your life where you still rely on something external to manage your internal state?

7) What new practices—breathwork, stillness, movement, creativity—could help you feel regulated and alive?

8) What beliefs do you hold about sobriety? Are they rooted in judgment, fear, or curiosity?

9) What does your soul actually need in the moment you reach for escape?

10) If you no longer feared your feelings, how would your relationship with substances change?

CHAPTER 79

GENDER

YOUNG SOUL

As a young soul, your sense of self is deeply fused with the body. You take your form to be your identity. And when your internal experience doesn't match the outer presentation, you assume it's all a big mistake. A cruel cosmic error. This friction—between your perceived gender and your assigned one—feels unbearable. You believe it must be fixed at all costs. You look to the world for solutions: surgeries, hormones, new names, new labels. Seemingly anything to feel like you belong to yourself.

The deeper spiritual roots of this tension are not yet visible to you. You haven't yet been taught to view your life challenges as part of a soul contract. You don't yet realize that your gender identity is not a flaw—it's part of your curriculum. You've come into this life with a very specific initiation: to accept yourself, fully and without exception. That's not a punishment. It's an accelerated path. But as a young soul, you focus more on the outer form than the inner growth. You want relief. You want validation. You want the conflict to end—on your terms.

This isn't to say your feelings are invalid. They're not. Your distress is real. But the way you interpret that distress is still based on the assumption that the body is who you are. And so you fight it, edit it, sculpt it, or reject it entirely. You don't see that the very discomfort you're trying to erase is the portal to your transcendence of the physical. You haven't learned to be with your experience as it is—so you try to become something else.

When you're in the minority, it doesn't make it easier when you live in a world that doesn't know how to hold your complexity. You search for belonging, not knowing that the deepest belonging comes from within. As a young soul, you think the answer is to make the world see you. But the real liberation begins when you start seeing yourself—beyond the flesh, beyond the labels, beyond the need to explain.

There's a certain irony here: you fight to be normalized by society, unaware that normalization robs you of the very spiritual gift you opted in for. On the surface, no one *wants* a hard life—but from a soul perspective, challenge is grace. And challenges are inevitable. What you attempt to smooth over in one area will be reintroduced through other forms of suffering. You can't escape your growth. You can only choose whether suffering deepens you or distracts you.

Eventually, life forces a deeper inquiry. You realize the pain isn't just from your body or your identity—it's from being at war with yourself. And the only way to win is through acceptance. Not passive resignation, but spiritual surrender. That's the path of the old soul.

Old Soul

As an old soul, you no longer mistake your body for your identity. You see it as a vessel—temporary, purposeful, and sacred. You understand that any discomfort you feel around gender is not an error, not punishment, but a path to accelerated liberation. The friction you feel is not a curse. It's a blessing. A fast-track out of attachment to form.

You know that the world is obsessed with categories, binaries, and labels—but you no longer need them. You've made peace with the fluidity of your experience. Whether you identify with your assigned gender, feel in between, or beyond all categories, you don't use any of it to define your worth. You're not here to fit in. You're here to recognize your true essence, which is love. And few challenges force you to love yourself unconditionally faster than living in a world that doesn't know how.

So you walk your path with humility. You don't shame your past self for needing to alter, explore, or question. You bless those versions. Every stage of your journey has brought you closer to the truth: you are not your body. You are the awareness experiencing it.

Similarly, you hold space for others, regardless of where they are on the spectrum. You don't push your views. You emanate acceptance for whatever station someone is at in their journey. Your presence itself is liberating. You model a kind of peace that comes not from external conformity, but from internal clarity. You don't care who someone appears to be—you sense who they *are*.

At times, it's hard to watch young souls amplify problems that—energetically speaking—only exist because they keep naming, defending, and fighting them. You see how much suffering is generated by clinging to identity, by reinforcing separation through language. But instead of reacting, you remember that whatever you give your attention to, you strengthen. So you don't engage in argument or try to fix anybody's path. You stay rooted in the deeper truth that peace comes when the narrative quiets. When attention shifts from the label to the light beneath it. And sometimes, your greatest offering is your silence. Not because you don't care, but because you care enough not to feed what isn't real.

Ultimately, the variety of gender experiences is not a social confusion—it's part of the cosmic dance. The infinite expressing itself through infinite forms. The more you let go of rigid definitions, the more love takes center stage.

PROMPTS

1) In what ways have you tied your identity to your body or gender?

2) What discomforts or challenges have you faced around being seen for who you are?

3) How has your relationship with gender shaped your self-worth?

4) What parts of your gender experience feel most difficult to accept?

5) How do you respond to others who express gender differently than you do?

6) What would it feel like to be completely at peace with your gender expression—without needing validation?

7) Where might your attachment to form be limiting your spiritual growth?

8) What if this exact experience of gender was designed to accelerate your awakening?

Chapter 80

Body Alterations

Young Soul

As a young soul, you're still deeply identified with your body. You believe it represents who you are. So when your self-image feels incomplete, insecure, or undefined, you turn to body alterations as a way to fill that gap. Tattoos, piercings, injections, implants—these become physical expressions of internal stories you haven't yet healed or seen clearly. Whether the alterations are decorative, rebellious, commemorative, or "just aesthetic," the underlying driver is either a longing to be seen, to control how others see you, or to fix something you don't know how to love.

You might say you're doing it for yourself—and in a way, you are. But which self? The one that feels unworthy without enhancement? The one still aching to be special, beautiful, tough, or understood? Even if no one else sees the change, your altered body becomes a mirror for an identity you're trying to construct. You're trying to anchor yourself in something fixed. But ironically, you've chosen the body—a constantly changing, impermanent form—to do it. This sets the stage for a lifelong uphill struggle that you cannot win.

You're so accustomed to chasing meaning outside of yourself that even emotional healing gets externalized. You ink your grief onto your skin, hoping to carry it more beautifully. You pierce your pain through your nose or belly button, hoping to reclaim your body. You sculpt and inject and color and carve, trying to match a version of yourself that feels more complete. But the real you isn't broken. It's just buried under layers of conditioning and unresolved emotion.

At this stage, permanence feels powerful. A tattoo says, "This matters. This is me." But permanence is an illusion. You don't need to have lived very long to recognize that your moods shift. Your tastes change. Your beliefs evolve. For some, faster. Others, more slowly. But change is inevitable. Yet you're banking on your current self to speak for your future self—without realizing that your future self may want nothing to do with this phase. It's not wrong to mark your body—but it's rarely as conscious as you believe.

You might say you like the aesthetic. But liking something is not the same as being free from it. That "liking" comes from a conditioned version of you—an image, a snapshot, a temporary resonance. You think being present means indulging that impulse. But true presence includes awareness of change. You may not see it now, but much of your aesthetic preference is just attachment dressed up as taste.

Some of your choices are spontaneous—done under the influence, or in emotional states you never paused to question. Others are deeply emotional, like commemorating loss or reclaiming power. But even these are rooted in the need to hold on to something. A loved one. A feeling. A story. The irony is, if you were fully present, you wouldn't need the permanent mark. You would carry their essence in your energy field, not your skin.

Culture validates your choices. Everyone's doing it, so you feel justified. It's even considered art. But art is fleeting, while living art breathes. When it becomes fixed, something in you starts to decay. The tattoo ink that embeds into your lymph nodes, the metals that burden your bloodstream, the surgical risks you normalize—none of this gets factored in when you're chasing identity. You don't yet see how it can drain your life force in the process.

Ultimately, what you're really trying to do is solve an inner dissonance through external means. You don't feel enough, or seen, or expressive—so you alter your container. But this tells your nervous system: "I'm not safe unless I look a certain way." Over time, this unconscious messaging builds shame, not self-worth. And the more changes you make, the more you crave others' reactions to reinforce your self-image. Your self-concept becomes outsourced.

If you look more closely, you can tell: you crave uniqueness, but you're following trends. You crave meaning, but you're clinging to symbols. You desire freedom, but you're binding yourself to the body. Every mark, every modification, is a tether. You're fighting the real reason you came here for: to evolve beyond the flesh. Not to punish it—but to no longer mistake it for who you are.

One way or another, life makes you realize that no matter how much you change your appearance, the dissatisfaction returns. The novelty wears off, the mark fades into normalcy, and the same old emptiness resurfaces. You tell yourself you just need another piercing, another tattoo, another tweak—but each addition only deepens the dependence. The body becomes a project that never ends, a canvas of unresolved longing, where every new alteration silently declares: *I am still not enough.*

And still, none of this makes you wrong. This is your lesson. This is your mirror. You have to go through it to outgrow it. There is nothing ever wrong with you.

You just are who you are at various stations of life. You make your marks now, not realizing they're a timestamp of your soul's current stage. And one day, you'll look back and smile—not in shame, but with gentle compassion. Because you'll have learned: your wholeness never needed to be etched in ink. It was always here, waiting for you to remember. And with that, you embark on old soul terrain.

OLD SOUL

You no longer mistake your body for your identity. You see it as a sacred vessel—temporary, purposeful, intelligent. You've realized that every time you alter your form, you're reinforcing the illusion that something is missing. And you know now: nothing is missing. Not from your skin. Not from your essence. You've begun to live from the inside out.

When you feel the urge to alter your body, you pause. Not because you're repressed or rigid, but because you understand energy. You've learned to question your impulses. *Is this coming from truth—or from pain? Is this a desire for freedom—or pointing to something in me I haven't forgiven?* You don't suppress your desires, but you investigate them. Most pass right through you when you give them space.

It's clear to you that body modifications stem from unresolved emotion—grief, shame, rage, yearning—and from a bigger disconnect to the impermanence of life and your own evolving nature. And rather than needing a permanent reminder, you've learned to alchemize those feelings through presence. You observe them, feel them fully, and then you release them. You don't turn your skin into a diary of your wounds. You let your being radiate the healing instead.

Even your aesthetic preferences have softened. You can enjoy beauty, but without the urge to own it. You've become less interested in curating an image, and more interested in emanating a frequency. You trust that if your energy is clean, people will feel it. You don't need tattoos to say what your presence already states loud and clear: *I am enough.*

You understand that every modification carries energetic consequences. Every puncture, injection, or implant interacts with your nervous system, your meridians, your immune response. You're more sensitive now—not fragile, but attuned. You feel when something lowers your vibration. And the idea of injecting ink or plastics into your body feels discordant. It's not about rules. It's about resonance.

You don't shame others for where they are. You've been there too. You remember what it was like to chase identity, to grip symbols, to mark milestones on your body because you hadn't yet found stillness in your soul. You see the innocence in it—but also the confusion. When you're free inside, there's nothing left to prove.

Old souls treat the body with reverence. Not as an object of vanity, but as a temple of awareness. You don't embellish it—you honor it. You let it speak without needing to decorate or distort it. You nourish it, rest it, listen to it. You understand it's on loan from nature, and you intend to give it back with gratitude—not graffiti.

You've come to see that everything is impermanent—your moods, your beliefs, your relationships, your body. And because of that, you don't stamp your pain. You don't etch your preferences. You trust that who you are today is not who you'll be tomorrow. You let the present self live lightly on your skin.

And then you notice something beautiful: the less attached you are to your image, the more radiant you become. You glow not because of what you wear or how you decorate yourself—but because of your full acceptance of who you are, as you are. Your authenticity becomes your magnetism. And it cannot be fabricated.

Over time, you realize that true freedom is not in altering your form, but in dissolving your identification with it altogether. The body is not your identity but your ally, a companion for your soul's journey. Instead of modifying it to match fleeting self-images, you cultivate presence so deeply that the urge to alter dissolves. What remains is simplicity, ease, and reverence—for the unmarked, unadorned vessel that already carries the imprint of the divine.

BODY ALTERATIONS CHART

It's important to remember that there is no right or wrong outside of yourself. There are no external voices that have the authority to tell you how to live your life, and believing that there are is one of the fundamental lessons of detachment on your journey of self-realization. There is only your inner voice, and that's all the guidance you need.

To what degree you're able to hear it and follow it, can vary greatly from person to person. And while a person might exhibit great awareness in one area of life, they might have pronounced blind spots in other areas. The following chart illustrates the difference between how young souls and old souls approach the topic of body alterations.

Young Soul (Identity Projection)	**Old Soul** (Divine Acceptance)
Alters body to gain approval, control, or status	Honors body as it is, without needing to change it
Driven by insecurity, rebellion, or unresolved trauma	Grounded in self-respect, presence, and wholeness
Uses external change to soothe internal discomfort	Seeks internal healing to transform outer perception
Seeks uniqueness through appearance	Expresses uniqueness through energy and presence
Body becomes a canvas for unresolved identity	Body becomes a vessel for soul embodiment and co-creation
Feels pressure to conform to trends or ideals	Feels no urgency to alter what is naturally sacred
Relies on modification to feel powerful or attractive	Finds power and beauty in authenticity
Interventions often create new dissatisfaction	Acceptance fosters lasting inner peace
Believes changing the body will change self-worth	Knows self-worth is independent of external appearance
Treats form as a problem to fix	Treats form as a miracle to honor

© 2025 Cirak

Prompts

1) What past emotional states have influenced your desire to alter your appearance?

2) Do you believe your body needs to change in order for you to feel lovable or confident? Why?

3) What is your relationship to your physical body: gratitude, frustration, pride, shame, neutrality?

4) What part of you do you think a tattoo, piercing, or surgery would express or fix?

5) Have your aesthetic tastes or preferences changed over time? How does that affect your view of permanence?

6) If you didn't care what anyone thought of your appearance, what would change?

7) What are other, non-physical ways you can express or process your emotions?

8) How would it feel to fully accept your body as it is—not forever, but just for today?

Chapter 81

Aging

Young Soul

As a young soul, aging feels like an inconvenience, a defect, a tragedy to be delayed for as long as possible. You don't talk about it. You don't think about it. And when it shows up on your skin, in your joints, or in the mirror, you do everything in your power to cover it up. To you, aging is a failure of control, an insult to your identity, your beauty, your plans.

In fact, you live as if you'll live forever. You accumulate like there's no tomorrow. You plan your life as though time is unlimited. But you also procrastinate, postpone, and defer the things that matter. You act both as though you'll never die and as though you'll never really live. You cling to youthful appearances while mentally fast-forwarding through decades. One part of you is rooted in the future, building a fantasy of immortality. Another part is stuck in the past, mourning every wrinkle as a loss. What's completely missing is the now.

You fall for the promise of eternal youth—serums, surgeries, fillers, lasers—anything to erase the evidence that you are changing. But the more you resist change, the faster it comes. Your fixation on "not aging" becomes its own energetic weight. The stress, the comparisons, the quiet belief that you're not good enough as you are—all of it compounds and exhausts your system. Ironically, it's the obsession with staying young that accelerates your aging the most.

You look at the elderly and feel disconnected. You may pity them, ignore them, or avoid them altogether. They remind you of what you're not ready to face. You see them as less useful, as burdens. Society reflects this: you tuck your elders away in homes, avoid difficult conversations, speak of death in euphemisms. You've inherited a view of aging that sees it as decline, not deepening.

In a society that sidelines the elderly, you unconsciously absorb the message that aging means becoming irrelevant and invisible. You become driven to prove your vitality—working harder, looking sharper, staying active for appearances' sake. It's not wrong to care for your health. But your motivation isn't peace—it's denial.

Of course, you can't be in denial forever. Your energy wanes. Your roles shift. Your reflection becomes harder to recognize. And that's when the deeper work begins—if you let it. The pain of aging becomes your invitation—not to fight harder, but to surrender more fully. To stop running from the inevitable and start listening to what this passage is trying to teach you: Slow down. Let go. Be here.

Old Soul

As an old soul, you don't give your attention to aging. You welcome your body and its faculties every day, as they are. You're here to experience, not to preserve. You rarely catch yourself aging, because you're always in the now. And when you see some signs, they simply mark the shifting seasons of your soul's journey. Like autumn leaves, you've learned to find beauty in the falling away.

You don't resist the mirror or the milestones. In fact, you've stopped counting. You no longer track birthdays, anniversaries, or the progress of any timelines. You don't think about how long you may have left—it's always about how present you are right now. This detachment from linear time grants you an ageless energy. You feel clearer, calmer, more radiant—not because you've done anything to your face, but because you've released the mental stress of needing to control it.

You're not fooled by a culture obsessed with youth. You know that peace makes people glow far more than Botox. You don't need to chase youth because you emanate vitality naturally when your system is not at war with itself. You live simply. Eat well. Rest deeply. Move gently. Laugh often. And most importantly, you don't attach to outcomes. That's what keeps you young. It's that simple.

You honor your body, but you don't worship it. You treat it with reverence, not neurosis. And when it begins to decline, you don't panic—you listen and give it what it needs. You've learned how to support your body by favoring natural rhythms over rigid regimens. You spend time outdoors, you fast when you need to, you stretch, hydrate, nourish, and ground yourself. Not to stay young, but to stay aligned. Your lifestyle is a quiet devotion, not a desperate intervention.

You don't see elders as irrelevant—you see them as living examples of the soul's journey. You recognize the sacredness in worn hands, the wisdom in slow speech. You sit with dying people without flinching. You've made peace with the inevitable. In fact, the truly old soul isn't afraid of death—they're ready for it. Their challenge isn't resisting age—it's staying fully present until their time is up.

You no longer treat age as a countdown, but as an expansion. Every wrinkle feels earned. Every slowdown is an invitation. You create beauty not with cosmetics, but with your energy. Your frequency shapes your face. And the older you get, the more your soul shines through.

Aging Chart

There is no peace to be found when your sense of self depends on constant comparison to others, or to the stories in your head. Nothing surfaces this more than birthdays and other milestones. The following chart highlights the differences in how young vs old souls experience aging.

Young Soul	Old Soul
Sees aging as faulty, decline, tragedy	Sees aging as natural, divine, beautiful
Clings to youth through products, surgery, and denial	Welcomes change like shifting seasons, with grace
Lives in past regrets and future fears	Moves lightly in the present, detached from linear time
Measures worth by vitality, productivity, or appearances	Measures worth by presence, authenticity, and resonance
Pities or avoids the elderly, seeing them as irrelevant	Honors elders as carriers of wisdom and soul depth
Motivated by denial—fighting against decline	Motivated by devotion—caring for body with reverence
Fixates on milestones, birthdays, timelines	Stops tracking time, lives with timeless energy
Feels irrelevant or invisible when youth fades	Feels radiant from within, energy shines regardless of age
Seeks control over the body, fears its decline	Listens to the body, supports it with natural rhythms
Sees time as an enemy to fight	Sees time as a companion, presence as true eternal youth

© 2025 Cirak

PROMPTS

1) What are your earliest memories of how aging or older people were perceived?

2) How do you feel about your current age, and what judgments have you absorbed about it?

3) In what ways do you resist the passage of time, physically, mentally, or emotionally?

4) What have you been putting off, as if you have endless time?

5) What fears arise when you contemplate aging or death?

6) Have you known someone who aged gracefully? What was their secret?

7) What would it mean to live in deeper alignment with the present moment?

8) If you released your fear of aging, what might become possible for you?

9) What wisdom has only come to you with age, and how can you honor it?

Chapter 82

Death

Young Soul

As a young soul, you don't think much about death—at least, not directly. You keep it in the background, shrouded in avoidance. It's something that happens to other people, far away, in some distant future you never plan for. Your days are spent accumulating—money, experiences, possessions—as if you're going to take it all with you. You plan your life like you'll live forever, but deep down, there's a fear you can't name. You dread the end, so you distract yourself with beginnings.

The irony is that your fear of death seeps into everything you do during life. You over-plan, over-buy, and overthink—driven by the unconscious terror of your own impermanence. You associate death with failure, loss, and—most of all—the unknown.

When someone you love dies, you're shattered. Not just from grief, but from confusion. You've spent your life avoiding death—so when it comes close, you have no framework to hold it. You feel like life has malfunctioned. There's no room for reverence, only resistance. Funerals are awkward, sanitized, rushed. You're taught to move on, to cheer up, to go back to work. Society has no language for real endings—because it's terrified of them.

This fear also fuels your spiritual bypassing. You might adopt beliefs about souls and afterlives, but not in a way that frees you. Instead, you cling to them as escape hatches. You don't want to feel the pain of mortality, so you smother it in stories. But they're hollow, unless you do the inner work and face the truth: you will die. Everyone you love will die. And it is not a mistake. It is part of the design.

What you don't yet see is that fearing death keeps you from living fully. When you resist endings, you dull your beginnings and contort the journey. When you cling to the physical body, you forget the soul. Death isn't here to torment you—it's here to remind you to wake you. But you have to stop running. Until then, you will live a half-life, chasing permanence in a world that offers none.

Old Soul

As an old soul, you've stopped avoiding death. You don't glamorize it, but you don't shrink from it either. You've sat with it. Looked it in the eyes. You've grieved losses and maybe even faced your own impermanence. And in that confrontation, you found acceptance and peace. Death is no longer your enemy. It's not even a disruption. It's returning to a place you never left.

You inhabit your form gently, knowing it's temporary. When it starts to fade, you listen. You give it what it needs. And when the time comes, you release it like a leaf letting go of the branch. You're not eager to leave, but you've learned how to let go and trust that you'll land where you're supposed to.

Ultimately, you know you cannot die. The body may fall away, the mind may dissolve, but the witnessing presence remains untouched. You've experienced glimpses of this stillness—in meditation, in grief, in awe. You've sat with the sensations that arise when contemplating your exit, and you've released the blockages that once kept you from meeting it fully. You no longer fear your expiration date. You walk with time. And this surrender gives your presence a timeless glow.

When someone dies, you mourn with reverence, but without resistance. You sense and celebrate their transition. You know they've returned to Source, the place beyond all suffering. Because you no longer cling to form, you can feel their essence everywhere. Death does not separate—it only shifts the nature of the relationship.

Because you've made peace with death, you live more fully. You waste less time. You speak more truth. You don't wait to be ready—you understand how precious your time in form really is. Each day is a miracle. Each goodbye could be the last. But this doesn't make you anxious—it makes you more present.

You're not afraid of the end. Your only prayer is that you remain awake all the way through. And you've learned something most cannot see until the very end: that dying is not the opposite of living. It is the completion of it.

And in that final breath, what matters most is not how long you lived—but how fully you loved, how gently you let go, and how clearly you remembered who you truly are.

DEATH CHART

Death is one of the great taboos. There are significant differences in how people and cultures process one of its members leaving their body. Some allow for more emotional processing, others less. Either way, establishing a healthy relationship towards death lies with the individual. Nothing brings out your connection, or lack thereof, with Source energy more than death.

Young Soul (Fear of Death)	Old Soul (Return to Source)
Sees death as the end or a failure	Sees death as a return to wholeness
Avoids thinking about mortality	Embraces mortality as part of the soul's design
Clings to youth, health, and legacy	Releases attachment to form and permanence
Experiences death as tragedy	Experiences death as transition
Fears the unknown, loss of control	Welcomes the mystery with reverence
Measures life by achievements, time	Measures life by presence and growth
Feels betrayed by illness or aging	Sees illness and aging as initiations
Holds onto people and stories tightly	Releases with love, trusts the soul path
Views death as separation	Knows death as reunion with Source
Fights death to feel in control	Surrenders to death in peace and trust

© 2025 Cirak

Prompts

1) What fears do you hold about death that you avoid?

2) How does your fear of dying shape the way you live?

3) What might shift in your life if you fully accepted that everything ends?

4) Who or what have you not yet grieved—and can you take the time now?

5) What would it feel like to welcome death as a peaceful transition rather than a loss?

6) What belief, identity, or attachment is ready to die now, so that you can live more fully?

7) What experiences have brought you closer to accepting mortality?

8) How might your relationships change if you treated each goodbye as sacred?

9) What qualities would you want to embody in your final years?

SPIRITUAL

Chapter 83

Awareness

YOUNG SOUL

You often treat awareness as something to *do* rather than something to *be*. You scan your mind and body, trying to track every thought and sensation as if vigilance were the same thing as consciousness. You make checklists in your head: *Am I being mindful? Am I staying present? Am I catching myself enough?* This feels like growth, but in truth, it's exhausting—because the one "checking" is just another layer of mind.

When you analyze your interactions, replay conversations, or obsess about how to do better next time, you call it awareness. But it's really overthinking in disguise—an attempt to manage life rather than meet it. You confuse analyzing yourself with knowing yourself. Instead of resting in presence, you loop endlessly through the mental theater of judgment, trying to perfect your performance.

There's often an image you want to uphold. You want to be seen as self-aware, emotionally intelligent, conscious.

You talk about your triggers, your shadow, your inner work. But beneath it lies the pressure to match some ideal of calmness or wisdom. Again, you're not being true to you.

You're also likely to use awareness as a reason to criticize. You notice other people's unconsciousness and ridicule it to feel superior. But the instant awareness becomes comparison, it is no longer awareness—it's simply more judgment.

Because you still identify with your thoughts, you assume awareness must *come from* the mind. You recite affirmations, cling to teachings, or push yourself harder in meditation. But awareness slips through your fingers precisely because you keep *trying* to find it. Like trying to fall asleep by effort, it doesn't work this way.

Even your healing is busy. You journal, breathe, chant, track, visualize—layer upon layer of doing, hoping stillness lies on the other side. But presence is never earned—it appears in the absence of striving. Yet this is the one thing you cannot trust—that you already are what you are chasing.

Often, you confuse awareness with vigilance. You scan for flaws, symptoms, problems to fix. You call it being conscious, but it's actually anxiety disguised as spirituality.

You don't yet believe life could unfold in your favor without your constant interference.

Even when you hear "be here now," you distort it into another commandment. You suppress thoughts of past and future, not realizing that those thoughts still appear only in the present. By rejecting them, you reject reality as its happening.

Nothing is more detrimental to your mental, emotional, physical, and spiritual wellbeing than saying no to right now. Deeper awareness stays elusive when you're in constant resistance, absorbed by the noise in your head, giving your attention to all the things that keep you attached to the surface.

Ironically, glimpses of true awareness do find you—in silence, in nature, in stillness. But instead of letting them dissolve you, your mind rushes to replicate, label, or even monetize the experience. You lose the silence because you keep wanting to understand it.

The friction from keeping yourself separate form life eventually grows unbearable. The constant pursuit in your head and wears you down. Only then does a more subtle truth dawn: awareness is not another thing to do. It's what remains when you stop trying.

Old Soul

As an old soul, you know awareness is not achieved through effort. Rather, it arises naturally when striving falls away. As such, you've stopped seeking awareness as a goal and begun resting in it as your natural state.

You feel awareness as space. Not mental sharpness or emotional intelligence, but the container through which life flows. Thoughts pass, sensations shift, identities dissolve, yet something remains—silent, stable, untouched. That presence is who you are.

Becoming more aware of yourself means dissolving the layers of conditioning that block you from looking deeper within and recognizing that there is no "you"—there is only your growing awareness of your body, mind, the masks you wore, the cultural scripts you absorbed, the trauma you resisted. All of it softens in the light of non-judging presence. Awareness itself is not a healing force; it makes space for it. All your cells light up when not depressed by your personal narrative. Your natural state is to be healthy and happy.

That said, at first, greater awareness can feel heavy. You see the grief, the anger, the illusions you avoided. You understand why people cling to ignorance. But as you surrender to the discomfort, what felt like a curse becomes liberation. Weight lifts. Aliveness surges. Awareness burns through illusions by simple exposure.

Humility follows. With nothing left to defend, you stop justifying yourself. You stop labeling life as good or bad, healed or unhealed. Awareness is the bridge where judgment used to divide. You no longer feel like you have to fix others; you can simply let them be. This shift from manipulation to allowing is at the very heart of being a witnessing presence.

Your being grows still, and from this stillness, a vast intelligence flows. You hear not only words but the silence behind them. You sense energies before they're spoken. You trust your body's quiet knowing before the mind explains. You act from alignment, not control. Awareness makes room for your conscience.

There are countless other benefits. In pure awareness, time dissolves. Past and future used to dominate your life experience, with yesterday's traumas and fear of tomorrow's unknowns driving your decisions and goal setting. Even a simple birthday party would put you in a state of comparison with others, where they're at, where you should be by now. Life was a pressure-filled time bomb, quite literally.

Now, you recognize past and future as thought-forms, appearing only now. Almost your entire personal narrative about who you were, where you came from, and where you're going has fallen away. You live not in the chronology of your mental plans but in the nowness of each new moment. Here, the subtle sensations of your body become even clearer. But whether awareness contracts in fear or expands in love, you no longer judge—you simply notice. Both become equal teachers.

That's why, even in chaos, you remain rooted. Pain can move through you, but it does not define you. Thoughts may arrive, but you no longer believe them. Action arises—not from compulsion but from clarity. What others may call "superhuman" is simply the absence of pretense. It is reality lived raw.

Full awareness lives beyond language. There's no need to talk about it, because your presence carries it more powerfully than words. You transmit it through silence, through gaze, through the energy you embody. Awareness is no longer what you practice. It's a constant state.

And so the paradox completes: what you once sought as the pinnacle of spiritual achievement turns out to be the most ordinary thing of all. Awareness was never absent—it was only obscured. Now you live by it. Now you are it.

Chart

With greater awareness, you no longer act out blind patterns and instead make yourself available to co-creation with life. The following chart shows how young vs old souls understand and develop their awareness.

Aspect	Young Soul Awareness	Old Soul Awareness
Definition of Awareness	Constant mental monitoring to stay in control	Natural presence beyond thought; effortless noticing
Source of Awareness	Mind-based vigilance	Spacious, non-reactive consciousness
Primary Goal	To improve, fix, or prevent suffering	To witness what is, without resistance or agenda
Relationship to Thoughts	Believes thoughts are truth and must be managed	Witness thoughts as passing clouds, not personal
Reaction to Feelings	Tends to analyze, criticize, resist, or suppress	Allows sensations to arise, be felt fully, and dissolve
Control Pattern	Use awareness to become better, more spiritual	Releases control and lets awareness guide
Common Trap	Spiritual hypervigilance and inflation of self	Over-identifying with emptiness or premature detaching
Energy Signature	Tense, forceful, seeking safety through knowledge	Calm, relaxed, expansive, grounded in presence
Practice Orientation	Applies tools & techniques to "achieve awareness"	Lives from awareness as a baseline state of being
Integration Threshold	May notice inner patterns but still resists discomfort	Welcomes all experiences as expression of consciousness

© 2025 Cirak

PROMPTS

1) When you say "I want to be more aware," what exactly do you mean?

2) How do you confuse awareness with vigilance, control, or self-monitoring?

3) In what situations do you "perform" consciousness rather than rest in it?

4) How do you use awareness as a way to judge others or yourself?

5) What practices help you fuel *being* rather than *doing*?

6) Can you describe a moment where you felt awareness without effort?

7) What shifts when you stop trying to become more aware, and simply notice what's already here?

Chapter 84

Thoughts

Young Soul

You live almost entirely in your head. The stream of thoughts running through your mind feels like *you*. You rarely pause to ask where these thoughts come from or whether they're true. If a thought appears, you give it authority. You make it important. You make it real. If it's loud, it must be urgent. If it's fearful, danger must be near. You obey each one like a command. And so, your mind doesn't just run your life—it drains the vitality out of it.

When you identify with thought, everything becomes personal. Any feeling that stirs in you seems like proof that life is happening *to* you. You live in constant victimhood, convinced the world is conspiring against you. You don't yet see that most thoughts are just artifacts of memory, mood, unprocessed emotion, and cultural programming—none of which are you. Still, you believe them as though they were wisdom.

You assume problems are solved by more thinking. So when confusion, anxiety, or overwhelm arises, you analyze harder, searching for answers in the very place that created the noise in the first place. But the more you think, the more stuck you feel, the more disconnected you become from yourself.

Perhaps you've tried meditation—but only to make thoughts stop. Stillness becomes another outcome to achieve, another form of control. When the mind doesn't quiet, you conclude you're failing. But that's missing the point: freedom isn't the absence of thought. It's the absence of identification with thought.

Perhaps you've experimented with "positive thinking," trying to replace negative loops with uplifting affirmations. Yet, once again, all you're doing is forcing optimism over unresolved pain, displacing stress with fancy mantras. Underneath it all, you remain in resistance, using new thoughts to escape old ones. Even your spirituality can become another mental game, entangled with words and concepts.

This addiction to thinking breeds a fear of silence. You get so used to noise that you feel naked, unsafe, and empty without it. You associate stillness with passivity or nothingness, so it's better to cling to knowing—even when knowing hurts. You don't notice that nearly all your thoughts are recycled. They revolve around other people's opinions, past regrets, imagined futures. You chase peace through the very mechanism that robs you of it.

This craving to think also feeds a false sense of control. You consume knowledge, analyze endlessly, anticipate every possibility. But the more you try to prepare for life, the more life shows you its unpredictability. The universe reflects your attachment to certainty by flooding you with uncertainty. It's a maddening loop. Again you try to outthink it, not realizing thinking is the very trap.

At the core of all this lies the grandest thought of all: your personal story. Who you are, what went wrong, what you must become. It is woven of lack, fear, and control. Your suffering is rarely from life itself—it's from your beliefs about it. Even healing becomes a mental project. You study, reflect, and reframe, but always from the head. Thinking trumps embodying, surrendering, allowing. Even your longing for peace becomes another thought. But peace does not live in the mind. It comes from the *absence* of mind.

OLD SOUL

You no longer believe everything you think. You see how thoughts arise from biological, psychological, emotional layers—and even from pure consciousness itself. But you no longer mistake those thoughts for yourself. They are simply patterns of energy passing through. Some are useful. Most are noise. Your well-being no longer depends on their content, but on your relationship to them.

You've recognized that if you can notice a thought, you cannot *be* the thought. If you can notice your feelings, you are not your feelings. You're the awareness of them. So, when fear arises, you don't react and resist. You locate and observe the associated sensations. And in that direct contact, the charge loses its power and the energy leaves you. All thoughts and feelings dissolve. Your body experiences the power of presence in a tangible, felt way the mind never can.

Consequently, you no longer lean on thinking as your main tool. Instead, you trust clarity to arise in the stillness behind the thoughts, not from stacking more ideas on top. You don't need to figure everything out to feel safe. That was the old illusion. Now, guidance emerges intuitively, through presence and connection to Source.

Silence has become your refuge. What once terrified you is now home to your peace and freedom. In stillness, you touch a knowing beyond intellect that appears when you stop pushing. You no longer seek to silence the mind. It quiets automatically when you let it be. When you hold compassion for it. When you see how it tries to protect and predict. You thank it for its service, but you don't hand it the keys. You've grown comfortable with mystery. And paradoxically, the more at ease you are with not-knowing, the more life reveals its simple truth.

As your awareness grows, thoughts grow clearer, sharper, more creative—an instrument of expression of the formless taking shape. Even when trivial or anxious thoughts arise, they no longer attach to you. Even when mental noise returns, you simply pause, return to the body, observe sensations, and re-center. Thoughts may continue, but they're tiny and insignificant on the vast backdrop of presence. Your stability no longer depends on the "right circumstances," but on the timeless awareness that sees through them.

That does not mean you should diminish or degrade your mind. You honor its gifts—its ability to recall, calculate, articulate, organize. But you no longer ask it to reveal the ultimate mystery of who you are. That belongs to awareness itself.

Ultimately, awareness is not something to be measured by how little you think, but by how gently you return, again and again, to the touch of your breath, to the ground beneath your feet, to the green of the trees, to the aroma of your morning coffee. Each return builds presence. Each surrender deepens freedom. In this way, life flows through you, not as a collection of ideas, but as universal truth.

THOUGHTS CHART

Your relationship with your thoughts dictates how you engage—or not engage—with each and every situation. The following chart contrasts how young souls vs old souls make use of thoughts and how that influences they're view of the world.

Young Soul	**Old Soul**
Identifies with every thought	Observes thoughts as passing clouds
Believes thoughts are facts	Sees thoughts as mental noise, not truth
Tries to control or suppress thinking	Allows thoughts to rise and fall without interference
Uses thought to escape feelings	Uses presence to feel what's beneath the thought
Thinks more = understands more	Knows clarity arises from stillness, not analysis
Analyzes problems endlessly	Listens for inner guidance instead
Ruminates on the past or worries about the future	Returns gently to the present moment
Seeks mental solutions to emotional pain	Recognizes thinking can't resolve what presence can heal
Attaches to the story in the mind	Detaches from stories and returns to awareness
Chained by thought loops	Freed by non-identification

© 2025 Cirak

Prompts

1) Which thoughts do you believe without question?

2) How do your thoughts try to keep you safe or in control?

3) What thoughts make you feel small or limited?

4) What's your relationship to silence?

5) How often do you confuse thinking with "doing something productive"?

6) What would happen if you stopped believing every thought? Have you tried?

7) When have you had a moment of clarity that came *without* thinking?

8) How does your body respond when you're caught in looping thoughts?

9) What does it mean to observe your thoughts rather than identify with them?

10) What new relationship would you like to have with your mind?

11) What current or new practices can you strengthen to take power back from your mind?

Chapter 85

Attachment

Young Soul

You cling to what makes you feel secure—people, possessions, goals, identities. You don't even see it as attachment. You call it loyalty, ambition, or passion. You think emotional intensity means love, and that controlling shows you care. When things are taken away, you panic. When relationships shift, you feel betrayed. Your sense of self is built on what you own and how the world reflects you back.

You chase outcomes, believing that finally getting what you want will bring peace. But it never does. Even when you succeed, you live in fear of losing it. You attach to praise, to success, to the approval of others. You cling to your story, your pain, your labels, your wounds. And when life doesn't go your way, you interpret it as personal failure—or proof that life is unfair.

You form identities out of your job, your relationships, your past. You say *my* job, *my* partner, *my* failure, *my* success, as though you are all those things. But all your "stuff" just weighs you down. It begins to own you. You attach to things to avoid suffering, not realizing that clinging is what creates your suffering. Your entire world is truly a reality of your own making.

Instead of pausing to ask why everything feels so hard—and if your lens on life has anything to do with it—you grip tighter, trying to manage the chaos, to stay in control. You continue seeking stability and fulfillment in the external world, even as it continually changes. And so you end up in constant battle with the very reality you've created.

At this stage, you believe detachment is cold. Letting go feels like weakness or abandonment. The idea of surrender terrifies you—like disappearing, or becoming invisible to the world. Yet it is your attachment that keeps you small, reactive, and trapped.

Only when something breaks—your heart, your health, your plans—do you pause and glimpse a stillness beyond the struggle. The glimpse doesn't last long—you quickly call the noise back. But it marks the beginning of old soul intuition: that maybe peace doesn't come from holding on, but from letting go.

OLD SOUL

You've learned that attachment is the energetic root of suffering. It binds you to the past, hijacks the present, and distorts the future. Even spiritual goals—awakening, healing, manifestation—can become attachments. So you notice what you cling to, not to judge yourself, but to loosen your grip. Detachment—done lovingly and with full presence—has become central to your path. Because you've realized: nothing outside of you is truly yours, and nothing can complete you because you're already complete.

Detachment doesn't mean withdrawal. It doesn't mean distancing yourself. It means intimacy without possession. You can love fully without clinging. You can care deeply without controlling. You can create, dream, connect—and still remain free. You allow things to pass through your life without becoming your life. There are no outcomes. There is only continuous co-creation.

You notice when identity tries to rebuild itself through attachment. But you're quick to release identification because you know firmly what it feels like to be at peace. In fact, you can move with and through change exactly because you let yourself feel fully. What used to be feel unbearable dissolves the moment you stop clinging to it, leaving behind a resonance that guides you forward.

This is how the universe works: The tighter you grip, the more life resists. The more you let go, the more synchronicity flows. Letting go doesn't mean giving up—it's participation at the deepest level. Far from making you less human, detachment makes you more open, more intimate, more alive. You love without trying to keep. You serve without trying to prove. You show up without needing to control. What remains is presence—spacious, free, and unstoppable.

Prompts

1) What in your life are you afraid to lose? What emotions arise when someone or something important drifts away?

2) How do you define yourself through what you have or who you're with?

3) What story do you tell yourself to justify holding on? Do you ever confuse detachment with indifference?

4) How would it feel to fully love something or someone without needing to keep it?

5) Where are you being invited to surrender, but still resisting?

Chapter 86

Identity

Young Soul

As a young soul, you believe you are your body, your personality, your accomplishments. Your sense of self is constructed entirely from the outside in. You define yourself by your appearance, your profession, your relationships, and the roles you play in society. What others think of you feels like truth. Their praise becomes your oxygen; their rejection becomes your downfall. You live with a constant need to prove that you matter—because somewhere, deep down, you're not sure that you do.

It's not your fault. From the moment you're born, you're taught to identify with your name, your gender, your background, your strengths, and your flaws. Nobody tells you that these are just costumes for the soul. So you believe the story. You cling to it. You defend it with your life.

You also become enamored by the external physical plane. And why wouldn't you? Earth is a dazzling place.

The senses are intoxicating. There's color, music, flavor, emotion, beauty. The body itself is a marvel—sensitive, sensual, responsive. Who wouldn't be seduced by such a playground?

But something always feels fragile. Everything you identify with eventually changes. Your body ages. Your relationships evolve. Your personality reshapes. When something ends—a job, a relationship, a phase—you see it as a crisis of identity. *Who am I now?* It shakes your sense of self. You feel lost, unsure, or threatened—not realizing it's the attachment to a false self that's suffering, not you. But you haven't yet discovered the deeper *you*. So you keep rearranging the pieces of your life, hoping the new configuration will finally be solid.

Yet, it never is. Life keeps pointing you to a deeper place, a deeper truth, but you're not ready to listen. It's much more compelling to uphold everything you think you have and are, than to let go of this supposed "false" self. How can letting go of yourself lead to finding yourself? It doesn't make sense. And as long as you're in your head about it, it won't. You only pay attention when you burnout and break down from trying at add to yourself. That's when your lens on life starts to shift.

But even when you begin to awaken, there's a new trap waiting: the spiritual persona. You swap worldly identities for sacred ones—the empath, the intuitive, the enlightened one—even the old soul. You want to be seen as evolved, unshakeable, above the drama. But if you look closely, it's the same need for identity wearing a new robe. You're still trying to be someone instead of letting yourself be who you are beyond the labels.

Until you break that illusion, you're not truly free. Only when the cracks become wide enough, do you catch a glimpse of the light. You see that who you are can't be named. That you are the awareness behind every experience. And from that moment, the true unwinding begins.

Old Soul

As an old soul, you no longer confuse yourself with your roles, thoughts, or form. You've worn the masks of parent, partner, healer, creator, success story, failure story, you name it. You've won and lost, risen and fallen. And through it all, something in you has remained unchanged: the witnessing presence behind it all. That's who you are.

You no longer need a label to feel real. You don't introduce yourself with titles or accomplishments. You show up in essence. You've detached from the story you used to tell about yourself—because you see how small it is compared to the vastness of your true being. You feel less like a separate self and more like a current moving through life.

This shift doesn't make you aloof. It makes you a guiding light. You can still engage in the world—you create, express, and connect—but from freedom, not identity. You've made peace with being undefinable. You don't seek to be understood. Your truth doesn't require translation. It speaks for itself in your energy field.

The less you cling to form, the more you enter flow. Even thoughts begin to feel optional. You choose what to engage, and let the rest pass like water under the bridge. You trust yourself to show up and respond to life instead of reacting to it. You sense the divine intelligence in all things and no longer need to "be someone" to feel valuable. You long ago dissolved the illusion of separateness.

And as your sense of self continues to soften, you glimpse unity. Not conceptually—but viscerally. You don't just *know* you're connected to everything—you *feel* it. The boundary between self and life gets thinner until all that's left is being. You are the space through which life expresses itself. You simply *are*.

What once felt like a solid self is now more like a frequency, a resonance moving through the form dimension. You don't tell people who you are—you radiate it through your presence. Even the impulse to correct others' perceptions falls away. You've realized that being misunderstood is harmless—and being at peace is priceless.

When people encounter you, they sense something that cannot be understood. It's something deeply at peace. The kind that needs nothing to complete it. The kind that reminds them of their own true, shared essence.

IDENTITY CHART

The following chart contrasts how young vs old souls relate to identity.

Young Soul	Old Soul
Builds identity through roles, labels	Sees identity as temporary and fluid
Seeks validation to feel real	Anchors self-worth in presence
Defines self by success, status, group	No longer defined by form, affiliation
Clings to identity for safety	Dissolves identity to access truth
Takes things personally	Views life from awareness of self
Protects the self-concept at all costs	Allows the self-concept to unravel
Needs to "be someone" in the world	Content as no one, doing what arises
Uses identity to control perception	Releases self, embodies authenticity
Suffers when identity is threatened	Finds freedom in identity's collapse
Lives through the mask of "me"	Lives from the stillness behind all

Prompts

1) What roles or labels have you most identified with in your life—career, relationship, personality traits?

2) When something external in your life changes (a job loss, breakup, physical change), how do you respond?

3) In what ways do you seek validation, approval, or recognition from others? What might be underneath that?

4) How do you define "who you are" when no one else is around?

5) Have you ever used a spiritual identity—"healer," "empath," "old soul,"—to feel more valuable or special?

6) What would remain if all your roles, preferences, and traits were stripped away? Who or what would you be?

7) Describe a moment when you felt completely at peace, without needing to prove or explain yourself. What allowed that sense of freedom?

8) How might your life feel different if you stopped trying to "be someone" and simply rested in being?

Chapter 87

Intelligence

Young Soul

You've been taught that intelligence is measurable. You believe it's about how much you know, how fast you think, how clearly you speak, or how well you can prove your point. So you chase intellectual certainty. You want to be the smartest person in the room—the one with the correct answer, the airtight logic, the impressive vocabulary. Intelligence becomes something you wield like a sword. It gives you a sense of control over life, over others, and over your own simmering uncertainty.

Analytical intelligence is your comfort zone. You dissect problems, create frameworks, and categorize everything. You trust what can be seen, named, and quantified. You prize logic, science, and precision—and quickly dismiss anything that can't be proven or explained. Your mind moves fast, but your awareness is narrow. You know how to break things apart, but not necessarily how to integrate them.

You often undervalue emotional intelligence. Emotions confuse you or seem like distractions from the "real" work of thinking. You may even call them irrational or weak. When someone cries or expresses deep vulnerability, it makes you uncomfortable. You haven't yet learned to sit with feelings without trying to fix or escape them. You're used to analyzing, not empathizing.

Your body is a tool, not a teacher. You push through fatigue, ignore pain, and override intuitive signals. You view rest as laziness and physical sensitivity as a flaw. Bodily intelligence—like knowing when to pause, when to move, or when something feels off—isn't something you trust yet. You live mostly in your head, disconnected from your inner wisdom.

Socially, you may be charming or persuasive, but there's often a hidden agenda: to win approval, gain influence, or position yourself for dominance. You read people to get ahead, not necessarily to connect. You may have mastered the social script, but you approach things guarded, managing impressions rather than cultivating authenticity. You use relationships to affirm your identity, not to deepen your understanding of others.

Your creativity is driven by a desire for recognition. You want to stand out, to be admired for your originality. You may be prolific, but the state of consciousness of the artist always comes through. Your work carries the weight of performance, expectation, and self-consciousness. You haven't yet tapped into the deeper source of creation that moves through you rather than from you. Art becomes a way to prove your uniqueness, not a way to bring form to divine inspiration.

Intuition, if acknowledged at all, is hit-or-miss. Sometimes you follow a hunch, but often mistake fantasy or impulse for true inner knowing. You may label a desire as "divinely guided" because it feels exciting or dramatic. You haven't yet learned to listen deeply, or to discern the quiet pull of the soul from the emotional tugs of the self.

Your moral intelligence is shaped by rules, traditions, and external systems. You tend to see things in black and white—right or wrong, good or bad, spiritual or not. You follow a code of conduct without understanding its roots. You haven't yet developed the capacity to hold paradox, context, or nuance in ethical matters. Your judgments can be harsh because they arise from fear, not understanding.

Even your spirituality may be intellectualized. You collect teachings, quote scriptures, and pursue knowledge—but you're often disconnected from the direct experience those teachings point to. You prefer certainty, even in spiritual matters, and may latch onto rigid beliefs to feel secure. You haven't yet realized that intelligence cannot grasp the divine; it can only learn to step aside.

Eventually, your mind becomes exhausted. All the thinking, arguing, achieving, and proving brings little peace. You begin to sense that something is missing—something deeper, more integrated. The intellect alone is not enough. It can justify anything, and that no longer feels like a trustworthy foundation. So you begin to wonder: *What if wisdom isn't loud, fast, or impressive? What if it's subtle, quiet, and felt?* And with that, the old soul listening begins.

Old Soul

You've come to see intelligence not as what you know, but how you relate to your circumstances. It's not about speed, cleverness, or correctness—it's about depth, discernment, and alignment. You still value logic, but you no longer idolize it. The mind has its place: practical tasks, clear communication, execution of insight. But it no longer runs the show. You've seen how the "smartest" people can be the most disconnected—and how true wisdom lives in silence, presence, and simplicity.

Analytical intelligence now arises from spaciousness. You still seek clarity, pattern recognition, and precision—but everything arises from presence. Intellect alone no longer dominates your assessments. You let in the mystery. You've made peace with not knowing. In fact, if you're a more seasoned soul, *not knowing* is your preferred state. You don't chase answers. You receive downloads. And so, the mind becomes a loyal servant to something far more alive.

Your emotional intelligence runs deep. You've learned to sit with discomfort—yours and others'—without flinching. You don't fix, avoid, or suppress. You tune in and feel what's unspoken. You hold space without controlling the outcome. And even the simplest encounter becomes sacred when you meet it fully present, deeply human, and completely open.

Your body is no longer a vehicle to push through, but a finely tuned instrument. You've learned to read its subtle signs. A shift in breath. A ripple of tension. A pinch in the gut. You don't need to decode it mentally—you trust that every sensation holds wisdom. Somatic intelligence guides your decisions more than logic ever did. When your body says no, you honor it. When it lights up, you follow.

Socially, you show up bare. No masks, no agenda. You've stopped performing, managing impressions, or hiding behind charm. You are transparent, authentic, energetically honest. You speak only when the moment calls, and you're unbothered by silence. You feel resonance more than approval. And when something is misaligned, you know it before words arise.

Creativity has become a devotion. You no longer create to impress. You create to honor what wants to come through. Ideas arise from stillness, from dreams, from flow. You've learned that originality is a side effect of alignment—not the goal. Sometimes your art is beautiful, sometimes strange—but always alive. You don't control it and don't pretend you can.

Your intuition is steady and refined. You no longer confuse it with emotion, fantasy, or fear. You know how it speaks—through resonance, imagery, sensations, inner knowing. And even though it's quieter than the mind expects, you've experienced it enough times to trust it fully. The mind can analyze later.

Your moral intelligence is no longer reactive. It's fluid and relational. You don't fixate on rules or labels. You feel into the energy behind actions. You can hold contradiction and complexity without falling into judgment. You don't ask, *Is this right?* but *What's true in this moment?*

Your spiritual intelligence is the degree to which you are embodied. That means listening to trees. Crying during silence. Welcoming mystery. You no longer need credentials. You simply walk the path and let intelligence move through your whole system. Through the body, the heart, the breath, the silence. You've learned to listen with your whole being. You're no longer here to be right. You're here to be real. That's what makes you wise.

Intelligence Chart

Growing up in a world that emphasizes mental acuity, it can be challenging to find back into your body and start trusting its innate wisdom. At every milestone, you are rewarded for being cerebral. Embodiment is a foreign concept. Yet, all the answers you seek arise within. The following chart contrasts how young vs old souls make use of their intellect.

Young Soul	Old Soul
Equates intelligence with intellect	Sees intelligence as multidimensional
Seeks to appear smart to gain approval	Values wisdom over appearance
Trusts facts, logic, and external data	Listens to intuition, emotion, energy
Uses knowledge to control outcomes	Uses awareness to align with truth
Fears unknown; clings to being right	Welcomes not-knowing as a gateway
Learns to perform or compete	Learns to evolve and contribute
Measures worth by achievements	Knows worth is intrinsic and constant
Overidentifies with mental speed	Honors the intelligence of stillness
Analyzes to avoid feeling	Feels fully to access deeper knowing
Lives from the head	Lives from body-mind-soul wisdom

© 2025 Cirak

PROMPTS

1) Which form of intelligence have you relied on most in life, and why?

2) In what ways have you used intellect to avoid feeling, vulnerability, or uncertainty?

3) Do you trust your emotions as valid sources of insight, or do you tend to override them?

4) How often do you listen to your body's signals, and what happens when you don't?

5) What does intuition feel like in your system, and how do you differentiate it from impulse or fear?

6) When do you create from a need to prove something, and when do you create from presence?

7) How do you respond to others who express forms of intelligence different from your own?

8) In what ways do you still seek external validation for being "smart" or "right"?

9) Which type of intelligence is quietly asking to be honored more fully in your life right now?

Chapter 88

Listening

Young Soul

One of the most limiting beliefs of being a young soul is thinking you're listening when you're actually just waiting to speak. You think you're taking in what the other person is saying, but in truth, your mind is racing—judging, comparing, planning your reply. You believe you're being patient, that staying quiet while someone else speaks is the same as listening. But really, you're just waiting for your turn to assert yourself. Listening becomes a covert strategy—an attempt to validate your worldview while appearing reasonable and attentive.

Even your questions aren't always questions. They're rhetorical traps designed to steer the conversation toward the conclusion you've already drawn. You're not really hearing the other person—you're translating their words into your private language and discarding whatever doesn't fit. And if silence lingers, the urge to fill it becomes unbearable. Better to speak nonsense than risk the discomfort of nothing at all.

Then there's the matter of speed. You want others to get to the point—your point, preferably. You finish their sentences, not out of closeness but out of impatience and projection. You assume you already know where they're headed. And when they correct you, it irritates you. Now the script is broken, and control has slipped away. To a young soul, true listening feels inefficient.

The same pattern plays out inwardly. The subtle voice of intuition doesn't stand a chance against the mental narrator constantly demanding clarity, certainty, and direction. Inner listening is drowned out by outside distractions. You interpret your feelings instead of feeling them. You avoid discomfort instead of meeting it.

Eventually, life catches you off guard. A failed relationship, a devastating pause, or an encounter with someone who listens so deeply it disarms you. And for the first time, you glimpse that listening might not be about collecting information or preparing replies—but about releasing the need to be right.

That moment leaves a mark. Something in you realizes how rare true listening is, and how hungry you are for it. You begin to wonder: *what would it mean to listen not as a strategy, but as a practice of presence?* That wondering is the first glimmer of your old soul.

OLD SOUL

You no longer listen to respond. You don't even listen to understand in the usual sense. You listen to be with. The words spoken are like ripples on the surface, while your attention rests in the stillness beneath. You are focused on the experience the other person is seeking to have and supporting it. The audible content matters very little. You hear what isn't being said.

There is no urgency. No compulsion to fix, guide, or reshape the moment. Everything is just perfect as it is. Because when you listen with pure presence—when you're zoomed in close enough—there is no room for anything else but the sheer is-ness of right now. Any thoughts that it should be different have no breathing room. Only the true simplicity of life remains.

And with that, listening is no longer a self-justification tactic. You're all about being in receiving mode, tuning into the unknown. You've realized most people simply want to feel seen and felt, not solved. The best way to honor them is to acknowledge them in their whole being. And the best way to do that is with your full presence.

So you listen with your whole body—relaxed, open, and reflective.

Language has lost its spell. Words are empty containers until awareness gives them context. You're not caught in their literal meaning anymore. You listen to the vibration, to the resonance, to the soul in the flesh suit who's speaking.

You've also learned to listen inwardly without forcing answers. Intuition arrives quietly. Sometimes it takes its time, and even if it doesn't, it's just as meaningful. You are no longer restless in silence. You trust that what needs to be known will reveal itself in time.

You also notice how listening transforms relationships. People soften around you. They feel more themselves, less guarded, because your listening isn't about you. It's not even about them—it's about presence itself. Your listening creates a mirror of safety, and in that safety, truth emerges naturally.

True listening dissolves the illusion of separation. The boundary between speaker and listener blurs. What remains is awareness listening to itself, through two voices, one silence.

Listening Chart

Listening is one of the most undervalued traits in modern society that loves to pro-occupy itself with noise and that encourages self-assertion. The following graphic illustrates the difference between how young souls and old souls value and experience listening.

Young Souls	**Old Souls**
Listening as control and strategy	Listening as presence and being
Hearing through filters of belief and personal narrative	Hearing beneath words into silence and vibration
Interrupts, finishes sentences, impatient to be heard	Patient, open, no urgency to respond
Silence feels unbearable, quickly filled with noise	Silence is spacious, welcomed as part of listening
Questions are rhetorical, steering toward own conclusion	Questions arise gently, serving the other's unfolding
Focus on defending or proving oneself	Focus on creating safety and allowing authenticity
Translates others' words into private language	Receives others' words in their own meaning
Impatience with slowness or meandering	Natural receptivity to rhythm and flow
Listens outwardly but not inwardly	Attuned to inner voice, intuition, subtle sensation
Listening as a tactic for control	Listening as communion, dissolving separation

© 2025 Cirak

Prompts

1) Do you often find yourself rehearsing a response while someone else is still speaking?

2) When was the last time you truly let someone finish—not just their sentence, but their energy?

3) What does silence bring up in you?

4) Reflect on a time you felt deeply heard. How did that feel?

5) How do you listen to your own inner voice—through analysis, interruption, or patient stillness?

6) What if most conversations are less about transferring information and more about revealing vibration?

7) Where do you notice yourself rushing others, and what fear sits beneath that urgency?

8) How do you experience the "space between words" when someone is speaking?

9) What truths emerge in you only when you slow down enough to really listen?

10) How would your relationships change if listening became less about control and more about presence?

Chapter 89

Stillness

Young Soul

Stillness makes you uneasy. It feels like a void—empty, dull, lifeless. You've been conditioned to keep moving, keep achieving, keep reaching for what's next. When there's nothing to do, you feel restless or anxious, as if something is wrong. So you reach for your device or fill the silence with noise, the space with tasks, the pause with planning. You don't see your constant seeking as avoidance—you see it as effort, as problem-solving, as the way forward.

It's no wonder stillness feels like a threat to your identity. You associate it with passivity or failure. If you're not progressing or producing, who are you? You fear being forgotten, left behind, or exposed. So you stay busy, even when your body and mind are tired. You keep going, even when your spirit longs to stop. You don't yet know that presence isn't the opposite of progress—it's the foundation for it.

Sometimes you call your stimulation "learning" or "seeking"—a documentary, a podcast, a book. But it's the same loop in disguise. You crave clarity, yet in accumulating knowledge, you crowd it out. You long for peace, but your pursuit of it becomes stressful. You say you want truth, but you rarely sit still long enough to let it reveal itself.

Stillness exposes you to yourself—and that's the real discomfort. In the quiet, you begin to feel things you've kept at bay: grief, fear, longing, doubt. The stories that hold your life together begin to dissolve. Your false self—the one you've spent years establishing for the world to admire—starts to leave you. And that's terrifying. You don't want to let the old version die. So you run. You distract. You "work on yourself" endlessly. You may even talk the spiritual talk, but beneath it all, you're still avoiding what unsettles you most: letting yourself be.

From where you stand, stillness is confusing. Any space that isn't filled feels dead. You haven't yet experienced the intelligence of pause. You don't trust that deep healing could happen without great effort. Or that peace could come without earning it.

Even your healing is crowded with doing. You chase breakthroughs, insights, altered states. You think the more you process, the faster you'll "get there." But the seeking deepens the illusion that something is missing. Even when you try stillness, it's often a technique to fix your state—not a willingness to see things as they are.

You may have glimpses. After a long run. Sitting in traffic. Watching trees sway. For a moment, something slows... but then the mind returns: *This can't be it. It's too simple. Too quiet.* You still expect fireworks. You want big truths, mega revelations, not small silences.

Still, there's a faint memory, a deep longing. A pull toward surrender, toward not pretending anymore. You may not speak it aloud, but part of you is tired of running. Nothing "out there" makes you feel whole. The noise no longer soothes. The goals feel hollow. And so something inside you finally asks: *What if I just stopped?* And in that moment, stillness has already arrived.

Old Soul

Stillness is your sanctuary. It's not where you go to escape—it's where you return to rest, recharge, remember. You no longer need a quiet room or a meditation cushion. You find stillness in the supermarket line, in the space between words, in the water running over dishes. It is the backdrop of form.

Far from being passive, stillness is potent. Alive. Awake. The most powerful forces in nature—healing, growth, creation—don't come from striving. They emerge from stillness. Knowing this, you stop trying to fill silence with effort. You wait, you listen, you trust. What arises in stillness is more intelligent than anything your mind could force.

You no longer believe that doing more means living more. In fact, the more still you become, the more vivid life becomes. You greet moments with curiosity. You feel into conversations. You let emotions arise and pass. Stillness hasn't dulled you—it has sharpened your ability to truly meet each and every moment.

Others may not understand that divine guidance is the most reliable compass. But your body does. Your nervous system knows. When you stop resisting the moment, your heart opens, and clarity flows in—not as thoughts to think, but as an inner knowing you receive. It's not effort. It's resonance.

You've stopped seeking. You've seen how seeking fractures your presence and delays your peace. You've stopped trying to become someone, stopped trying to get somewhere. You've realized: the moment you stop striving is the moment you're arriving. Presence is the only destination there is.

Stillness is where integration happens. Not through thinking about what you've learned, but through letting it settle. It works for everything. From studying for an exam to processing traumas. Instead of rushing to understand, you let the answers reveal themselves. You know now that inner wisdom doesn't require doing. It just requires space.

Stillness has become your most honest mirror. It reveals when you're attached, when you're trying, when you're posturing. But it doesn't shame you. It reflects you with compassion. In that reflection, the false self falls away and only your true self remains. It's so simple. And it works.

You hold space differently now. You don't interrupt silence to fill it. You don't speak up in order to fix things. You allow space in conversation, in healing, in decision-making. You know that stillness communicates more than words ever could. It speaks the language of frequency, of depth, of Source.

Your stillness no longer depends on your environment—it's the quality of your being. You carry it into traffic, into conflict, into creation. Even when the world around you spins, you exist in stillness. You are stillness. And in that, you've become unshakable.

PROMPTS

1) What sensations arise in you when you're in stillness?

2) How often do you distract yourself, even in subtle ways, from just being?

3) What do you believe stillness says about you—are you lazy, unproductive, or free?

4) What fears do you associate with doing nothing?

5) Can you remember a time when stillness taught you something your mind couldn't?

6) In what ways have you tried to "earn" peace rather than simply receive it?

7) What emotions surface when you stop distracting yourself and simply sit in stillness?

8) How would you design your life if stillness were a regular companion, not a rare visitor?

9) What is one small daily activity where you could invite more stillness?

Chapter 90

Acceptance

Young Soul

You think acceptance means giving up. Admitting defeat. Making peace with something you don't like and pretending it's okay. You think, *If I accept this, I'll be stuck with it forever.* To your mind, acceptance sounds like self-betrayal. You think it means you've failed. Or worse—you've agreed to a life you don't want.

So, you resist. You fight it. You try to fix, push, argue, reframe, and analyze your patterns. You chase clarity through books, coaches, or mental gymnastics. But none of it sticks. It can't stick, because beneath all the effort is one silent belief: *I can't accept this. Not yet. Not like this. I want my version.* And so you stay stuck—prolonging everything you don't like with your resistance to it.

Your resistance reaches into all corners of life. You resist your sadness, your fears, your doubts, your helplessness. You resist the traffic, the weather, the line at the coffee shop. You want to jump over all of it, bypass it, reason your way around it. You don't understand why you can't "figure it out." It looks like everyone else has.

You don't realize you can't figure out what you're unwilling to feel. You haven't yet understood that you're resisting your feelings about your circumstances—not the circumstances themselves. And so obsessing over the external world keeps you occupied. Meanwhile, your unconscious patterns play on repeat and drain your energy.

You tell yourself you're being positive. That you're focusing on what you want, not what you don't want. But your positivity isn't based on presence or connection to Source—it's built on avoidance, on mentally pushing away uncomfortable thoughts and feelings. It's a far cry from recognizing that true expansion comes from feeling your feelings fully, to release stuck energy and finally move forward.

But your mind keeps getting in the way. It thinks that accepting something makes it permanent, when—from an energetic standpoint—the opposite is the case. As the saying goes: *What you resist, persists.* And young souls resist almost everything—pain, discomfort, uncertainty, endings. Even the weather. Even traffic. That's why so much of life feels like a fight. You're entangled in the belief that your environment has to match your expectations for you to be at peace.

ACCEPTANCE

And so, you continue to manifest from this place. You envision a better world, one more aligned with the version of yourself you aspire to be. But it's all built on the same faulty foundation: *I cannot accept myself as I am.* Thus, the very energy behind your efforts to create change is tainted with self-rejection. At the deepest level, you're still saying no to yourself. No to your feelings. No to the now. Imagine the message your body receives when you say: *I don't want to be here. I don't want to be who I am.* The universe simply echoes that vibration back.

Until you cease being at war with your own reality, your nervous system stays dysregulated. You live in your head, spinning stories about why life isn't working, why you're not there yet, why it's so hard. You try to "work on yourself," imagining that one day you'll become this perfected version who has it all together. But this mindset doesn't take you forward. Until you stop running from who you are now, you remain stuck.

Acceptance doesn't mean settling. On the contrary, it's what gets you unstuck. When you stop resisting how you feel, you come back into your body. You come back into the now. You become available to consciously co-creating with life again. The moment you stop trying to be somewhere else, everything starts happening for you here.

Old Soul

You've stopped resisting what's already here. Not because you've given up, but because you've learned that resisting something that has already happened changes nothing, other than creating upset for yourself. Nor do you believe that accepting something makes it permanent. Instead, acceptance is the first—and fastest—step toward real transformation. It brings you back into relationship with life, into sync with yourself.

You've also long understood that acceptance isn't a mental strategy. It's not about reinterpreting the story or reframing it to see it positively. Acceptance is something much deeper and more potent. It's the act of allowing yourself to fully *feel* what's arising—without rushing to fix, escape, or spiritualize it.

When something painful happens, you no longer react from the mind. You tune into the body. You observe the sensations, feel the contractions, listen to what wants to express itself. You give your experience space—whether it's comfortable or not, makes no difference. You know that the light of your awareness liberates energy. That one conscious breath is more honest than any thought.

Healing isn't about changing your experience—it's about letting it complete. When you let it move through you,

ACCEPTANCE

clarity returns. The story loses its charge. You're no longer attached. What once felt overwhelming now becomes the invitation to deepen your connection with yourself.

Furthermore, when you stop pushing against reality, your nervous system settles. Your field clears. You begin to receive insight—not from mental analysis, but straight from Source. The next step arises organically. You don't need to plan it. You *feel* it. You take inspired action—not as a reaction to life, but as a result of living in sync with it.

When you no longer need a better version of yourself to be okay, you stop chasing the future at the cost of now. Instead, you've found peace and freedom in letting yourself be. And from there, clarity and direction arise all on their own. The irony is, acceptance doesn't delay your evolution—it accelerates it.

As an old soul, you've internalized the seasons of life. That form is impermanent. That pain is not forever. So you don't panic when discomfort arises. You stay open. You let it be. And because of that, nothing sticks. Feelings flow through you like clouds across the sky. And you remain still, spacious, unmoved. You welcome sensations, knowing they bring insight into what resonates and what doesn't. There's no drama. No judgment. Just presence.

ACCEPTANCE CHART

Being at peace with who you are is the fastest path towards soul maturity. The following chart illustrates how young souls and old soul understand acceptance.

Theme	Young Soul (Resistance)	Old Soul (Acceptance)
Core Belief	"This shouldn't be happening."	"This is what's here—let me meet it fully."
Orientation	Against reality	Aligned with reality
Emotional Response	Reactivity, frustration, blame	Openness, curiosity, allowing
Mental Habit	Rumination, fixing, controlling	Observing, witnessing, spaciousness
Action Source	Fear, urgency, self-protection	Clarity, presence, inner guidance
Relation to Pain	Avoid or fight it	Feel it fully, let it pass
Time Focus	Past/future (regret, worry)	Present moment awareness
Inner State	Tension, resistance, fragmentation	Coherence, flow, stillness
Identity Perspective	"This is happening to me."	"This is happening for me."
Outcome Over Time	Energetic depletion, repeated lessons	Inner peace, freedom, flow, dissolution of self

© 2025 Cirak

PROMPTS

1) What life situations do you still struggle to accept?

2) Does acceptance feel like giving up or losing control?

3) What part of you believes that if you accept something, it will never change?

4) What might shift in your life if you allowed your feelings to move through you without analysis or judgment?

5) In what ways has resistance kept you stuck in patterns you long to move beyond?

6) Can you recall a time when true acceptance brought unexpected clarity or momentum?

7) How does your nervous system respond when you stop trying to change and simply allow?

8) What would it look like today to stop resisting what is?

Chapter 91

Imagination

Young Soul

Imagination is your escape hatch. When reality feels boring, stressful, or limiting, you drift into fantasy—imagining better outcomes, grander versions of yourself, or dramatic confrontations that never happen from which you emerged victorious. It gives you a sense of control, a place where you're the hero at the center of attention. You imagine success, romance, revenge—whatever the moment demands to soothe your unmet needs.

However, you rarely notice how much energy you expend on scenarios that don't exist. Instead of using your imagination to shape a new reality, you use it as a form of resistance to the current one. You use it to reinforce your version, your identity. You visualize how others see you, how you wish they would see you, and how you can prove yourself to the world. You rehearse conversations to win them over, arguments to justify yourself, and futures where you have finally arrived. But all of it is driven by the same underlying story: that who you are now is not enough. Your imagination becomes a tool of ambition and comparison, not insight. You don't yet realize how deeply it's intertwined with your personal narrative.

Sometimes your imagination turns dark. You project fears into the future and live them as if they're real. You obsess over what might go wrong, what others might think, or how badly you'll fail. You might call this "thinking ahead" or "being realistic," but really, it's your nervous system playing out worst-case scenarios in a twisted attempt to deal with the unknown and feel safe. Your imagination becomes a fear loop, amplifying your need for control.

You also easily confuse imagination with intuition. A random thought or feeling pops in, and you assume it's a message from the universe. But it's likely just artifacts from your unconscious mind, shaped by desire or fear. Without a well-developed awareness muscle that can help you discern, you chase every impulse that feels exciting or "aligned," only to crash later in disappointment. You haven't yet learned the difference between a mind-generated fantasy and a vision straight from Source. So you misinterpret imagination as divine guidance, when it's often just noise.

You use daydreams the way you might use social media or substances—to distract from boredom, discomfort, or silence. It feels like you're doing something creative, but mostly you're lost in thought, avoiding stillness. Instead of discovering what's really inside you, you overlay imagined stories. You borrow images of success, beauty, or heroism and make them your own private theater. You don't yet notice that much of what you imagine isn't truly yours—it's borrowed conditioning, recycled desires used by others to sell you something.

Over time, you begin to see that imagination—when used to escape or control life mentally—simply reflects your current state of consciousness. So, you start to ask: *Is there a place from which imagination arises all on its own? What messages would it carry?* And with that, you step onto old soul terrain.

Old Soul

Intuition is one of the ways Source shows you things. Not as proof, but as invitations to the co-creative process. That doesn't mean you blindly follow every image or idea, but you listen. You feel into the texture of it. If it's infused with clarity, gentleness, and resonance, you know it's worth exploring. If it's agitated, lack-driven, or fear-based, you know it's a projection. This discernment didn't come from books—it came from years of tuning into your body and inner truth.

As such, you no longer use imagination to escape reality—you use it to deepen your relationship with it. You know it's not just fantasy, but a gateway between worlds: where insight arrives, symbols speak, and visions form before they manifest through you. It's why you trained your energy field to be still and receptive, so you can tell when something shines through from the divine. You let images come to you, not from you.

Sometimes imagination arrives as metaphor: a vision during meditation, a sudden transcendence while walking in nature, a dream with a message you feel is more than real. You no longer dismiss these or over-analyze—you treat them with reverence. You explore them, sometimes excitedly, knowing that truth often speaks in symbols. If you're a truly old soul, you hold space and just let the image do its work.

Your imagination is essential to your co-creative powers. It allows you to receive and consistently hold frequencies until they take shape. You're not "manifesting," you're in direct relationship with the formless. You no longer visualize to *get something*; you imagine as a way to channel and interact with the cosmic desire to express itself as form. When your imagination is clean, unforced, and resonant, it carries energetic precision. It sends a clear signal. And the physical world responds.

You've also discovered imagination as a healing force. A vision of validating your younger self, or seeing light where once there was darkness, can re-pattern the nervous system. These images aren't "pretend"—they shift energy, restore coherence, and open space for renewal. Imagination, like anything infused with awareness, is medicine.

Beyond the personal, you see how imagination weaves humanity together. Collective myths, archetypes, stories, and even visions of the future—all arise through the shared imagination of countless souls. You recognize that every image you hold feeds not only your life but the collective dream of the species. So you contribute consciously, aware that every thought counts.

At the end of the day, your task is to keep the vessel clear. Tend to your emotional, mental, and energetic hygiene, knowing that a distorted imagination distorts your receiving antenna. You've matured beyond both fear-fueled fantasy and personal desire-based manifestation. Now, imagination is a sacred place where you listen, receive, and create in communion with something much vaster than yourself, of which you, too, are an expression.

PROMPTS

1) How do you currently use your imagination, more for escape, control, or creation?

2) What recurring fantasies or fears play out in your imagination? What deeper needs do they point to?

3) What's the difference between a thought you generate and a vision that arrives?

4) How clean is the channel of your imagination, emotionally, energetically, mentally?

5) What does it feel like in your body when imagination is aligned with Source vs self?

6) In what areas of life are you being invited to co-create through vision rather than effort?

7) How might you use imagination as a listening space, not a projection screen?

8) How can you contribute to the collective imagination with images of healing, harmony, and awakening?

Chapter 92

Manifestation

Young Soul

As a young soul, manifestation is exciting because it feels like control. You think: if I can master the technique—vision boards, affirmations, scripting—I can have everything I want. And that's the key word: *want*. You manifest from the place of personal desire, often unaware that your desires themselves are shaped by wounds, conditioning, and comparison. What you're asking for may not actually serve your soul, but your mind believes it will fill the gap.

You treat the universe like a vending machine. Insert the right vibration, say the right mantra, focus hard enough—and you'll get the car, the job, the partner. It's not that this doesn't work. It can. But when it does, you often find yourself still dissatisfied. Because what you created came from the version of you that felt incomplete. You manifested your preferences, not your truth. The reality remains that you can't fill an inner void with external goods.

There's also urgency to your "co-creating." You don't realize you're actually controlling. You visualize to avoid uncertainty. You try to override divine timing with deadlines. You compare your manifestations to others who seem successful and spiral into doubt. This creates a paradox: the harder you grasp, the more distant things become. The more intensely you try to manifest, the more misaligned your energy gets.

You want to believe you're spiritual. But most of your desires are still rooted in *more*. More status, more beauty, more validation, more comfort. Even the desire to "serve humanity" can become self-centered if it's motivated by identity or self-importance. You don't yet realize that true manifestation isn't about getting what you want—it's about becoming a match for what wants to move through you.

Sometimes you lean on rituals as if they hold magical power—burning candles, repeating mantras, arranging crystals—believing the act itself forces the universe's hand. The problem is not the ritual, but the desperation underneath it. Instead of aligning your state, you cling to superstition, hoping technique can override your disconnect with truth.

Another trap is dressing up fear as positivity. You paste affirmations over your doubt, repeating "I am abundant" while your mind is bathed in lack. Rather than release resistance, you suppress it. This makes manifestation feel like yet another mask worn to convince yourself and others you're okay.

Jealousy spikes when you see others "manifest" what you want. You secretly resent them or assume they know a secret formula you missed. You compare timelines, imagining you're behind. In truth, your envy reflects the same illusion that fuels your desire: that you're not good enough, that life is withholding something from you.

Sometimes you work yourself to exhaustion trying to manifest—journaling every day, visualizing until your mind aches, demanding synchronicities as proof. But the more effort you exert, the less flow you feel. Burnout is the body's way of showing you that manifestation, when forced, only widens the gap between you and the unfolding of life.

Eventually, you notice something. You might get what you asked for—but it fulfills the outer picture, not the inner longing. You feel the thrill of attaining, but not the peace of attunement. You begin to suspect manifestation isn't about forcing reality into your image. It's about letting in what you cannot imagine.

Old Soul

As an old soul, you've stopped manifesting from lack, fear, or control. You no longer ask the external to fill a hole in your identity. You know that what you truly need can't be found in outcomes. Instead of trying to manifest a *thing*, you instead focus on becoming an open vessel. You stop declaring, *This is what I want,* and start asking, *What wants to come through me?*

You've realized that when you manifest from self, it is limited by your level of consciousness. When you visualize from a constricted identity, you only call in more experiences that reinforce that version of you. So you've worked on dissolving the layers of conditioning, the false self. You've released attachment to your desires—not because they're wrong, but because you know they constitute a fraction of the whole picture.

When you feel desire, you don't chase it. You sit with it. You let it clarify itself. You ask, *Is this coming from love or from fear? From wholeness or from lack? From my mind or from deep within?* Crafting clarity around what motivates you creates a shift in your vibration. Your energy becomes cleaner, lighter, more magnetic. You're no longer broadcasting chaos and confusion.

You've made peace with not knowing. You don't need to see the whole stairway. You just need to take the next step from within. You understand that surrender doesn't mean passivity—it means total cooperation with life's intelligence. You stop trying to *imagine* what the future could look like, and start allowing yourself to *receive* what your current self could never have predicted.

This is the paradox of high-level manifestation: the less you try to manifest, the more effortlessly life begins to arrange itself around you. Opportunities find you. People appear. Events align. Not because you planned them—but because you trust timing. You trust the process. You don't need to micromanage God. When you're rooted in being, life flows toward you, and you flow with life.

Sometimes you're guided to act boldly. Other times, you're guided to wait. You no longer dismiss the subtle nudges that defy logic, because you've come to recognize intuition as the language of the soul. What the mind deems irrelevant may be the key to the unfolding. You've worked hard to refine your inner listening—not mistaking impulse for intuition, or trying to force flow. You understand that the mind shouts, but the soul whispers.

You've also learned that gratitude itself is manifestation. Not the kind where you fake appreciation to get more, but the authentic recognition of what already is. Gratitude tunes your vibration to acceptance and sufficiency, dissolving the very lack that once drove your desires. Suddenly, when you feel like you have enough, what emerges is the clearest signal of what you're ready to receive.

Ultimately, the most miraculous manifestations come not from wanting, but from your willingness to wait for the right moment to arrive. And for you to maximize your manifestation powers, there can be not an inkling of urgency, expectation, or impatience in your energetic field. Even the slightest attachment to *how* and *when* causes your receiving frequency to dip.

Manifestation at the highest level requires your sense of self to step aside and allow life to happen. You can feel the truth in this because you've never manifested great things when you were trying to fix things. You manifest great things when life's intelligence can move through you because you stopped getting in the way.

And when you no longer manifest from the self, your creations serve the whole. They're for the elevation of consciousness. That's why they carry so much power. You've merged your personal will with divine will. And that makes your vibration irresistible to the universe.

Manifestation Chart

Even when you've understood that you live in a vibrational universe, what you create is still a reflection of your level of awareness. The following chart contrasts how young souls and old souls make use of their manifestation powers.

Theme	Young Soul (Self Manifestation)	Old Soul (Source Co-Creation)
Core Motivation	To get what I want and feel in control	To align with Source and serve the whole
Source of Desire	Lack, fear, comparison, story of "me"	Soul, intuition, resonance
Orientation	Control, force, performance	Flow, surrender, receiving mode
Method	Visualization, rituals, affirmations	Presence, embodiment, stillness
Role of Emotion	Manipulate feelings to manifest	Feel fully to become energetically clear
Relationship to Outcome	Attached, pressured, disappointed easily	Detached, trusting, at peace with all outcomes
Identity Perspective	"I create my reality."	"I align with the reality meant for me."
Time Focus	Future-based: "When I get this, then I'll be happy."	Present-based: "I am already whole."
Energetic Pattern	Wanting, desiring, grasping, pushing	Allowing, opening, receiving
Outcome Over Time	Short-term gains, long-term dissatisfaction	Sustained fulfillment, deep alignment

© 2025 Cirak

Prompts

1) What have you been trying to manifest lately, and what deeper feeling are you hoping it will give you?

2) In what ways have your desires been shaped by past pain, social comparison, or unhealed identity?

3) When you think about surrendering control and letting life guide you, what emotions arise?

4) What beliefs or assumptions are limiting what you think is possible for you?

5) Where in your life do you still confuse effort with alignment?

6) What would it feel like to be deeply available—but not attached—to what wants to move through your life next?

7) When have you mistaken impulse for intuition in manifestation? What was the result?

8) How do you experience gratitude—as a strategy to get more, or as genuine resonance with what is?

9) In what ways do you cling to rituals or "formulas" as if they hold the power, rather than your state of being?

10) If you stopped asking life for anything, what might you finally become available to receive?

CHAPTER 93

FLOW

YOUNG SOUL

You've rarely, if ever, experienced flow. You've heard the word tossed around—usually in reference to athletes or artists—but it's never felt available to you, let alone something you could call upon at will. Your life moves in fragments—thoughts colliding, tasks heavy with hesitation, confusion, or resistance. There's no glide, no rhythm, no natural momentum. Only effort. Only pressure. Only trying.

You don't yet understand what blocks flow, so you don't know how to allow it. Your inner world is loud—commentary, judgment, projection, planning. You narrate your every move, editing each moment. Your attention flickers between past and future, memory and anticipation, with no presence in sight.

Even when the moment opens briefly, you don't trust it. The present feels too empty, too quiet, too uncertain. You search for somewhere else, someone else, something to control. You grip life mentally, steering and calculating every step. Letting go feels like laziness, failure, even death to the self-image you've worked so hard to shape. So you keep injecting preferences, fears, expectations—not realizing it's your very interference that breaks the flow before it begins.

Sometimes bursts of productivity or creativity arrive, but they are initiated with great effort and end in depletion. You assume that's normal—push harder, recover later. You believe pressure drives performance, not noticing that you're swimming upstream against a current you don't even know exists.

To you, true flow sounds like fantasy. A grace reserved for the gifted few. But that's only because your reality is shaped by interruption. You resist what is, trying to replace it with what you think should be. You live in your head, not your body. In ideas about the past and future, not presence.

You also mistake stimulation for flow. You chase dopamine spikes, novelty, and intensity, then call it being "in the zone." But you're not in sync—you're intoxicated. Flow isn't an excited mind. Flow is the *absence* of mind. And that scares you, because it dissolves the very self you're still trying to build.

Even when ease appears, you analyze it—trying to repeat or capture the formula. But flow isn't a formula. It's a natural byproduct of awareness. Without awareness, you lack the foundation for flow to take hold. The problem is, you don't yet know how to step aside.

Eventually, you grow tired of the grind. You notice how clunky life feels—how much you strain for so little yield. You wonder if there's another way. But it's hard to grasp the paradox: flow begins where the self ends. So, as long as your self is still under construction, you keep resisting. You remain a stranger to flow—and flow a stranger to you.

Old Soul

Flow is no longer a mystery. It's the natural state when you no longer interfere with life happening. The more aware you are, the less "you" there is in the way. Thoughts may arise, but you don't hold them. You no longer narrate the moment—you *are* the moment.

You've lived the futility of control. You've seen how pushing and planning create only friction. You've understood the paradox: it's through stillness that momentum builds. When you stop chasing outcomes, something larger takes over. Flow isn't something you must generate. Flow is something you allow yourself to join.

It begins with acceptance—not mental reframing but embodied surrender. You say yes to life, even when it's uncomfortable. You stop resisting your emotions. You stop editing your experiences. The absence of resistance is the opening into the greater current.

You know that flow is not a privilege. It's available to everyone in every act—washing dishes, walking to the market, sitting in stillness. Flow comes from living in alignment. The more relaxed your system, the more harmoniously life moves and you move with life. Nothing extraordinary is required. Just non-interference.

When flow wanes, you don't panic. You listen. You notice where tension has entered your body—a fearful thought, a grasp for control, a subtle contraction. You observe, you release, and flow returns. It's that simple.

You also know that reactivity blocks flow more than anything. Every attempt to control clogs the current. Surrender clears it. So you stop dramatizing setbacks. In fact, in your mind there is no such thing as a setback. You have no unmet beliefs to get upset about. There is only life happening. *This is what's happened. Let's see what happens next.*

The deepest flow states aren't euphoric highs. They're spacious, timeless, still. You move without effort. Act without thinking. You're not chasing intensity—you're inhabiting being. And in that being, life expands—elegant, precise, effortless. You realize how little the mind knows, how little needs to be managed, how intelligent the present moment is when you trust it.

Flow Chart

The following chart illustrates how young souls and old souls understand flow.

Young Soul	Old Soul
Tries to control outcomes	Trusts the unfolding of life
Seeks peak performance	Moves in harmony with Source
Lives in the mind	Lives through embodied awareness
Pushes through tension	Listens for energetic alignment
Interprets flow as rare or elite	Recognizes flow as natural state
Reacts from urgency	Responds from inner stillness
Distracted by mental chatter	Rooted in present-moment awareness
Struggles to replicate success	Allows each moment to be unique
Confuses force with strength	Understands surrender as power
Measures by results	Measures by presence and ease

© 2025 Cirak

Prompts

1) When was the last time you experienced true flow, and what conditions made it possible?

2) In what areas of life do you try to control or predict outcomes the most?

3) What thoughts or habits interrupt your flow?

4) What scares you about surrendering to the moment?

5) What would it look like to trust life to move through you without your interference?

6) Can you recall a moment where letting go led to unexpected ease or insight?

7) How would your day change if you approached each task without resistance?

Chapter 94

Spiritual Bypass

Young Soul

When you first discover spirituality, it feels like a lifeline. After years of chasing outcomes, suffering through challenges, and wondering why life is so hard, you stumble upon something that promises peace, clarity, even transcendence. Naturally, you become enamored with the topic. You read the books, learn the phrases, attend retreats, and announce you're "on the path," while everyone else is still lost. But things get complicated quickly.

As with any new chapter, you don't begin clean. You bring your old self along. Your old mode of attaching to labels and avoiding feelings carries forward and finds a way to articulate itself in this new framework. Much of your "spirituality" becomes a way to avoid pain, bypass emotion, or reinforce identity. It's the same dynamic as before, just in a different wrapper.

You use spiritual language to mask discomfort. *Everything happens for a reason*, you say, while sidestepping grief. *It's their karma*, you tell yourself, as you dodge compassion or responsibility. You urge others to *let it go* before you've learned to feel and release your own wounds. You rush to forgiveness without passing through anger. You perform presence without actually being present. Spirituality becomes a new control system to override emotion, deny vulnerability, or feel superior without facing your shadow.

Soon, you begin to imagine yourself further along than others. You talk about being *high vibe* or *above drama*, even though you're still caught in reactivity and suppression. You distance yourself from people who *don't get it* and may even judge others for doing what you only recently stopped doing. You call out their bypassing, toxic positivity, or false light—forgetting how much those tools taught you.

But this frustration reveals a deeper truth: you still believe there's a *right* way, and other paths are *wrong*, instead of simply incomplete. You haven't yet embraced the full spectrum of human learning and that everyone evolves in their own way, in their own timing.

That includes you. Eventually, you, too, mature. The bypassing gets old. The repeated mantras ring hollow. The forced positivity feels heavy. Maybe life humbles you.

Maybe pain breaks through the mask. Either way, the spiritual persona begins to fade and the old soul path begins.

Old Soul

You no longer see bypassing as failure or use it as a reason to condescend—it's simply a phase. You remember what it was like to use spirituality as a shield. A sincere attempt to escape pain, transcend chaos, or find safety in a confusing world. Every soul passes through it. It's part of your awakening process and every stage is divinely orchestrated.

So when you see others doing it, you feel compassion, not judgment. You know real growth doesn't come from being shamed—it comes from feeling seen as you are. By modeling calmness, grounded embodiment, and sincerity, you let your energy speak louder than your words. You become a mirror, not a critic.

You're also awake enough to notice if bypassing tries to creep back into your ways—an impulse to feel superior, a flash of spiritual ambition, a temptation to hide behind noble language. But you don't criticize yourself for these patterns. You witness them gently, smiling at their transience. You observe sensations and return to yourself. No story. No attachment. Just presence.

You see the larger picture now: everyone is doing the best they can with the awareness they have at this time. If they could choose differently, they would. Bypassing isn't fake—it's simply a nervous system still sorting itself out, not yet ready to feel. And readiness is not a virtue—it's just timing. You trust that timing in others as you do for yourself.

For old souls, labeling people as "asleep," "inauthentic," or "behind," no longer feels authentic. It hurts too much to give your energy to such weighty accusations. The illusion of hierarchy has long fallen away. But, even with this, it took a while to get here. One of the main challenges of older souls is navigating a world build by and for younger souls, without getting frustrated, feeling alienated, or thinking you're better. Nor can you disregard the inherent responsibilities of being embodied, such as maintaining health and wellbeing, and seeing others in their highest light. No matter how enlightened, you cannot get ahead of yourself and your physical existence. The work of aligning truly never ends.

Today, you enjoy the benefits of living a Soure-led life. Your world is based on love, clarity, simplicity, freedom. A freedom that honors all stages of the path—including the messy, the misguided, and the conditioned ones. You no longer need people to wake up. You simply love them where they are.

Spiritual Bypass Chart

It's easy to judge others for being different than you, for not being as far along. Regardless of soul age, your primary task is to learn to stay focused on yourself. This is your life to live and you are 100% responsible for your vibration. The following chart highlights the differences in how young souls and old souls evolve in their spirituality.

Young Souls	**Old Souls**
Spirituality used to override feelings	Spirituality embodied as full presence
Mantras and phrases replace feeling	Feelings allowed to arise and pass
Pain avoided through "positivity"	Pain welcomed as part of healing
Superiority via "high vibe" identity	Humility through shared humanity
Forgiveness rushed to skip anger	Forgiveness arises naturally after releasing stuck energy
Persona of calmness	Authentic calm from inner alignment
Judgment of others' path	Compassion for all stages of the path
Spiritual control replaces old control	No control—trust in life's unfolding
Seeking safety through bypass	Safety in honesty and embodiment
Growth measured by image or language	Growth measured by depth of surrender

© 2025 Cirak

Prompts

1) In what ways have you used spirituality to avoid pain, conflict, or uncomfortable emotions?

2) When have you mistaken spiritual language or behavior for genuine inner transformation?

3) Do you ever feel superior to others who seem "less conscious"? What part of you needs that story?

4) Have you judged others for bypassing, even while doing it yourself?

5) How might bypassing be a necessary and natural part of someone's spiritual path?

6) What would it look like to offer compassion instead of correction when you see someone bypassing?

7) Are there areas of your life where you still use spirituality as a shield rather than a mirror?

8) Can you allow all stages of the journey to be sacred, including the messy, misguided, and performative ones?

Chapter 95

Psychedelics

Young Soul

You hear that psychedelics open you up—to healing, to consciousness, to God. The promise is magnetic: a rapid shift, a mystical journey. Finally healing from trauma, breaking free from limiting beliefs, escaping the flatness of ordinary life. You're told you can meet your higher self, transcend suffering, and taste enlightenment. Who wouldn't want that?

But psychedelics are a shortcut. And young souls love shortcuts—not because you're lazy, but because you're still young. You're still learning to move with life instead of against it. You want the end before you've lived through the middle. You're still chasing end results, trying to skip your evolution and bypass the journey. And while your desire to heal is sincere, the method betrays a hidden truth: you don't believe you're good enough as you are.

In other words, you want to heal and free yourself, but you're running from the one thing that matters most in this endeavor: accepting yourself as you are. And that's the real problem. Underneath the noble intention to awaken or evolve, there's a quiet panic: *I need to change because I judge/deny/can't deal with certain parts of myself.* Psychedelics offer the illusion of transformation without requiring you to feel every part of the process. But only full self-acceptance—as you are, where you are—without amplification or distortion of your feelings, releases you from your entanglement with them and moves you forward.

As a young soul, there's a cosmic law you haven't yet touched: the energy behind your action is contained in the outcome. If you move from fear, unworthiness, or grasping, that vibration imprints itself onto every result. If your choice is born from rejection of self, it will multiply into more rejection—even if wrapped in cosmic visions and self-love slogans. One seed of self-rejection bears many fruits. Soon, your entire orchard becomes something you didn't mean to plant. You wanted liberation, but you've built an empire of relentless longing.

You may say you're "doing the work" or "seeking truth," but beneath it, you're still trying to escape the present moment. You want to be someone else—someone healed, powerful, awakened, unburdened. And psychedelics feed that fantasy.

Even when you have glimpses of what's possible, when you fall back to baseline, there's a chance you feel even more broken than before, deriding yourself for not living in that state. The visions become ideals. The uninhibited "you" that touched unconditional love becomes the standard against which you now judge your everyday self. All you can think of is getting back to that place. You've just added more layers of subtle violence to your being.

And then there's the word that keeps coming up: *integration*. It sounds gentle, spiritual, wise. But it's just the attempt to stabilize what was opened too soon. You forcefully cracked something open—in your nervous system, your psychic defenses, your energetic boundaries. It didn't come as a result of micro-tuning yourself towards light, love, and acceptance, using everyday situation as your mirror. It came from self-rejection, from going to extremes to get away from who you currently are. Nothing is more disruptive to the divine timing of your unfolding.

These fragments can heal, yes—everything eventually does. But healing a blown-open system often takes months, years, even lifetimes of deep rest, somatic repair, and spiritual reorientation. It's a lesson that comes with a cost your younger soul couldn't foresee. And that's not your fault. Surrounded by other young souls, you weren't told any of this going in. But the aftermath is yours to carry. And often, that burden grows heavier when you can't admit that the "medicine" has created another, deeper wound.

So you continue to insist you're progressing—to yourself and others. Saying otherwise would be a blow to the massive desperation and expectations that back up your actions. But that's all surface. Energetically, you're actually moving in the opposite direction. You wanted to escape suffering, but you've deepened it by reinforcing the idea that you're not enough as you are. The entire journey becomes another chapter in your book of avoidance. And the only thing that finally brings clarity is the burning of that book—the moment you realize none of it is needed. That the shortcut didn't save you. That what you sought was never out there. It was always already here.

That's the real gift—when the whole search dissolves. When the pursuit fades. When you're left with nothing but your right now and the remnants of all your efforts. That's when you start to see the deeper truth: *I don't need to go anywhere. I just need to be here.* It's not a glamorous insight. But it's real.

From there, a new kind of old soul intelligence begins to emerge—one that comes not from abandoning yourself, but from trusting life as it is, not as you wish it to be.

OLD SOUL

You've gone down the psychedelic path before—if not in this lifetime, then in others. You've felt the pull of transcendence, the desire to escape the mundane. You've tasted altered states, touched the beyond, and returned disappointed or disoriented, wondering why the beauty didn't last. And now, you know: it's not about what you glimpse. It's about what you're willing to stay with. And that is always who you are now.

You've come to see that the drive to "awaken" through any forced method—be it drugs, withdrawal, or other extreme practices—is itself motivated by lack, by feeling like you're not good enough, and that it carries the potential to create an even bigger wound. Not because awakening is wrong, but because trying to rush it violates the pace of the soul, as reflected in the cosmic mirror. You've felt what happens when you override the body, when you push the psyche beyond what it's ready to hold. It doesn't lead to liberation. It leads to fragmentation.

You understand now that there is nothing to achieve. No badge, no identity as a "conscious" person that will bring lasting peace. That whole game belongs to an earlier chapter of your journey. It was a necessary chapter—one filled with seeking, striving, and spiritual hunger. But now you see clearly that peace is not about getting anywhere. It's about wanting to be here.

You recognize that every act is shaped by the consciousness from which it was born. If you manifest from an unconscious belief that you are not enough, the essence of that belief will live on in the experience you create. Even if you encounter love or oneness or your uninhibited self, your body remembers that you did not trust it without a chemical push. Your nervous system absorbs not just what happened, but *why* it happened. And true healing only begins when you're honest about that.

The word *integration* has lost its significance for you. You hear it and sense the bypass. Not always—but often. You know that young souls typically use the word to try to make sense of something that overwhelmed them. The real integration is not journaling or joining a circle—it's rebuilding trust with the parts of you that were pushed too far, too fast. And that's slow work. Sober work.

You don't judge those who seek. You remember what that felt like—to want freedom from suffering so badly that you'd do anything for it. But now, you move differently. You no longer need to be cracked open. You need to sit still. To be kind. To listen. You've stopped chasing awakening and started embodying presence. It's quieter here—which is what you were seeking in all that noise. And it's far more real and powerful.

You've come to see that the design of life is not random. The slowness, the repetition, the ordinariness—it's not meant to punish you. It's meant to purify you. It's an extremely meticulous and detailed process. The level of detail speaks to the love and attention that has gone into designing it. It teaches you to find beauty in the details. To love what's in front of you. To stop rejecting what already is. To stop using God as a drug. Enlightenment isn't an elevated state—it's your ability to stay where you are when nothing feels special.

Ultimately, being with yourself *as you are* is the doorway to all the states you once tried to force. Safety. Insight. Expansion. Love. They come—not from chasing them—but because you allow them to arise in you when you get out of your own way.

As an old soul, you're no longer a seeker—you're a participant. You observe. You accept. You meet yourself again and again. And you smile. Because you remember: the mistakes and detours weren't just part of the path, they *are* the path.

You trust that what's real doesn't need to be induced, it just needs to be received. And in that trust, something ancient awakens. A stillness so deep it unravels every fantasy you once mistook for truth. And now, you walk the real path. The one that doesn't require you to leave, because you're already home.

Psychedelics Chart

Partaking in psychedelics can have a significant impact on the trajectory of your life, as all energetic manipulation does. The following chart contrasts how young souls vs old souls view psychedelics.

Perceived Goal	Taken via Psychedelics	Underlying Energetic Cost	Soul-Aligned Alternative
Experience ego death	Forced through chemical override	Bypasses inner readiness; reinforces self-rejection	Presence through stillness, meditation, and humility
Feel more Source	Artificial merging with divine	Unstable expansion; lacks integration	Daily practice of surrender
Heal trauma	Emotional flooding without true safety	Creates dependency on peak experiences	Heal slowly through somatic+energy work
Access mystical insight	Psychic flooding, illusion of knowing	Spiritual arrogance or fragmentation	Let truth arise from silence and service
Break free from identity	Temporary escape without grounding	Dissociates from the human experience	Release self through sustained awareness
Accelerate awakening	Manipulated peak state	Egoic impatience masked as progress	Trust divine timing & wisdom of limitation
Unlock creativity	Chemically induced novelty	Undermines organic inspiration and flow	Co-creation with Source
Transcend suffering	Quick bypass of discomfort	Skips karmic lessons, repeats patterns	Learn in presence with what is
Gain spiritual status	"Trip" becomes an identity narrative	Feeds sense of self, need to feel special	Live your truth, let your presence teach
Shortcut growth	Mind-altered progress w/o roots	Leads to confusion, crash, or addiction	Choose the slow path of integrity & self-trust

© 2025 Cirak

Prompts

1) Whenever you've sought transformation, were you moving toward truth—or away from discomfort?

2) What motivations have fueled your interest in altered states, and do they feel rooted in self-love or avoidance?

3) How does your nervous system respond when you imagine forcing a breakthrough?

4) What messages are you sending to your body when you pursue awakening through chemicals or extremes?

5) What part of you feels the need to "become" someone else to be whole?

6) Have you ever mistaken intensity or vision for genuine growth?

7) How has the idea of "integration" played out in your life? What has truly helped, and what has not?

8) Can you identify ways in which your past "spiritual" efforts were fueled by self-rejection?

9) What does it feel like to truly be with yourself, without trying to change anything?

10) What might shift if you trusted that everything you're seeking already lives within you?

CHAPTER 96

REGRESSION

YOUNG SOUL

The idea of past lives sounds absurd to you. It doesn't even register as something worth considering. You were raised in a world that rewards logic, endorses science, and praises provable facts—things you can measure, define, and see with your own eyes. To mainstream culture, reincarnation sounds like spiritual nonsense, something only delusional or eccentric people believe in. You lump it together with horoscopes, fairies, and conspiracy theories. If anyone brings it up, you roll your eyes or change the subject.

Even if you're curious about spirituality, regression sits in the farthest corner—out there with the most "woo-woo" ideas. It's just too abstract, too untethered. You're trying to ground yourself, not float away into La La Land. You're drawn to cognitive therapy, life coaching, maybe some mindfulness or yoga—things backed by data, recognized by institutions. The idea that your emotional wounds might trace back to another lifetime feels incomprehensible.

Ironically, to a young soul, past life regression sounds like escapism, a way to avoid dealing with real problems. And because your identity is still tightly bound to this life—your name, body, image, history—the suggestion that you've lived before, or will again, doesn't just sound ridiculous. It sounds threatening. It undermines everything you've been taught about who you are.

The deeper issue is that you still see yourself as a fixed personality moving through a single, linear life. You haven't yet sensed your infinite nature. The idea that awareness extends beyond form—beyond memory, gender, culture—is too destabilizing. Even if you flirt with spiritual ideas, you want results now. You're not ready to consider that your current life is just one page in a much longer book.

And so, you completely miss the point. You assume past-life exploration is about indulgence or importance. You don't yet see that true regression is not about collecting identities, but dissolving them. You haven't quieted enough to feel the infinite thread that runs through your being. That awareness will come. But for now, regression still feels like a fantasy from the fringes.

Old Soul

As an old soul, you know the concept of past lives is all about continuity. You've lived enough to sense that your consciousness does not begin and end with this body. You're no longer driven by what is considered "real" and what isn't. You no longer judge your feelings as right or wrong, true or false. You allow things to be, including whatever wants to express itself through you.

So when regression arises—through memory, meditation, or guided practice—you're not inclined to cling to it as proof of anything. You're aware that facts and knowledge are just illusions, something your younger soul self once idolized, but that you've since transcended. So you hold any rationalization lightly, and let regression serve as a window into unresolved threads that still ripple through your present.

If an image presents itself—a battlefield, a monastery, a family scene—you take it not as literal history, but as energetic teaching. What matters isn't *when* it happened, but *what it reveals now*: the unfinished grief, the repeating pattern, the karmic entanglement that wants to surface.

In this way, regression serves the energetic release of old patterns. You recognize that the unconscious material of the soul often disguises itself as anxiety, aversion, or inexplicable attraction. By revisiting these deeper layers, you bring them into awareness, where they can finally dissolve. You don't dramatize them. You just need to witness them. Awareness creates the space for healing to occur.

You've also realized that regression is not about gaining new identities, but about dissolving them. When a memory surfaces, it's not an invitation to say *"I was that"*—it's an opportunity to release attachment to the story altogether. The point is not to take on another costume, but to recognize the one constant through it all: the awareness that witnessed every role, every triumph, every failure. Regression doesn't expand who you think you are—it strips away who you're not.

As an old soul, you know that what carries forward across lifetimes is not titles, possessions, or personalities, but frequency. What you refine in love, presence, and truth remains. And what you resist keeps recycling. Regression is simply one way to accelerate your own clearing, helping you embody more fully who you already are beyond form.

And so, past lives are not about the past at all. They are about freeing yourself in the present—untangling the knots that keep you from resting in the timeless self. You don't need regression to know who you are, but it serves as a reminder that you are ancient, infinite, and always in the process of becoming.

Prompts

1) What is your honest reaction when you hear someone talk about past lives?

2) Do you feel curious, skeptical, or resistant—and why?

3) Can you remember a moment when your sense of self felt larger than this lifetime?

4) How would your identity shift if you deeply believed you had lived before?

5) What parts of you are still tightly attached to this life's story?

6) How might past-life stories help you soften judgment or increase compassion toward yourself or others?

7) What would it mean if regression were less about proof and more about dissolving identity?

8) How might trusting soul continuity change the way you meet everyday struggles?

Chapter 97

Multiverse

Young Soul

The multiverse is a compelling concept—especially because it comes dressed in the language of quantum physics, which feels more credible to you than the mystical overtones of past-life regression. You may encounter it in documentaries, podcasts, or late-night conversations with friends, but also hear bits and pieces from more renowned sources. Either way, something about it excites the mind, and that's something you always feel drawn to.

But something about it doesn't reach deeper. It remains an intellectual thrill, an abstract puzzle. You imagine parallel lives—what if you had taken that job, stayed in that relationship, moved to another city? These thought experiments bring a rush, but they don't free you. They trap you further in comparison: the self you are against the selves you wish you could have been. The multiverse becomes a stage for regret and fantasy, another distraction from the life that's actually unfolding here and now.

Unlike regression, which feels ancient and imaginary, the multiverse feels modern, even scientific. It doesn't ask you to believe in karma or reincarnation—only in possibilities. But that's the trap: you stay in your head, spinning scenarios, instead of sinking into your body, where real transformation happens. You imagine "better" timelines without shifting the frequency that creates your present one.

And that's where the multiverse concept loses its grip. Because you still perceive life as linear, choices feel final—like doors that close behind you forever. The idea that parallel paths exist all at once feels far-fetched and too abstract to wrap your head around. You believe you are the sum of your past, pushing toward a fixed future, and that effort is the only way forward. The subtle idea that your consciousness aligns with one of infinite timelines doesn't register.

Even when you hear about quantum theory or the observer effect, you collect them like shiny facts. You think you're exploring reality, but you're still trying to control it. You chase new timelines while living in the same one, because your energy hasn't shifted. You're still moving from fear, lack, and separation.

Only when all this mental seeking grows exhausting, do you realize more knowledge doesn't bring freedom—it binds you tighter to the insecurity of all the things you don't know. Your outlook on life becomes dominated by "not enough" and "what if."

As a young soul, you want to hack your way into another reality, but you can't even rest in this one. So the multiverse stays a curiosity, not a revelation. You can't sit still enough, long enough, to notice that multiple timelines are accessible now—not through thinking, but through being.

Old Soul

For you, the multiverse is no longer a theory. It is felt. Not in the head, but in your field of awareness. You've lived so many versions of yourself—even in this life alone—that you no longer cling to a single identity. You've acted from fear and watched reality respond with constriction. You've chosen from peace and seen pathways open with ease. The multiverse isn't "out there." It's vibrational, here, now.

You sense that every thought, feeling, and choice is part of the tuning fork that you are. Whatever frequency you inhabit—from presence to avoidance, from love to fear—constitutes the timeline you inhabit. What many call fate is just the accumulation of unconscious choices.

Regression asks you to look back. The multiverse asks you to wake up now. It doesn't require belief, only presence. When you shift your state, reality reorganizes. You don't need visions of parallel lives to know they exist—you feel the vast field of possibility opening each time you return to stillness.

There is nothing mystical about this. When you're angry, life mirrors resistance. When you're grateful, doors open. This is not ideology but lived experience. The multiverse isn't proven through facts. It's tuned into through frequency.

You are no longer seduced by the fantasy of becoming the "best version" of yourself. You exited that game long ago. You aren't chasing an ideal—you're listening for vibrational alignment. Which version of you feels aligned with truth, with peace, with love? That's the one you inhabit.

The paradox is that the more deeply you surrender to this moment, the more other timelines reveal themselves. You see them all, like distinct layers—accessible, if you choose to tune yourself accordingly, primarily through surrender and presence. And so, even the multiverse becomes less about possibilities and more about giving yourself permission to trust life as it is, knowing that infinite paths are contained within it.

REGRESSION VS MULTIVERSE CHART

Sometimes, the idea of parallel realities is easier to explore because the mind does not get caught up on linearity, as it might with regression. This chart contrasts how young vs old souls understand regression vs the multiverse.

Aspect	Regression (Past Life)	Multiverse (Quantum)
Origin of Concept	Spiritual traditions	Quantum physics
Rooted In	Memory and karmic continuation	Parallel possibilities and entanglement
Common Associations	Therapeutic healing, reincarnation	Timelines, choices, data streams, observer effect
Young Soul View	Dismissed as fantasy or superstition	Intriguing but theoretical and abstract
Old Soul View	Emerges after dissolution of self	Felt as vibrational alignment and frequency
Energetic Orientation	Backwards in time, linear	Sideways or expansive, nonlinear
Mode of Access	Meditative states, guided therapy	Presence, attunement, energetic shifts
Emotional Impact	Healing but fragmented	Empowering when embodied
Relation to Identity	Tied to past stories of the self	Identity dissolves into fluid states
Spiritual Implication	Realigns past with present understanding	Reveals infinite versions of now

© 2025 Cirak

PROMPTS

1) What does the word "multiverse" mean to you? An escape, a curiosity, or something else?

2) When have you fantasized about a different version of your life, and what energy was behind that desire?

3) Can you recall a decision that radically altered your timeline? What inner state were you in when you made it?

4) How do you feel when you consider that other versions of "you" might exist right now?

5) In what ways do you try to control your path instead of aligning with it?

6) What would it mean to stop chasing the "best version" of yourself and instead choose the most aligned one?

7) How does your emotional state affect what shows up in your life?

8) Are there choices you've made from fear that you can now release without regret?

9) Can you feel multiple possibilities coexisting in this moment? Which one feels most peaceful to inhabit?

Chapter 98

Meaninglessness

Young Soul

There comes a point in your journey of self-realization when the life you built begins to crumble. It happens—not because it was bad or you made a mistake, but because it was never truly yours.

At first, as a young soul, the letting go feels like relief. You've been working on yourself, stepping off the hamster wheel, and moving toward this mystical thing called enlightenment. You're doing it—you're finally unhooking from the conditioning. But then the space that opens feels vast and cold. You start releasing what no longer serves you—only to realize it was all you ever knew.

This is when existential panic sets in. You've been told to trust the process, to let go of attachments—but no one warned you you'd fall into emptiness. It's not just the job or the beliefs or the relationship falling away. It's your identity. The scaffolding of your entire worldview collapses. And what's left? A silence so deep it feels like death. And in many ways, it is—the death of the self you spent your whole life building and defending.

Your first instinct is to fill the void with something new. A new mission. A new philosophy. A new spiritual story. But in striving, nothing sticks. You've seen too much, let go of too much, to go backward—yet you're not ready to move forward. You dangle in the unknown. You might call it depression, burnout, confusion. But what you're really experiencing is the Dark Night of the Soul.

For some, it arrives like a sudden avalanche. For others, it unfolds slowly, peeling back layers over years. Either way, it shakes you to your core. Many a young soul turns back—reaching for the familiar comforts of distraction, identity, belief, ambition, or control. You may delay the process. But you can't unsee what's been seen.

The dark night isn't just suffering—it's total dismantling. And once it begins, it's hard to return to a life rooted in illusion. You may try. You may reattach to roles, ideas, or relationships that once gave you meaning. But they no longer hold the weight they once did. More and more, they feel hollow. The soul no longer accepts substitutes.

Many stall here. They bypass. They numb. They intellectualize. They medicate themselves out of the void instead of entering it. And so the dark night drags on, sometimes for decades, and even lifetimes, because the one thing it demands—radical surrender—is the one thing your identity cannot provide.

You might mistake the dark night for a psychological crisis and try to fix it through will or analysis. And while it may overlap with depression or trauma, it cannot be resolved with strategy or drugs. It doesn't resolve through solving—it resolves through letting go and taking a leap of faith. It ends not through striving, but by dying to the person you thought you were.

So yes, you can turn back temporarily. But the spell has been broken. You can no longer fully believe in the old self. And eventually—when you're ready—life will bring you back to the threshold, so you can discover who you truly are.

Old Soul

As an old soul, you no longer fear meaninglessness. You recognize it not as a threat—but a sign of freedom. The moment you stop needing life to "mean something," you can finally relax. The search ends. You stop assigning value to things that can be lost—which is everything. You stop worshipping permanence. And in the stillness that remains, a deeper truth emerges: you are meaningful simply because you exist.

You no longer resist the void. You know it isn't empty—it's more alive than anything else. It's Source. It's the fertile unknown, the cosmic intelligence where everything new begins. So you stay connected, even when the mind fidgets and complains. You trust the unfolding and let the mystery speak, even when you don't always understand it.

You don't need to interpret every emotion or event. You don't need to extract meaning from every challenge. What matters isn't what's happening—it's how present you are with it. And paradoxically, it's in this surrender to meaninglessness that the deepest meaning begins to bloom.

You may still use words, metaphors, and frameworks, but you can drop all stories at a moment's notice and return to the stillness from which all things arise and revert back to. You're finally free—not because you solved anything or have all the answers, but because you no longer need to know.

It's in the space of not-knowing that true co-creation flourishes. When you don't impose meaning onto life, you let meaning reveal itself. You shape reality through alignment and resonance. You become available to what wants to move through you. You become a channel for the unknowable.

The more you trust this, the more graceful your life becomes. That doesn't mean everything is perfect—but you've let go of the search. And in that letting go, you've discovered the ultimate meaning: presence, peace, and being.

PROMPTS

1) What parts of your life once gave you meaning that no longer feel aligned? How have you responded to this misalignment? Have you taken action or still ruminating about what to do?

2) Have you recently or at an earlier point in life experienced a sense of existential confusion or meaninglessness? Was it short-lived or did it endure? What changes did you make in response to it, if any?

3) How do you respond to the unknown? Where do you feel it in your body? Do you try to dispel that feeling or sit with it?

4) What role has your identity played in creating a sense of purpose for you? Where did that identity come from and which parts of it are truly yours?

5) What beliefs about success, love, or spirituality are you currently re-examining? Are there any you want to let go of?

6) Can you recall a time when letting go of meaning actually brought you peace? What prevents you from experiencing that more often?

7) What does it mean to you to live from resonance rather than reason?

8) How do you feel about the idea that meaninglessness can be a doorway to Source? Does it seem foreign and abstract, or do you intuit it as truth?

9) What might it look like to live each day without needing to prove anything to anyone, including yourself? Can you spend a day finding meaning in nothing but pure presence?

CHAPTER 99

MEDITATION

YOUNG SOUL

Young souls tend to dismiss meditation. It feels too impractical, requires too much time, and seemingly offers little immediate benefit. In a world that bombards you with message of quick fixes and instant results, meditation feels woefully outdated.

Then one day, as life grows noisy, stressful, overwhelming, and you come to it more seriously. You've heard that meditation can calm your nerves, sharpen focus, reduce anxiety. So, you give it a try. You sit, close your eyes, and immediately run into the very thing you were trying to escape: your thoughts. They don't stop—if anything, they get louder. You might be inclined to label meditation as a hoax and set it all aside. Or you assume they're doing it wrong and double-down with effort.

That's when meditation becomes another goal, something to master. You want to "quiet your mind" and "achieve inner peace," so you chase stillness by counting breaths, listening to guided audios, chanting mantras, visualizing energy flowing through your chakras. You measure progress by how long you can sit, how calm you feel, how little you fidget. Secretly, you hope it will fix you, make you more evolved, more spiritual, and deliver the insights and transcendent state everyone keeps raving about.

The first time you experience bliss, you're ecstatic. Finally, it's working. But from then on, disappointment abounds. You keep trying to get back there—not realizing that striving creates more distance. So you turn to structure—apps, timers, incense, postures. Meditation becomes another self-improvement task. Another checkbox. And when nothing profound happens, you wonder why everyone else seems to be having breakthroughs while you sit there restless and confused.

Years can pass. You sit regularly, but your life hasn't changed. You still react. You still judge. You're still anxious, distracted, entangled. The peace you chase keeps slipping away. You thought you're evolved, but underneath, you're still rejecting parts of yourself. You've been using meditation to rise above your human messiness, unaware it's another form of self-abandonment.

After much trial and error, a deeper question arises: What if meditation isn't about effort or escape at all? What if striving itself is what keeps you stuck? This is when your old soul life begins.

Old Soul

You've learned that true meditation has nothing to do with controlling your thoughts. It's not about suppressing the mind or chasing peace. It's about letting everything be exactly as it is—within and around you. You sit to meet yourself fully. You allow thoughts and feelings to arise and pass. You notice sounds, sensations, memories, distractions. And you stop fighting any of it.

You no longer meditate to get anywhere. You meditate to be here. You're not trying to become enlightened, more spiritual, or to transcend your humanness. You're simply letting life move through you without resistance. And the quieter you become inside, the more clearly life speaks.

You may still choose to sit formally, but you no longer need to. Every moment becomes meditation when you're fully present. Walking, eating, listening—even feeling anger—is a doorway to awareness. Your only job is to notice how you feel. Noticing keeps you on the side of awareness.

With meditation as your core practice, the wisdom of Source begins to express itself through everything you do. The way you say "Good morning" and mean it. The way you yield to others in traffic, even if you have the right of way. The way you listen, tuned to the energy behind words. The way you walk into a room, establish calm, and point out solutions that benefit everyone. The way you are always open, in receiving mode, giving shape to the formless in your own unique way.

You also carry deep compassion for those just starting. You remember when meditation was about fixing yourself—when you tried to escape pain in the name of peace. That all fell away when you stopped needing to improve yourself and started allowing yourself to be. So now, you hold space for others. You don't shame them for striving. You know they'll discover—through their own exhaustion—that peace is not a reward for effort, but the balance that remains when effort dissolves.

You no longer sit to control or manipulate your energy, but to become more intimate with it. If sadness arises, you give it space. If joy comes, you let it bloom. You no longer label your experience as good or bad. Everything is allowed to be. Everything belongs. Every moment comes to life when you meet it with presence, regardless of its contents. Everything has its place and purpose when perceived with awareness. There is total peace when you no longer need anything to be different. Meditation is the practice of acceptance.

Eventually, the lines blur. Meditation is no longer something you *do*. It's who you are. You speak, walk, and respond from stillness. From fullness. From wisdom. From infinite love, in the way only Source can love.

Meditation isn't the path to freedom: it's your natural state.

Meditation Chart

Unconsciously, meditation can become a crutch. But with awareness, a crucial tool for spiritual growth. The following chart contrasts how young souls and old souls make use of their time on the cushion.

Young Souls	Old Souls
Goal is to master or achieve	No goal—simply presence
Chase peace or bliss	Rest in what is, regardless of state
Measure progress by duration of calm	No measurement—depth felt in immediacy
Use apps, timers, rituals as crutches	Every moment becomes meditation
Escape pain or discomfort	Meet pain and joy equally
Identify with thoughts, try to quiet them	Observing thoughts without attachment
Strive for best self or enlightenment	Letting self fall away into stillness
Discipline mistaken for depth	Depth revealed through surrender
Meditation as a checkbox task	Meditation as natural state of being
Temporary relief, little life change	Lasting transformation thru presence

© 2025 Cirak

PROMPTS

1) What motivates you to meditate? Are you seeking to escape something, fix something, or connect more deeply?

2) What do you expect to happen when you meditate, and how does that expectation shape your experience?

3) When you sit in silence, which sensations or emotions come up for you? Which ones do you tend to avoid?

4) Can you recall a moment when you experienced effortless presence? What did it feel like in your body?

5) What would it mean for you to meditate without trying to improve, fix, or change anything?

6) How might you bring meditative awareness into everyday activities like eating, walking, or washing dishes?

7) The next time you meditate, what would shift for you if you stopped expecting a certain experience, and just let whatever comes up be?

NOTE: For a detailed explanation of how to learn to observe your thoughts and feelings, be sure to consult the CORE PRACTICE chapter at the beginning of this book. You will also find a link to online resources to assist you in your practice.

Chapter 100

Presence

Young Soul

You don't live in the present moment. You live in the future you want to reach and the past you wish you could fix. Your thoughts bounce between planning, replaying, anticipation, and regret. You may not even realize it, but you're almost never here. Presence feels boring, impractical, or even dangerous—what if you stop paying attention to the plan you've created and things fall apart?

Presence requires trust, and, as a young soul, you don't trust life yet. You think you have to predict and hold it all together. If you don't think, worry, plan—who will? You're still operating from the illusion of control. You're afraid that letting go means giving up on the life you're pursuing.

You've heard about "being present," but who has time for that when there are things to fix, futures to build, problems to solve? You have a big vision for your life to pursue. Presence, to you, is something for monks or people who have the privilege of slowing down. Not you. Not now.

But this resistance to presence keeps you stuck in everything you're trying to get away from. The very thing you think will waste time—stopping, breathing, feeling, listening—is what would actually restore clarity and flow. But you're too busy chasing the future to notice. You haven't yet discovered that stillness is not the opposite of momentum. It's the source of it.

You continue to believe your value lies in your ability to manage, prepare, and stay one step ahead. You equate stillness with laziness, and presence with passivity. You think you're being responsible by constantly thinking ahead, but your mind is in a constant loop of imaginary scenarios. This moment right now feels like an obstacle to the better one you're trying to reach.

When something bad happens, you immediately assign blame, analyzing it to death. Or you try to escape, either mentally or physically by distracting yourself with something new. You scroll, you binge, you vent. Anything but sit still. Silence feels threatening, even a little depressing. It's much more compelling to fill your day with stimulation—just enough to keep your discomfort at bay.

You don't realize how much of your suffering comes from resistance to your suffering. You think it's the situation that hurts you, but it's actually your inability to just be with it. You fight time. You fight your thoughts and emotions. You fight reality—the very reality you yourself have manifested from your lack, fear, and need for control. And then you wonder why life feels like such a personal struggle.

Even when you try to be present—perhaps during meditation or a yoga class—you're often just going through the motions. You're trying to "do it right" so you can get some result. Presence becomes a task to complete or technique to master. That's why bio-hack conventions are much more appealing than silent retreats. But there are no shortcuts. As long as your mind keeps interfering, wanting life to feel a certain way, you cannot find peace.

The fundamental challenge to being present is your deep identification with thought. You believe every thought is true and every feeling must be acted upon. Your thoughts are constantly whisking you away into the past and future. You don't realize you have the option to observe your thoughts without becoming them.

Of course, you can't live like this forever. Eventually, it dawns on you that thinking more doesn't solve anything. Trying harder just adds pressure. Wanting more just gets you less. You realize that the only thing you haven't tried is the one thing you've always avoided: being fully here. No agenda. No performance. Just presence. And that's when your old soul comes into view.

Old Soul

Presence is not a technique you apply. It's your natural state when you're no longer lost in thought. It's the ground that emerges when you stop needing to fix what is or control what comes next.

You no longer believe that life happens in the mind. You feel it in your body, in your breath, in the subtle shifts of awareness that occur when you stop resisting and start flowing. You've learned that peace isn't found in getting everything right—it's found in relaxing into what's already real. And when difficult emotions arise, you meet them with space. Instead of reacting out of habit or fear, you locate them, observe them, and watch them dissolve.

You are so much wiser now. You've learned that resistance prolongs suffering. But pain held in presence becomes wisdom. You notice how clearly life speaks when you stop interrupting it. You trust the unfolding. You allow silence to stretch. You don't need to fill every moment with productivity. You've realized that being is your most productive state. Far from being passive—presence is profoundly creative. It's the space where Source energy, inner truth, and clear action merge.

You no longer need to narrate your life. You don't rush to label every experience or justify every choice. You're comfortable with not knowing, with the continuity of life. You know that presence reveals itself when you stop trying to get somewhere. You've seen that your most aligned actions arise not from overthinking, but from deep listening. The mind may still offer commentary, but you don't fight your thoughts—you simply stop giving your attention to those that don't serve you.

Presence simplifies everything. What once felt overwhelming now feels manageable. What once triggered you now moves through you. You see how much of your former suffering came from resisting the reality that you ultimately created. Now you meet every moment with openness. That doesn't mean you like everything—it means you don't argue with what has already happened.

You've discovered that the more present you are, the more opportunities flow. Relationships deepen. Creativity expands. Colors feel richer, sounds more alive, touch more sacred. You experience life with a vibrancy for which there are no words. It can only be felt.

Presence is timeless. Minutes can stretch into eternity. What once felt like a fleeting moment now feels infinite.

The less you seek to be elsewhere, the more life takes care of itself. Presence connects you not only to life as it is unfolding, but to the eternal backdrop against which all moments play out.

Don't abandon life—let it move through you. In that total surrender, you finally come home.

Presence Chart

The following chart shows how young and old souls experience presence.

Young Souls	Old Souls
Distracted by past and future	Fully rooted in now
Presence is boring, lazy, impractical	Presence is natural, vital, creative
Constant loops of planning & regret	Silence & stillness felt as wisdom
Control comes from thinking ahead	Trusts life to unfold, no control needed
Relief thru distraction & stimulation	Finds peace in being, no escape needed
Presence as task or technique	Presence as essence, beyond practice
Identifies with thoughts and feelings	Observes thoughts w/o becoming them
Fears letting go— life will collapse	Letting go as freedom, letting life flow
Must make life happen	Being is most fertile ground for action
Believes stillness wastes time	Stillness is the source of clarity & flow

PROMPTS

1) When do you most often get lost in thought?

2) Describe a recent moment when you felt fully present. What allowed that to happen?

3) What thoughts or beliefs make it difficult for you to trust the present moment as it is?

4) What emotions tend to arise when you stop distracting yourself? Can you welcome them without judgment?

5) What's one area of your life where you could practice greater non-interference—and just let things unfold?

6) What would it look like to live one full day rooted in presence—not forcing, fixing, or chasing anything?

7) How might your life change if you stopped equating productivity with constant effort?

8) Can you remember a time when stillness revealed insight or clarity you couldn't reach by thinking?

9) What fears arise when you consider fully letting go of control?

10) How does it feel to imagine presence not as a task to do, but as your natural state to return to?

www.ingramcontent.com/pod-product-compliance
Lightning Source LLC
Chambersburg PA
CBHW022220090526
44585CB00013BB/448